D1453538

National histories
and European history

National histories
and European history

Edited by

Mary Fulbrook

Reader in German History, and
Director, Centre for European Studies
University College London

UCL
PRESS

D
228
. N 375
1993

© Mary Fulbrook, 1993

This book is copyright under the Berne Convention.
No reproduction without permission.
All rights reserved.

First published in 1993 by UCL Press

UCL Press Limited
University College London
Gower Street
London WC1E 6BT

The name of University College London (UCL) is a registered
trade mark used by UCL Press with the consent of the owner.

ISBN: 1–85728–075–X

A CIP catalogue record for this book
is available from the British Library.

Copy-edited and typeset in Palatino by
Grahame & Grahame Editorial, Brighton

Printed and bound by Biddles Ltd,
King's Lynn and Guildford, England

Contents

Preface

The majority of the essays in this volume originated as papers delivered to a collaborative conference on "National Histories and European History" which took place in London in February 1992. The paper by John Breuilly was originally delivered at a conference in Oxford in June 1992, while that by Jude Bloomfield was specially commissioned for this volume.

The conference was a joint endeavour of the Association for the Study of Modern Italy, the German History Society, the School of Slavonic and East European Studies of the University of London, and the Society for the Study of French History, in association with the UCL Centre for European Studies. I am extremely grateful for the enthusiastic co-operation of these organizations, and for the accommodation and administrative support provided by SSEES. The conference was also supported by a generous grant from the British Academy, for which I would like to express thanks on behalf of all the participating societies.

Finally, my particular thanks to Professor Norman Davies for delivering a keynote address to the conference; to Dr Kathleen Burk, Professor Ian Kershaw, and Dr John Breuilly for chairing sessions; to Professor Shelley Baranowski, Dr Christopher Duggan and Dr Rainer Schulze for their contributions on the panel; to Radojka Miljevic and Heidi Berry for administrative and secretarial assistance; and to all those individuals who attended the conference and commented so fruitfully on the first drafts of the papers, contributing to what will no doubt be a long-running intellectual debate on a topic of major contemporary significance.

Mary Fulbrook
UCL Centre for European Studies
October 1992

Notes on contributors

Mary Fulbrook is Reader in German History, University College London, and Director of the UCL Centre for European Studies. Her books include *Piety and politics: religion and the rise of absolutism in England, Württemberg and Prussia* (1983), *A concise history of Germany* (1990, updated 1992), *The divided nation: Germany 1918–1990* (1991), and *The two Germanies 1945–1990: problems of interpretation* (1992). She is Joint Editor of *German History*. Her current research is on political culture in the GDR, and history and national identity in the two Germanies.

Roland Axtmann is Lecturer in Politics and International Relations at the University of Aberdeen. His research interests focus on historical and comparative political sociology, and regime formation and breakdown. He is currently completing a book on globalization and democratic politics in the European nation-state.

Lucy Riall is Lecturer in History at the University of Essex. She is currently completing a study of state-formation and policing in Sicily in the mid-nineteenth century, and is engaged in writing a textbook on the Italian Risorgimento. She also has research interests in the comparative study of national unifications, focusing particularly on Italy and Germany.

Clive Emsley is Professor of History at the Open University. His books include *Policing and its context 1750–1870* (1983), *Crime and society in England 1750–1900* (1987), and *The English police: a political and social history* (1991). He is currently engaged in research on crime and policing, especially in nineteenth-century rural Europe.

John Breuilly is Reader in History at the University of Manchester. His publications include *Nationalism and the state* (1982), *Joachim Friedrich Martens und die deutsche Arbeiterbewegung* (1984), and *Labour and liberalism in nineteenth-century Europe* (1992). He is currently involved in a research project on the comparative cultural history of mid-nineteenth century Hamburg, Lyon and Manchester.

Wendy Bracewell is Lecturer in History at the School of Slavonic and East European Studies, University of London. She has written a study of piracy and banditry in the Adriatic borderlands, *The Uskoks of Senj: banditry, piracy and holy war in the sixteenth-century Adriatic* (1992), and is currently working on problems of national identity among the South Slavs.

Martyn Rady is Lecturer in Central European History at the School of Slavonic and East European Studies, University of London. His publications include *Medieval Buda* (1985) and·*The Emperor Charles V* (1988). He has written several articles on the history and politics of Central and Eastern Europe.

Jonathan Morris is Lecturer in Modern European History at University College London. He is the author of *The political economy of shopkeeping in Milan 1886–1922: class, space and commerce* (1992). He is currently working on a comparative history of the European *petite bourgeoisie* between 1800 and 1933.

Dick Geary is Professor of Modern History at the University of Nottingham. His publications have been concerned primarily with the history of socialist theory, and European labour history, especially in Germany. His books include *European labour protest, 1848–1939* (1981), *Karl Kautsky* (1987), and *European labour politics from 1900 to the Depression* (1991). He is an Editor of the recently founded journal, *Contemporary European History*.

Martin Swales is Professor of German at University College London. His publications include books on *Arthur Schnitzler* (1971), *The German Novelle* (1977), *The German Bildungsroman from Wieland to Hesse* (1978), *Irony and the novel* (1979), *Thomas Mann* (1980), (with Erika Swales), *Adalbert Stifter: a critical study* (1984), *Goethe: 'The sorrows of young Werther'* (1987), and *Buddenbrooks: family life as the mirror of social change* (1991). He is currently completing a study of German realism in the European context.

Jill Stephenson is Reader in History at the University of Edinburgh. She is the author of *Women in Nazi society* (1975) and *The Nazi organisation of women* (1981), and is currently writing a book on *War and society in Württemberg 1939–45*, as well as a general history of Europe in the twentieth century. She is Joint Editor of *German History*.

Jude Bloomfield is Lecturer in Political Science (Modern European Studies) at University College London. She has published on cultural policy and cities in western Europe, and is completing a book on Communist theories of fascism and strategies of resistance in Germany and Italy in the 1920s. Her current research interests focus on European civil society and identity.

Douglas Johnson is Emeritus Professor of French at the University of London. He is the author of numerous books and articles on modern French history, including *Guizot* (1963), *De Gaulle* (1971) and *Michelet and the French Revolution* (1990).

National histories
and European history

CHAPTER ONE
Introduction: States, nations, and the development of Europe
Mary Fulbrook

In the closing decade of the twentieth century, dramatic changes are taking place in the nature of Europe and its constituent parts. On the one hand, often hotly contested moves towards closer economic and political cooperation in the European Community have unleashed heated debates about the character and scope of national sovereignty. At the same time, creeping and often unnoticed processes of transnational cultural integration and economic interdependence have been proceeding apace. Meanwhile, in a number of areas the forces of a newly awakened nationalism have erupted in the wake of fragmenting multinational polities. The Soviet Union has collapsed and been followed by the Community of Independent States; Yugoslavia has been fractured by warfare and violence on a scale which harks back to the years before·1914; Czechoslovakia has engaged in a more orderly and amicable process of divorcing its Czech and Slovak constituent elements. And in the centre of the redrawn map of Europe after the fall of the Wall, a virulent racism and hostility to foreigners has blazed up in the newly united Germany, particularly in the eastern areas of the former German Democratic Republic. In a variety of respects, both the definition of "Europe" and the nature of national identities have become topics of very direct political import.

Yet even quite divergent interpretations of European history have generally taken place within certain mutually accepted parameters, or implicit assumptions. One such parameter has been, for several generations, the nation state. Any survey of the history shelves

1

of bookshops and libraries will reveal the importance of nation state boundaries as the taken-for-granted unit of analysis: there are sections devoted to the histories of France, Italy, Germany, Britain, and so on. Within these sections, each volume effectively takes as its starting point contemporary political boundaries and imposes some form of chronological and thematic framework to shape what becomes a national "biography" (however contested the details of interpretation may be). The fiction of individual national biographies is effectively sustained by the analysis of military, diplomatic and trading relations between discrete nation state units. These units become the relevant actors on the international stage, spoken of in the singular and even given a gender ("France" decided it was in "her" interests, and so on).

Similarly, made up of nation states, Europe's history has often been written as that of the sum of national histories. To write a history of (at least Western) "Europe" has often been to write a history of developments in what are perceived as the more important states and their interrelations, along, perhaps, with a few general chapters based on thematic lines such as economic, social and cultural history. What is defined as "important" depends, often only implicitly, on assumptions about the "essential" defining characteristics of "Europe" – Western Christianity, the heritage of the Enlightenment, the centre of industrialization and "modernization", colonialism and Empire, parliamentary democracy, being some of the more favoured candidates, leading to the marginalization or complete exclusion of smaller or "peripheral" states and alternative topics.

But in a variety of respects, the nature of the entities which had been, in effect, taken for granted for more than half a century in Europe are in a process of major upheaval. These changes, which run in a variety of directions, prompt a reconsideration of the validity of the nation state as the obvious unit of historical analysis, or at least an explicit historicization of the nation state. A continent undergoing radical and as yet unfinished processes of transformation has become the object of new forms of inquiry and conceptualization.

The essays collected in this volume seek to contribute to these processes of reconceptualization. There are two major areas of inquiry which this book addresses. First, there is the nature of the historical development of the nation state itself. What processes were at work which contributed to the formation, first of discrete states as political units, and later as self-professing nation states seeking to define and propagate a national identity? Secondly, how should we begin to reconsider the changing nature of Europe itself over time, and seek to understand how general European trends, and the location of individual states within a wider European system, have shaped the distinctive patterns of its constituent parts? How did apparently peculiar "national", cultural and social characteristics relate to either broader European, or sub-national, local and regional factors? Finally, and put rather pointedly: is it the case that European history, far from being the sum of individual national histories, in fact constitutes an alternative framework within which different kinds of constituent parts may be identified and interpreted?

The formation of the European nation state

What is a nation state? We all assume we know what we are talking about, until we try to define matters more closely. The British government will talk about national sovereignty – until, as Jill Stephenson points out below, the Scottish start appealing over the head of the "national" government to the European Community, in pursuit of Scottish "national" interests. As the Berlin Wall was breached, East and West Germans appealed vociferously to their common national identity – until the hard facts of economic collapse and social disintegration in the east began to prove the almost insurmountable difficulty of fulfilling former Chancellor Willy Brandt's exhortation to "let grow together that which belongs together". And generations of observers have puzzled over the existence of a Swiss national identity, as the citizens of this tiny, bee-hive-like confederation of cantons go about their business in four official languages and many mutually unintelligible dialects.

Historically, the formation of *states* with a centralized government administering and controlling a clearly defined geographical territory preceded the articulation of ideas of the *nation*. A number of factors are important in explaining the processes of territorial state formation in early modern Europe, out of the more diffused patterns of sovereignty evident in feudalism.[1]

Military competition and the threat or reality of warfare meant that those rulers who were capable of raising taxes and armies were more likely to survive (often literally!) than those who were not. More explicitly: success or failure in warfare, which was at least partly dependent on success in revenue-raising, helped to determine the pattern of which states persisted and which were incorporated as parts of other territories, as internal boundaries on the map of continental Europe were repeatedly redrawn over the centuries. Economic development was probably as important as military competition in the development of a state system in Europe. As Hobsbawm has pointed out, "looking back over the development of the modern world economy we . . . see the phase during which economic development was integrally linked to the 'national economies' of a number of developed territorial states as situated between two essentially transnational eras".[2] "International" relations had implications for internal political structures, or domestic patterns of state building. The exigencies of revenue-raising for the pursuit of warfare meant the development of more centralized administrative systems and bureaucracies. Domestic structures depended too on patterns of social, economic and political relations *within* emerging state territories. Rulers could build up their own bureaucracies, highly dependent on the central ruler, or they could seek to rule *through* pre-existing social and political structures on the land – or they could negotiate a new form of rulership entailing mutual compromises and changes. Which option was taken would depend on a variety of factors, including the co-optability or resistence to centralization of local elites, their own social and economic power bases and interests, the strength of their representative political institutions or estates, and so on.

It should be noted that the emergence of more clearly defined territorial states was not at first associated with the concept of a "nation", let alone with the idea, essential to later nationalist movements, that nation and state should be coterminous. With the expansion of the territorial area of early modern states, a variety of strategies could be employed to claim legitimacy within changing boundaries. Dynasty and tradition, hereditary rights and acquisition by marriage or conquest, might justify rulership united in one person over the most diverse territories, under the most diverse conditions, without any necessary attempt to claim or forge any common identity as a "nation". But while mediaeval Catholicism had provided a certain broad cultural umbrella for at least western Europe (and had provided a long-lasting base for cultural-religious fault-lines dividing "Eastern" from "Western" Europe, and indeed "Europe" from the "Orient"), in the more divided religious landscape of post-Reformation Europe, differences of religious confession played a major role in processes of state-building.

When and why did emergent European states become "nation states"? There now exists a considerable literature on the topic of nationalism and national identity.[3] The invention of the concept of the "nation" is a comparatively recent historical phenomenon, only gaining widespread currency in the early nineteenth century. But the new idea of "nation" could be very variously defined: from the mono-ethnic or linguistic conception of the *Volk*, who allegedly stemmed from the same biological roots and spoke the same language, through to what could be a multi-cultural, multi-lingual and often populist notion of the sovereign "people", united by common ideals and a common historical destiny, encapsulated in the slogan "We, the People". As Benedict Anderson has pointed out, the common aspect is less a substantive element or bundle of shared attributes (whether ethnicity, religion, culture, history, language or a selection or combination of these and other factors) than a more general sense of an "imagined community".[4]

For this to exist in the minds of participants, certain preconditions were essential. For example, communications, including printing and the mass circulation of published material, were prerequisites for the articulation and propagation of any concept of national identity – although preconditions should not be confused with causes. Moreover, the notion that such a thing as the imagined community of the nation existed did not necessarily entail the demand that it should be united within a unitary political unit under a common government. The reception of Herder's ideas of the German *Volk*, for example, were perfectly compatible with loyalty to the Prussian or Bavarian state. The essential precept of nationalist political movements, that the "nation" and the political territory, or state, should be coterminous, is of course a closely related but historically contingent development. And not all claimants to the status of nation also constructed successful states.

Part I of this book focuses on processes of state formation. Roland Axtmann surveys recent important approaches and debates among historically oriented social scientists. He devotes particular attention to Michael Mann's distinction between "despotic" and "infrastructural" power in seeking to develop a typology of states, and emphasizes the importance of analysing the relationships between subordinate and dominant classes as well as between elites and rulers. Axtmann argues that social history must be combined with political history; so too must the history of the constitution of the individual self. For – as explored in a range of studies since the path-breaking works of Norbert Elias, Michel Foucault and others – along with the emergence of the modern state went new forms of social discipline, codes of conduct and the internalization of self-control.[5]

These general themes reappear in different ways in the essays by Riall and Emsley. Riall starts by surveying the historiography of Italian unification, pointing out that while non-Marxist historians have tended to focus attention primarily on international relations (Great Power rivalry) combined with ideological factors (the triumph of liberalism), Marxist accounts have focused on internal class forces with an emphasis on the role of the bourgeoisie. In the context of wider debates over the peculiarities of different national histories, sparked by controversies over the alleged German *Sonderweg* (peculiar pattern of development) when compared to the "normal" histories of Britain or France, Riall is concerned to direct attention to patterns of political structure, and in particular to relations between central and local elites (centre/periphery relations) and between elites and subordinate classes (state/civil society relations). She argues that in Italy, the difficulties of state formation had much to do with the lack of a national elite having control over the regions, with a consequent struggle between central and local power holders. In many areas "the benefits of national unification or liberal government offered little incentive for the local elites to cooperate with the central authority", while "the powers delegated by the centre could be used to bolster the power of local elites in ways that were not always favourable to the central power".[6]

Emsley's attention is on changes from feudal patterns of social control in the countryside as the modern state develops. His analysis of gendarmeries in Europe shows that, while thin on the ground and relatively inefficient at their overt, explicit tasks of crime-prevention and policing, gendarmes played a highly important, if often only implicit, role in "internal colonization" and the "domestication of the peasant". Their task was effectively, by wearing the uniform and flying the flag, to mark out "national" (or "imperial") territory in areas where peasants had not formerly acknowledged national authority. Emsley argues that "Gendarmerie-style policing fulfilled a role largely different from that of the kind of policing which developed in states, or parts of states, where the population acknowledged some form of national identity."[7]

John Breuilly brings together a wide array of political, social and cultural factors in his detailed analysis of the complexities of German nation-state formation in the nineteenth century. Breuilly analyses the essential reconceptualization which was necessary of the distinction between public and private, and the nature of territoriality, sovereignty and boundaries, such that there was a concentration of sovereignty within a unified territory. He examines the interplay between conceptions of nationalism and the articulation of notions of national identity on the one hand, and on the other the political processes which brought about the formation of what has traditionally been seen as the first unitary German nation state in the German Empire of 1871. This state, however, viewed from the perspective of the exclusion of Austria from German affairs for the first time in a millenium, can also be seen as the first "division" of the German nation. As Breuilly points out, the southern boundary of the German Empire of 1871 (between Catholic, German-speaking Bavaria and Catholic, German-speaking Austria) had no "national" content whatsoever; and Bismarck, the architect of the first German "nation state", did not base his politics on any such idea. Ironically, too, the particularism and regionalism of certain localities with distinctive religious, legal or socio-economic traditions within the enlarged German states of the German Confederation after 1815 had played a role in national unification, as local interest groups might appeal to the wider national ideal as a means of freeing themselves from the more immediate interventions of regional state capitals. The articulation of national identity was of course facilitated *after* unification by the introduction of uniform educational and other institutions which transmitted a "national" culture.[8] Breuilly's essay provides a model of the sort of detailed historical analysis of social, political (both domestic and international), cultural and "mentalities" factors which is required to tease out the complexities of nation-state formation in any particular case.

Not all candidates for "nation" status became nation states – nor do all want to. There are potential benefits, as well as possible disadvantages, for communities which consider themselves to be nations to be incorporated as parts of a larger political whole – as, on some views, the British case may show.[9] Nor do political boundaries necessarily determine which communities will feel themselves to form a nation. How does a "nation" articulate its identity, and how do other identities – social, cultural, religious, regional – relate to, or cross-cut, notions of national identity?

One of the most frequently quoted comments on nationalism is the remark made by the French scholar Renan: "Getting its history wrong is part of being a nation."[10] It may be said that some versions of national history are more constrained by empirical material than others. We are all aware – or like to think we are aware – of obvious falsifications, imaginings, or more subtly, modes of what Hobsbawm has called the "invention of tradition". We are keen, too, to point to blind spots or what the Germans refer to as "blank areas" on the historical map – embarassing episodes or aspects which are conveniently left out of certain historical accounts for political reasons. But all writing of history is nevertheless informed by certain assumptions about what to select from the past, and how to characterize the identities and roles of key historical actors or groups. Any cursory glance at educational policies and controversies in quite different regimes, democratic as well as non-democratic, will reveal the key political importance of history in promoting a certain version of the nation's historical mission, its national myths about its past and its role and identity in the present. Whether one considers recent debates on the teaching of history in the National Curriculum in Britain, or virulent controversies over the Third Reich in the two Germanies during forty years of division, or conflicting interpretations of war-time resistance and collaboration in France, it is clear that – for all their basis in empirical material – historical interpretations often have as much to do with the present as the past.

Wendy Bracewell presents an intriguing analysis of the role of national histories in articulating changing identities among the South Slavs, particularly the Serbs and the Croats. She illuminates the variety of characteristics which may be identified as constitutive of a nation, and the ways in which definitions are employed to construct both narrower and more inclusive identities under changing political circumstances. Rajić's history of the Serbs presented their claims to nationhood despite (in Rajić's view) their enemies' lies and "their own ignorance of their glorious past". With Karadžić, there was a shift from a definition in terms of dynastic tradition and Orthodox faith to one based on language and descent, which in turn altered the boundaries between "Serbs" and "non-Serbs" – but which was inclusive of all who met the criteria, irrespective of social class. Among Croats, it was at first primarily the nobility who constitued the "political nation"; but when Croats needed Serbs as allies against the Magyars, Croat identity was reformulated under the wider concept of an "Illyrian" identity, covering all South Slavs. Since this attempted reformulation was not reciprocated by the Serbs, Illyrian identity in fact only served to unite the Croats – but now including the common people. Croat appeals to a wider "European" (Catholic, Habsburg, democratic) identity, further served to divide them from the "orientalist" (Byzantine, Orthodox, Ottoman, despotic) Serbs. Bracewell's analysis – in which she points out that neither history, nor identity, is entirely contingent – provides illuminating insights into the historical background to the current upheavals in what was Yugoslavia.

The changing character of the European system

Moves over recent decades among West European nations towards closer economic and political co-operation within the European Community have certainly suggested that a rethinking of national and European identities is in order. Certainly as far as West Germany from the 1950s to the 1980s was concerned, the growth of a (West) "European" consciousness and focus of identity appeared to provide a solution to the problems of a discredited German nationalism in a divided nation. For other states with less compromised pasts and provisional presents, an emotional transition to Euro-enthusiasm was less easy – arguments had rather to be based on the logic of the international economy, the advantages of moving to a single market, the alleged importance of not being "left behind", or "missing the train" when others forged ahead together. International interdependence was in any event increasingly clear when that ultimate symbol of national sovereignty, the (royal) mint and the coinage of the realm, seemed no longer under the control of national parliaments – when, as commentators liked to observe, the German Bundesbank had only to sneeze and the rest of Europe would catch a cold (or, as the British government found out, be forced to jettison its entire economic strategy and accept unwilling devaluation). The often rocky road towards a strongly contested notion of European integration, as well as more mundane EC directives on transnational issues ranging from the facilitation of labour migration to the quality of food additives and the purity of beer, opened a series of political debates on the relations between "Europe" and national sovereignties and identities.

It is nevertheless not impossible to imagine the following scenario for the twenty-first century. Despite the vociferous opposition of certain national political elites, or the votes cast in referenda or general elections by the citizens of different states, as a result of perceived economic, political and military exigencies over the decades, a United States of Europe was forged. Pro-European historians of the USE in the twenty-first century would write its history as that of the ultimate political unification of a previously definable entity, highlighting the battle of "progressive" forces in the face of "reactionary" provincial opposition. "National" identities would be relegated to the role of regionalism and even antiquarianism; a new "European identity" would be constructed, and its antecedents traced. The sense of being a citizen of Europe would be confirmed, not only through the spheres of culture and education, but also, very practically, through citizens' rights, or the application and experience of uniform economic and political regulations. Enhanced mobility, the growing acceptance of a multi-cultural, multi-ethnic, multi-lingual society, improved communications and the absence of internal frontiers, would soon make the enlarged social space encompassing what was defined as being "at home" rather than "abroad" as natural to Europeans as the geographical extent of the USA is to its citizens. A process of state-formation with the construction of a new identity would be in train, in many ways quite analogous to the earlier processes of nation-state formation on a smaller scale in Europe.

As a scenario, this is not at all implausible, and many elements are already clearly in place, although the unpredictability of politics and the scope for human intervention in a non-determined course of history means that – fortunately – history can only be written with the benefit of hindsight. Nevertheless, it provides an interesting perspective on the course of European history up to the 1990s, on the ways in which "Europe" has been defined, and the ways in which broader European developments influence and are influenced by national and regional developments. The second section of the book focuses on broader European perspectives.

Martyn Rady sets out from a critique of Wallerstein's highly influential world systems theory. Rady does not rest content with identifying empirical flaws of historical detail in Wallerstein's necessarily very wide-ranging conception of core and periphery, but rather goes on to propose an alternative interpretation of the longstanding fault-lines which have run across Europe for a millenium or more. Rady points out that the process of enserfdom in Eastern Europe pre-dated, and was not attributable to, changes in the structure of international trade. The key feature separating "East" from "West", for Rady, has to do with legal norms and institutions of local self-government. The relative absence of effective instruments of peasant autonomy and the extensive powers of local nobilities in the east facilitated the imposition of serfdom in ways not possible in the west. Rady seeks to elevate the legal division of Europe above religious or cultural divisions, identifying two major fault-lines: the River Elbe, which divided those areas where *Weistümer* (written customaries of law) existed from those where they were absent; and the River Rhine, marking the boundary of the reception of Roman Law and later the development of rationalistic natural law in the Enlightenment. Rady argues that long-standing differences in the relations between state and civil society in Eastern and Western Europe played an important role in the post-war experiences of the Communist states of the Soviet bloc, and that their reverberations have implications for the major processes of restructuring and democratization which are underway today.

The essays by Morris and Geary focus on the issue of regional and other factors affecting the political attitudes and strategies of the "European" petite bourgeoisie and working classes respectively. Morris' analysis of the European petite bourgeoisie highlights the diversity of experiences of this class during processes of modernization, and leads him to question the validity of comparisons at the national level. Rather, Morris stresses the salience of regional and local commercial environments as determinants of petit bourgeois politics, providing by way of detailed example a comparison of the shopkeeper movements in Paris and Milan during the period 1880–1905. Despite the frequently made global

generalizations about, for example, the importance of petit bourgeois anti-modernism in the origins of German Nazism, or the issue
of English exceptionalism, for Morris any "European history of the
petite bourgeoisie" must be developed on the basis of detailed local
studies and not as an aggregate of national histories. Moreover, it
may turn out that the petite bourgeoisies of, say, different national
capital cities have more in common with each other than with
compatriots in other towns.

Geary's detailed survey of the range and variety of working class
identities in Europe before the First World War similarly reveals
a "picture . . . of massive national and regional diversity". Geary
argues that "the prime determinant of at least the political identity
of workers is to be found *outside* the workplace in factors such as
residence, popular culture, the attitudes and behaviours of other
social groups, and above all the role of the state."[11] Insofar as
there are distinctive national patterns, these are shaped more by
the policies of the state than by any putative "national characters".

Nevertheless, the notion of the "peculiarities of national cultures"
has persisted. Martin Swales' analysis of German prose writing
within the general context of European realism challenges received
– and often normative – views of the allegedly aberrant traditions
of nineteenth-century German fiction. He argues that, while the
German prose tradition "is, indeed, particular", nevertheless "in
its particularity, it debates issues that are germane to the broader
European experience". While the accepted canon of European realism is a "realism of fact", the German tradition provides a "realism
of concept and idea, of discourse, of mental life". In an energetic
defence of the richness of this tradition against those detractors
who see it as "yet another example of the besetting German sin of
inwardness", Swales connects the cultural and symbolic sphere with
outer processes of socio-cultural change, and suggests that the German experience has much to offer in any contemporary rethinking
of identity, provincialism, nationality and European integration.

Jill Stephenson's focus is on the western periphery of Europe:
Britain. In the context of current discussions between Euro-sceptics
and Euro-enthusiasts which revolve around issues of identity and
sovereignty, Stephenson explores the peculiarities of this insular
state, which, unlike continental Europe, had not not been subjected
to invasion and military conquest since 1066. In examining Britain's
often problematic relationship with "Europe", Stephenson devotes

particular attention to the question of whether Britian is itself a multi-national state, and to what may be seen as a periphery within the periphery: Scotland. In ways strikingly reminiscent of the German localities of the nineteenth-century Confederation which – as described by Breuilly – appealed to ideas of a wider German nationality above the heads of powerful and interventionist regional state governments, so from the Scottish perspective there might be advantages in European integration which would remove certain powers from the Westminster parliament. Stephenson's wide-ranging analysis of Britain and Europe sets in a broad historical and political perspective some of the most important issues in understanding Europe in the 1990s.

Jude Bloomfield argues that the major changes which have been taking place in Europe over recent decades require new modes of conceptualization. Received theoretical approaches – whether the "additive approach" which sees Europe as merely the sum of its constituent states, or, at the other end of the spectrum, the type of global "world-systems" theory following Wallerstein – cannot adequately comprehend the character and dynamics of the "New Europe". Focusing particularly on the emergence of a new European "civil society", and analysing diverging ideas and cultural definitions of Europe, Bloomfield develops a vision of a multi-ethnic, multicultural Europe which poses new questions for theoretical analysis and empirical research. Finally, in a brief Epilogue, Douglas Johnson discusses the ways in which historians have shaped our perception of Europe's identity, past and future.

National histories and European history

The topics covered by this book range over a large historical and geographical arena, and clearly cannot claim to provide exhaustive coverage of all relevant aspects. Nevertheless, in discussing a variety of issues relating to our conceptualization of national histories and European history, they raise a number of important methodological and substantive points.

Traditionally, the nation state has provided the taken-for-granted parameters for the writing of history. But it should not be forgotten that the nation state is itself in fact only a comparatively recent product of history, which may in the event also prove to be relatively short-lived. While many aspects of the processes of state formation, and the articulation and propagation of varying versions of national identity, have been illuminated by recent research – and exemplified in contributions to this volume – the relationship between the emergence and possible superceding of nation states on the one hand, and developments within a broader European system on the other, still throws up many puzzles to which we have no adequate answers. There does seem to be some relationship between the formation of a system of multiple, discrete states and the distinctive pattern of capitalist development in Europe; and there similarly seems to be a relationship between the development of transnational trends and the renegotiation of the functions of nation states in late twentieth-century Europe. But these relationships are complex and not as yet fully understood; they are, moreover, further complicated by the persisting or renewed strength of a variety of nationalist ideologies which seem to bear little rational relationship to economic or political exigencies.

The writing of national histories may be the appropriate thing to do when nation states are the key political actors, definers of economic policy, and sources of socialization and culture – as they have been during the last century or so. And, after all, it is one of the functions of history to tell us how we got to where we are. The wary writer of a national history will seek to avoid teleology, and attempt to do justice to the diversity of strands of a story while charting a clear path towards the present through the thickets of historical detail.[12] But the nation state may not be the most appropriate unit of analysis for all purposes.

As the chapters by Morris and Geary show, in seeking to understand the varying political attitudes of pan-European classes, the salient unit for comparison may be that of a town, a region, a particular sub-culture; or it may be a much broader part of a continent, in ways explored in Rady's contribution. A narrow expertise in a particular area may blind the historian to ways in which that area is coloured by, and partakes in, wider trends, or is determined by its place in a wider system. Moreover – as many of the confusions of the German *Sonderweg* debate have shown – to understand what may genuinely be national peculiarities, every national history must, whether implicitly or explicitly, rely also on comparative history. Historical sensitivity will indicate where definitions of what constitutes the "nation" or focus of sense of identity have shifted (Croatia/Yugoslavia, Scotland/Britain, Bavaria/Germany – Germany/Europe?) and what the constitutive elements are deemed to be (language, religion, ethnicity, culture, common political goals or economic interests . . .). Such sensitivity will also enable us to rise above the prejudices of everyday political debate, in which different nations are often ascribed enduring national characters, and to think more flexibly about possible future rearrangements in political structures and constructions of identity.

To write a history of "Europe" as the twentieth century draws to an end is to write in a period of many uncertainties. As Norman Davies has pointed out,[13] previously received Eurocentric approaches, defining Europe as the model for all the world to follow – as the repository of "Western Civilization", the source of "Progress", Democracy, Religious Toleration, the Scientific Tradition, Philosphical Thought, Masterpieces of Art – have increasingly come into disfavour, as the perspectives of suppressed minorities have been re-articulated and the darker sides of European history brought into sharper focus. To write a history of Europe as simply that of the "Great Powers" and their interrelations is no longer adequate under conditions of increasing European integration. And the persistent identification of "Europe" with a (variously defined, but always allegedly superior) notion of "Western Europe" which relegates "Eastern Europe" into insignificance or complete oblivion, has – whatever its previous intellectual inadequacy – now been finally undermined by the collapse of the Soviet bloc and the disappearance of the Iron Curtain. A new, more comprehensive history of all-Europe – exploring historical "failures" as well as "successes", minority interests as well as dominant ones, continental as well as national and idiosyncratic topics, with full geographical coverage of all of Europe – is required; but, as Norman Davies has stressed, this is "easier said than done".

There is much that we still do not understand about how and why European states emerged, about the peculiar attractions of often undefinable notions of national identity, about the ways in which these are articulated, transmitted, received and changed, and about the current transformations in the European system. But it is clear that the development of more adequate historical perspectives is essential to any informed debate on contemporary transformations in what many now understand to be – in many different ways, and often for very different reasons – a common European home.

Notes

1. There is a large and expanding literature on theoretical approaches to the state and on the formation of the modern state, which clearly cannot be considered in detail here. For a range of classical and recent contributions on a variety of relevant aspects, see for example: P. Anderson, *Lineages of the absolutist state*, London, 1974; R. Bendix, *Nation-building and citizenship*, Berkeley, 1964; P. Evans, D. Rueschemeyer and T. Skocpol (eds), *Bringing the state back in*, Cambridge, 1985; D. Held et al. (eds), *States and societies*, Oxford, 1983; G. Poggi, *The development of the modern state*, London, 1978; C. Tilly (ed.), *The formation of national states in Western Europe*, Princeton, N.J., 1975.

2. See E. J. Hobsbawm, *Nations and nationalism since 1780*, Cambridge, 1990, p. 25.

3. See for a selection of recent important works, which will in turn provide a guide to further reading: Peter Alter, *Nationalism*, London, 1989; Benedict Anderson, *Imagined communities*, London, revised edn. 1991; J. Breuilly, *Nationalism and the state*, Manchester, 1982; E. Gellner, *Nations and nationalism*, Oxford, 1983; E. J. Hobsbawm, *Nations and nationalism*; Tilly (ed.), *Formation of national states*.

4. See Anderson, *Imagined communities*.

5. See, for example, Norbert Elias, *State formation and civilization*, Oxford, 1982; orig. 1939.

6. See below, pp. 61, 62.

7. See below, p. 87.

8. See also J. Breuilly (ed.), *The state of Germany*, London, 1992, for further exploration of the changing role of the national idea in modern German history.

9. The issue of national identity is extremely complex. Many citizens of contemporary multi-cultural, multi-ethnic Britain would identify with the claim to be "British", while not considering themselves to be "English", "Scottish", "Welsh" or "Irish". Similarly, many Scots and Welsh see no value in separatist movements. For a historical perspective, see Linda Colley, *Britons: forging the nation, 1707–1837*, Princeton, 1992. See also the chapter by Jill Stephenson in this volume; and Hobsbawm, *Nations and nationalism*, pp. 31–2, on the "threshold principle" for "viability" of candidates for nation state-hood.

10. Quoted, for example, in E. J. Hobsbawm, *Nations and nationalism*,

p. 12. See also Benedict Anderson, *Imagined communities*, pp. 199 ff. for an extended discussion of Renan's perception of the importance of "having already forgotten" certain aspects of history in constructing a national identity.

11. See below, p. 207.
12. For my own attempt at a national history of what is often seen as a peculiarly problematic case, see M. Fulbrook, *A concise history of* *Germany*, Cambridge, 1990, updated edition 1992.
13. Norman Davies, "Towards a new history of all-Europe", paper delivered at the conference on National Histories and European History, London, February 1992. See also Norman Davies' forthcoming *Oxford history of Europe*.

Part I
State formation and national identities

CHAPTER TWO

The formation of the modern state: the debate in the social sciences

Roland Axtmann

In the last twenty years or so, an increasing number of social scientists have discovered "history". Not only have they turned their attention to social structures and processes of the past, but they have also attempted to confront the methodological challenge of mainstream historiography. They accept that social phenomena or events can only be understood in their context in time and space; where and when social processes (or phenomena) occur affects both their course and the (structural) outcome. Because of this temporal and spatial context, they concede that social scientists have to move away from the idea of the possibility of a *general* explanatory theory of society (or politics, economics, culture) which would aim to explain, for example, the political system of Ancient China and that of contemporary Switzerland with the same set of categories and explanatory variables. They have thus emphasized the need for analysing the constructing, deconstructing and reconconstructing of patterns of social interrelationships (i.e., social institutions) through human agency within a specific temporal and spatial setting.

One of the subject-matters which has attracted much of the attention of historical social scientists has been the formation of "modern" political institutions within a clearly demarcated (sovereign) territory in the course of the transformation of the multiplicity of overlapping and divided authority structures of the medieval polity. In this chapter, I shall present some of the arguments advanced in this debate on the formation of the modern state.[1]

1   The typological approach

Such is the importance of the work of Max Weber to the renaissance of a historically oriented social science in the last twenty years or so, that both Weber's typological approach and his substantive research questions still inform many analyses of state formation. As is well known, Weber organized his empirical material by constructing ideal types. One of his most famous typologies was based upon the distinction between three different forms of justifying domination.[2] The hallmark of *traditional* domination is justification by belief in the sacredness of traditional orders and seigneurial rights handed down to the present from time immemorial: individuals obey out of piety. *Legal* domination, by contrast, is characterized by obedience to impersonal rules which have been stipulated in a legally correct form. *Charismatic* domination, finally, is justified by affectual surrender to the personality of the ruler and his extraordinary charismatic means of grace: individuals obey because they believe in the mission of the charismatic leader. These ideal types are constructed with an inbuilt logical dynamic. *Traditional* domination displays the tension between the sacredness of traditionally founded norms and the tradition-free arbitrariness of the ruler. In *rational-legal* domination, there is a tension between formal procedures based on abstract principles and regulated discretion on the side of the ruler allowing for material equity. In *charismatic* domination, the claim of the leader to absolute obedience is based on supposedly extraordinary charismatic qualities which are likely to prove too demanding for the charismatic ruler to live up to continually.

This typology was then further developed on the basis of the hypothesis that "every domination both expresses itself and functions through administration".[3] Weber maintained that historical reality involves the continuous, though for the most part latent, conflict between rulers and their staff over the control of the means of administration. Taking this power struggle as his starting point, Weber constructed typologies of political structures on the basis of the degree of concentration of political power in the hands of the ruler or, alternatively, the decentralization of political power and its delegation to administrative staff. This typological approach allowed Weber analytically to distinguish between traditional, legal-bureaucratic, and charismatic types of domination as well as to construct subtypes, e.g. patriarchalism, feudalism, Ständestaat and patrimonialism for the traditional type of domination.

Combining these two aspects of legitimation and organization, one arrives at a Weberian conceptualization of the state as that political organization whose administrative staff successfully upholds the claim to the monopoly of the legitimate use of force in the enforcement of its order in its territories and over people within them: "The modern state is a compulsory association which organizes domination".[4] To sustain domination and protect state power against internal as well as external challengers, states attempt to extract and mobilize resources from society. The core of any state is thus the network of administrative, legal, extractive, and coercive organizations. As a result, Weberian analyses of state formation focus typically, though by no means exclusively, on discussions of the (intellectual or cultural) principles underpinning claims to legitimate rule and the forces transforming these principles as well as the organizational changes in the transition from traditional to legal-bureaucratic structures of domination.[5]

Amongst historical sociologists, Reinhard Bendix was the most prominent adherent to Weber's approach. In *Nation-building and citizenship*, he analysed the causes that accounted for the political transformation of Western European societies "from the estate societies of the Middle Ages to the absolutist regimes of the eighteenth century and thence to the class societies of plebiscitarian democracy in the nation-state of the twentieth century".[6] Hence he discussed the formation and transformation of the traditional authority relations of the Middle Ages into the administrative-bureaucratic authority relations in the nation-state through the direct or indirect effects of the industrial and democratic revolutions in Western Europe. Bendix aimed at a crisp formulation of contrasting types and then, above all, at a historically adequate analysis of the structural tensions within each type and the processes that led to the transition from one type to the next. In Stein Rokkan's summary, "Bendix's analysis focuses on the tactics of centre-forming collectivities, dynastic bureaucracies and military organizations in breaking down local solidarities and creating direct links between the territorial nation and its individual subjects through the development of universalistic criteria of citizens rights and obligations."[7]

The same methodological concerns informed his study of *Kings or People* in which Bendix analysed political power and changes in the mandate to rule.[8] He distinguished two structural forms of political authority and the conditions of their legitimation: "traditional" monarchical domination based upon religious-sacral legitimation, and the "modern", rational-bureaucratic, form of domination with its legitimacy based on the claim to exert authority by popular mandate. He identified "national" intellectual elites, which were located in an international network allowing for the diffusion of values and ideas, and transnational learning more generally, as those modernizing agents who gradually undermined the prevailing "traditional", and typically sacral, legitimatory principles of domination by formulating rationally grounded and justifiable "modern" alternative interpretations.

There has been one major recent contribution which could be seen as a new typological approach. One of the issues addressed by Michael Mann in *Sources of Social Power* is the variations in state forms in pre-industrial Europe. He distinguished between *"absolutist"* and *"constitutional"* regimes. According to Mann, these regimes were subtypes of a single form of state: "a weak state in relation to the powerful groups of civil society, but a state that increasingly coordinated those groups".[9] Both regime types shared two principal characteristics:

> Their power was limited by their largely military functions and did not include a share in property rights, and they extracted fiscal revenues and coordinated their dominant classes primarily for military purposes. Their differences concerned merely the forms of coordination – one approaching organic unity, the other backing away from it . . . .[10]

In order to highlight the specific characteristics of the pre-industrial state more clearly, Mann distinguished between two forms of state power. The first kind of state power is *"despotic power"*. It refers to the range of actions that the ruler and his staff are empowered to undertake without routine, institutionalized negotiation with civil society groups. Where despotic state power is high, representation of civil society groups and their voluntary participation in the activities of the state are low. Despotic power is "power over" civil society. *"Infrastructural power"* is the second kind of state power. It is the capacity of central states, whether despotic or not, actually to penetrate the territory of civil society, and to implement logistically political decisions throughout the realm. The state has "power through" society, coordinating much of social life with its own infrastructures.[11] The pre-industrial state was infrastructurally weak, but whereas in "absolutist" regimes despotic power was (relatively) high, in "constitutional" regimes it was (relatively) low.

In an "absolutist" regime, the relationship between ruler and local power holders tends to be conflictual; the despotic claims of central government are high, but it does not possess enough infrastructural power to penetrate civil society and co-ordinate it according to its despotic designs. In a "constitutional" regime, the relationship between ruler and local power holders tends to be co-operative; despotic claims of central government *vis-à-vis* the local power holders are rare, but the penetration and co-ordination of civil society is higher than in the "absolutist" regime type, as central government substitutes a co-operative relationship with the elite groups in civil society for the lack of state-controlled infrastructural power.

By distinguishing between the two types of state power we are in a position to classify a variety of political structures.[12] For example, feudalism could be classified as a regime type with low infrastructural as well as low despotic power; Stalin's authoritarian regime, on the other hand, would show high levels of both infrastructural and despotic power. Absolutist monarchies would be classified as regimes with (relatively) high levels of despotic power and (relatively) low levels of infrastructural power, whereas liberal-democratic bureaucratic regimes of the twentieth century would show low levels of despotic power but high levels of infrastructural power. These distinctions allow us to analyse state formation by specifying the dimension on which "growth" occurs, on the dimension of either despotic or infrastructural power; to analyse the organizational mechanisms which generate and sustain either extension; and to discuss the interrelationships between the developmental processes of either or both levels. It also opens up possibilities for comparative research.

On the other hand, however, Mann's classification is also in need of refinement. As with Weber's typology in his sociology of domination in *Economy and Society*, it is constructed by focusing on the interaction of elite groups and neglecting the social relationships of the ruled amongst themselves and with these elite groups. This focus is justified in so far as the struggle between the centrality of royal authority and the locality of the landlord class is a major feature of recorded history. It was precisely the lack of infrastructural power which made it necessary for the ruler to delegate authority to local power holders. This delegation entailed the risk of the decentralization of political authority. However, the local landlord class established and enforced power relationships with the agrarian peasant producers. The struggle between central ruler and local power holders was centrally concerned with retaining control over the peasant producers on the part of the landlords and undermining this local power base on the part of the central ruler. Typically, the central ruler attempted to turn the peasant producers from subjects of a manorial lord into subjects of the state ("citizens"); the local power holders, in turn, attempted to retain control over their power base by securing their role as intermediaries between the state and their subjects. The relationships between the state and local power holders were thus not constituted in a self-contained social space. They were embedded in the overall power and conflict structure of society. Whether the tendency towards a conflictual or co-operative relationship between ruler and local power holders materialized in reality was co-determined by the patterns of social relationship between the rulers and the ruled as well as those amongst the ruled. Mann's typology, which is built around differing types of elite relations, would therefore have to be expanded to include differing types of class relations as well.

Turning now to the current social scientific debate on state formation, I shall focus specifically on two substantive research areas. Much of the debate has focused on the interrelationship between state formation and the development of capitalism. How important was the establishment of a multipolar European state system or, alternatively, a capitalist world-economy for either development ? In the next section, I shall present some pertinent arguments from this particular debate. In the following section, I shall sketch aspects of the debate on the interconnection of state formation and the rise of "disciplinary society".

2   State formation, variations in state forms, capitalism

Some historical social scientists noted that it was only in the West that there emerged the "modern" state, at the same time, moreover, in which the unique economic structure of capitalism resulted in massive economic development. In the tradition of Max Weber they asked why it was that both these structures emerged in the West and in what ways the processes of state formation and the capitalist market relations interacted.[13]

One argument put forward saw the political fragmentation of early medieval Europe as a necessary condition for the formation of a decentralized market system between AD 800 and 1000.[14] In a much condensed form, the argument runs like this. The power struggle between pope and emperor resulted in the impossibility of establishing an imperial system of domination, be it in the form of caesaropapist or theocratic rule. Rather, this confrontation enabled the formation of separate territorial states within Europe which were to become politically independent from imperial authority but whose autonomy would also thwart the church's own imperial drive. The church thus played an important role, both in making empire impossible in Europe and also in the formation of a multipolar state system.

But while it was instrumental in creating political fragmentation, the church was imperative for the normative integration of Europe at the same time. It gave people a sense of belonging to a single civilization, indeed, it defined and constituted this civilization as Latin Christendom in the first place. The church created and integrated this civilization through normative regulation: "Political and class struggles, economic life and even wars were, to a degree, regulated by an unseen hand, not Adam Smith's but Jesus Christ's."[15] For example, for complex economic chains of production, distribution and exchange across the continent to be established, there had to be a high degree of mutual trust and the general recognition of norms regarding property rights and free exchange. These were above all guaranteed "by the common social identity provided by Christendom".[16] Political fragmentation thus did not result in anarchy or *anomie*.

The state which evolved in this geographical and social space had severe limits imposed on its arbitrariness. On the one hand, it developed in the midst of a pre-existent civil society which comprised the church and its various organizations, as well as nobles, burghers and yeomen/peasants concentrated in manors, castles, cities, guilds and villages, and all of them engaged in networks of interaction which were either too localized for the nascent state to control or too transnational to keep within its territorial boundaries. Typically, this pluralism was strengthened through legal entitlements to representation and its institutionalization in estates assemblies. But state arbitrariness was also limited by the multipolar state system. Political competition between the members of this system offered civil society groups suffering under an arbitrary government the opportunity to "escape" to one of the state's political competitors. The mobility of people as well as capital thus limited the state's power to interfere in the activities of the most powerful civil society groups.[17] Given the existence of these civil society groups, their capacity to escape "despotism", and the transnational character of the economy of the feudal period, the ruler had to co-operate with these groups in order to extract money or other economic resources. And the mobilization and extraction of these economic resources was necessitated by military competition. As Mann put it, until well into the nineteenth century, "simply from an analysis of state finances, the functions of the state appear overwhelmingly military and overwhelmingly geopolitical rather than economic and domestic".[18] The revolution in military technology and the formation of professional and permanent armies and navies in the seventeenth century increased the fiscal pressures on the state which were transmitted through the international military system. The resultant collaboration of the state with the better-organized civil society groups, and especially with the landed nobility and with the commercial oligarchies in trading states, turned gradually into an organic unity between state and dominant classes. This collaboration was forthcoming on the part of the dominant classes because the state had provided useful services to these groups, for example co-ordinating and regulating their activities through the administration of justice and the military protection of their trading interests across a territorial space that they could not control themselves. This reliance on the state increased with the extension of class relations over a wider geographical terrain as a result of economic, capitalist, development: "Merchant and landlord capitalists entered and reinforced a world of emergent warring yet diplomatically regulating states. Their need for, and vulnerability to, state regulation both internally and geopolitically, and the state's need for finances, pushed classes and states toward a territorially centralized organization."[19] This meant, on the one hand, the formation of states of either the "absolutist" or "constitutional" type; on the other hand, the increasing confinement of economic interactions within national boundaries and, at the same time, the authoritative mediation of transnational economic relations by the state.

This narrative, then, has a clear starting point and termination. Medieval Europe was an entity composed of overlapping, intersecting and crosscutting networks of social interaction based on ideological, economic and political power. But the geographical and social space of each network differed such that "no single power agency controlled a clear-cut territory or the people within it".[20] Through the pressures exerted by the international military system, these networks became congruent within the territorial boundaries of the "organic state". A "national" state, a "national" economy and a "national" society (and, eventually, a "national" ideology/identity) came into existence. In this perspective, the analysis of state formation is centrally concerned with understanding the processes which resulted in social reality becoming territorially "fixed" within nation-state boundaries.

Military and geopolitical power thus play a large part in the explanation of these processes. Indeed, explicit reference is made to the militaristic theory of the state developed in Prussian and Austrian historiography around the turn of the century by Hintze, Gumplowicz, Oppenheimer and others. For example, Hintze had maintained that the formation of states and the development of their institutional orders were not determined by socioeconomic conditions but by their position within the state system. For Hintze, war was intrinsic to the European state system and operated as "the flywheel of the whole political enterprise of the modern state" by enforcing rationalization and intensification of state organization and, in particular, the interlocking of the political-administrative system of domination, the military, and the economy.[21] Increased economic growth by means of economic and commercial policies of the state and/or the exploitation of the population and the development of military and administrative institutions were complementary phenomena.

This militaristic/geopolitical perspective was also adopted by

Charles Tilly for whom "war makes states and states make war".[22] In his recent book, Tilly set out to explain the reasons for the great variations over time and space of state forms that have prevailed in Europe over the last millenium and for their eventual convergence on different variants of the national state.[23] He argued that:

> War and the preparation for war involved rulers in extracting the means of war from others who held the essential resources – men, arms, supplies, or money to buy them – and who were reluctant to surrender them without strong pressure or compensation. Within limits set by the demands and rewards of other states, extraction and struggle over the means of war created the organizational structures of states. The organization of major social classes within a state's territory, and their relations to the state, significantly affected the strategies rulers employed to extract resources, the resistance they met, the struggle that resulted, the sorts of durable organization that extraction and struggle laid down, and therefore the efficiency of resource extraction.[24]

Geopolitics, state making, class structure and class struggle are thus seen as interdependent, forming a complex, though historically specific, totality.[25] The emphasis on this interactive pattern sets Tilly's approach apart from Hintze's and moves him closer to that of Mann's.

Tilly distinguished between three modes of state formation: the coercion-intensive mode; the capital-intensive mode; and the capitalized coercion mode. In the *coercion-intensive mode*, the resource-seeking state had to operate in a setting in which resources were most often found in kind, dispersed in the countryside, embedded in agriculture, and controlled by landlords with considerable autonomous force. In this setting, one finds states being formed "on the basis of strong alliances between war-making princes and armed landlords, large concessions of governmental power to nobles and gentry, joint exploitation of the peasantry, and restricted scope for merchant capital".[26] In their effort to discipline and control these autonomous landlords as well as to squeeze the means of war from their populations and others they conquered, rulers set out to build massive authoritarian structures of resource extraction deploying a variety of mechanisms for this extraction: direct expropriation, co-optation, clientage, and/or heavy-handed taxation. However, with few cities and concentrated capital, the economy was based on coercive production and coerced appropriation of the agrarian produce. In sum, these states were externally militaristic as they had to conquer to gain resources and internally repressive as they had to coerce the direct peasant producers. Russia, the Ottoman territories, and Prussia serve as exemplars of such states.

If we translate Tilly's terminology into Michael Mann's, we could say that the state of the coercive-intensive mode increased its despotic power over civil society without being able fully to overcome the resistance of civil society groups to its attempts at infrastructural penetration (resource mobilization and resource extraction). The *capital-intensive mode*, on the other hand, was characterized by a higher level of infrastructural penetration and a low level of despotism. As much of economic production was market-oriented, resources were monetized, concentrated in cities and controlled by capitalists and financiers. Rulers entered into compacts with commercial urban oligarchies who were prepared to provide the state with capital resources in exchange for state protection of their (international) trading interests. The availability of capital resources allowed states to borrow, tax, purchase, and wage war without having to build bulky and durable structures of extraction. At the same time, these state structures were relatively representative, as representation of the capitalists was the most effective way of extracting resources for war. Northern Italy, the Netherlands, Venice, and Ragusa are exemplars of such small, city-centred, republican, and commercial states.[27]

In the *capitalized coercion mode*, finally, we find a blend of capital and coercive resources which could be mobilized. In this setting of a more even balance between capital and coercion, rulers "spent more of their effort than did their capital-intensive neighbors on incorporating capitalists and sources of capital directly into the structures of their states. Holders of capital and coercion interacted on terms of relative equality".[28] In England, for example, "[t]he commercialization of both urban and rural economies meant that taxation and borrowing for war went more easily, and with less state apparatus, than in many other European countries".[29] At the same time, however, this easy access to capital went hand in hand with a heavy reliance of the state on landlords for day-to-day (local) government of the realm which resulted in constraining *royal* autonomy but fortifying *state* power. In comparison, France's less capitalized and commercialized economy led to the build-up of a significantly bulkier central state apparatus than in England as a result of the endeavour to mobilize resources for the conduct of wars. In these two countries, as well as in Spain (after the merger of the more commercial Crown of Aragon with the more coercive-based Crown of Castilian) and in Prussia (after the acquisition of its Rhineland territories), "the coincidence of coercive centers with centers of capital facilitated – at least for a while – the creation of massive military force in a time when large, expensive, well-armed armies and navies gave those national states that were able to create them the overwhelming advantage in the search for hegemony and empire".[30]

The combination of a high degree of military power in external geopolitical relations of violence with a high level of infrastructural penetration of a commercialized economy gave the states in the capitalized coercion mode a competitive advantage within the state system. They out-performed, through greater efficiency and war-making capacity on the basis of a close "organic unity" (Mann) between state and dominant classes, all political structures which could not rely on access to both commercial and coercive resource mobilization and extraction. Since the eighteenth century, they thus ushered in a period of convergence of the various political structural forms on this type of state.

Tilly's explanation of state formation could be faulted on many accounts. Goldstone, for example, pointed out that "England's state was arguably shaped more by the Reformation (in 1531–34), by conflict over the religion of the dynasty (in 1688–89), and by conflict over the state between landlords and non-landlords (in 1828–32) than by military exigencies".[31] He also noted that though German unification in the nineteenth century could be told as the story of Prussia's growing military advantage, this was not the case in Italy where unification depended much more on domestic nationalist movements. In any case, why do "ideological" issues play no role in Tilly's accounts: religion (e.g. the Reformation) or nationalism? Why no discussion of the state-making impact of revolutions? On the other hand, Tilly's central argument that states depend on economic resources provided by dominant classes; that the most powerful national states depend particularly on capital resources and thus on capitalist development; and that the closer (or more "organic") the cooperation between states and capitalists the greater the ease with which resources can be extracted and mobilized, is well developed and finds support in Mann's analyses. Tilly's distinction between three paths to state formation is thus a useful starting point for a more detailed analysis of the European-wide experience of state formation.

In their discussion of state formation, both Mann and Tilly focused on the relations of states with each other in a multipolar state system and the relations of states with their dominant (and, in the case of Tilly, subordinate) classes. Neither of them analysed in any detail class relations and the structure and effect of trans- and inter-national economic relations on state formation processes. However, as Perry Anderson had earlier demonstrated, a concern with the effects of class relations on political structures had not necessarily to result in economic determinism.[32]

Analysing the "Lineages of the Absolutist State" in Western and Eastern Europe, Anderson argued, on the one hand, that they had to be located in the structure of class relations. In Western Europe, the "crisis of feudalism", as reflected in changes in the forms of feudal exploitation such as the substitution of money-rent for labour rent and rent in kind as the dominant groundrent, changed the forms of the feudal state. The disintegration of feudalism at the "molecular" level of the manor/village resulted in the displacement of political-legal power upwards to the "national" level. The absolutist state acquired many of the political-legal powers of the feudal landlords and became "a redeployed and recharged apparatus of feudal domination, designed to clamp the peasant masses back into their traditional social position".[33] Anderson thus characterized absolutism in Western Europe as the appropriate form of aristocratic domination in an epoch of transition to the predominance of the capitalist mode of production. In Eastern Europe, however, absolutism developed well before capitalism had spread beyond the River Elbe. Here, it was the constant seigneurial preoccupation with preventing labour mobility which lay behind much of the internal drift towards absolutism.[34] Yet, as Anderson was at pains to demonstrate, the development and structural peculiarities of Eastern absolutism could only be fully explained if the international state system in the seventeenth century, and in particular the expansionism of Sweden between 1630 and 1720, was taken into account: "It was the international pressure of Western

Absolutism, the political apparatus of a more powerful feudal aristocracy, ruling more advanced societies, which obliged the Eastern nobility to adopt an equivalently centralized state machine, to survive."[35]

Anderson thus combined class analysis with the analysis of the structure and dynamics of the international system. And Anderson was adamant that the interactions between East and West in those centuries was first and foremost political and military, rather than economic.[36] He thus took issue with Immanuel Wallerstein who, in focusing on the structure and dynamics of the European world-economy, interpreted the political institutional changes in the East as an effect of the penetration of the more advanced economic systems of the West into Eastern Europe.

Wallerstein discussed European state formation as an effect of the emergence and development of the capitalist world-economy since the "long" sixteenth century.[37] He conceptualized the state as dependent on economic and class forces operating on both the "national" and "world" level. According to Wallerstein, the structure and development of the political institutions are determined by the position of the respective countries within the international division of labour and by their function for the world market. He argued that in capitalism economic production is geared towards the realization of profit on the market. Oriented in its activities towards the world-economy, the capitalist class endeavours to exert political power to eliminate market competition and turns to the state to demand the establishment of market constraints by state intervention: "The states are created institutions reflecting the needs of class forces operating in the world-economy".[38] For state intervention on the world market to be successful the state apparatuses must have different strength. The higher the convergence of interests within the capitalist class from early on in its development, the stronger the state apparatuses.[39]

Wallerstein argued that the capitalist world-economy requires such an unequal distribution of state-constituted political-military institutions, since this allowed for a coerced transfer of the economic surplus from "peripheral" economies to the "core" of the world-economy through political-military power:

[I]f there is to be a multitude of political entities . . . then it cannot be the case that all these entities be equally strong. For if they were, they would be in a position of blocking the effective operation of transnational economic entities whose locus were in another state. It would then follow that the world division of labor would be impeded, the world-economy decline, and eventually the world-system fall apart. It also cannot be that no state machinery is strong. For in such a case, the capitalist strata would have no mechanisms to protect their interests, guaranteeing property rights, assuring various monopolies, spreading losses among larger population, etc.[40]

The "conditio sine qua non" of the existence of the modern world-system is therefore the development of relatively strong state apparatuses in the "core" of the world-economy, and relatively weak ones in the "periphery". Historically, however, this was evidently not the case. In 1550, the Netherlands, Northern Italy, and parts of Southern Germany were situated in the "core" of the European world-economy; but they did not have a strong state-machinery. In 1700, Prussia, Austria, and Sweden had strong state apparatuses, but did not belong to the centre of the world-economy.[41] Furthermore, how can we explain the strong Prussian state and the weak and highly fragmented state in Poland, both "peripheral" countries? Why did the Netherlands, England, and France – each of them a "strong" state in the core of the world-economy – develop different sets of political institutions? None of these problems can be sufficiently well explained within the functionalist framework of Wallerstein's world-system theory.

In this world system approach, then, it is argued that there is a coincidence of political and economic processes on the nation-state level and a correspondence of the international economic and international political systems on the "world level".[42] The case for such a congruence is argued by contending that economic differentiation within the world economy distributes unequally the potential for resources that can be mobilized by different state apparatuses. It thereby creates differential power capacities and stratifies the international political system accordingly.

The nub of this argument is the contention, first, that the fundamental connection between the parts of the world system is purely economic, and, secondly, that the domestic economy and/or the international economic positions of states determine their military strengths and international strategic importance.[43] The international system is primarily a world economy and owes its existence to the development and dynamics of capitalism. Since economic strength determines military strength it is futile to analyse the state or state formation from a geopolitical perspective. No additional piece of information could be gained from the geopolitical approach.[44]

Wallerstein's analysis thus forcefully raises the issue of the adequate level of analysis. For Wallerstein, the adequate analytical level is the capitalist world-economy and its specific division of labour. Bendix, Mann, and Tilly, on the other hand, would agree with Theda Skocpol that "[s]tates necessarily stand at the intersections between domestic sociopolitical orders and the transnational relations within which they must manoeuvre for survival and advantage in relation to other states".[45] For Bendix, as we have seen earlier, it is the location of states within an international system that facilitates the "intellectual mobilization" of modernizing elites on the basis of the international diffusion of ideas and values – though Bendix also accepts the validity of geopolitical approaches. For Tilly, it is the location of states within the geopolitical structure of the interstate system; and for Mann, it is the overlapping, intersecting and crosscutting ideological, economic, political and military power networks with their heterogeneous and disparate geographical and social reach. All these approaches share the view that political structures are not self-contained and evolutionary entities, but that, in order to understand their form and transformation, they have to be placed within specific interactive networks. The writing of the histories of the formation of national states in Europe is, of necessity, the writing of European, if not "world", history.

3   State formation and social discipline

In recent years, analyses of the interconnection between state formation and capitalist development were complemented by inquiries into the connection between state formation and the formation of a disciplinary society and disciplined subjects.[46] Max Weber had already discussed the connection between discipline and modernity in great detail in his studies on the sociology of religion. Pivotal to his discussion was his interpretation of ascetic Protestantism as a religious ethic which demanded "the disciplining and methodical organization of conduct".[47] The ethic of ascetic Protestantism led to the rejection of the world as an incomplete and contingent place. The form taken by the Puritans' world-rejection was, however, one of active rational world-domination since it was within the world that the religious believers had to prove their worth. This notion promoted bureaucracy as the tool of an all-encompassing rationalism of world-domination.[48] The development of the modern state as a compulsory legal-bureaucratic association, as indeed the "modern" world in general, was seen as inherently bound up with a particular kind of (secularized) ethical world view. Weber thus focused on the causal significance of the ethic of ascetic Protestantism for the methodical self-control of one's own life as well as the "secularization" of this religious ethic which allowed for all kinds of social relationships to become disciplined and organized.[49]

But the origins of modern discipline have also been located in structures and processes that had little do with a particular religious ethic. Such alternatives to the Weberian account were put forward by, for example, Norbert Elias and Michel Foucault. Both of them saw the rise of "disciplinary society" as related to the formation of the state. For Elias, the "civilizing process", which involved a transformation of violent bodies into restrained bodies, was closely bound up with the pacification of social space through the monopolization of physical violence by the state. According to Elias, such pacification allows for (geographically) ever larger and (socially) ever closer webs of interdependencies in which individuals are enmeshed. This lengthening of the social chains as well as the concomitant advance in the social division of functions make it ever more advantageous, and increasingly necessary, for individuals not to give way to spontaneous impulses and emotions, but rather to restrain their affects and exercise foresight and self-control in order to secure their social existence. In a society in which more and more people must attune their conduct to that of others, social integration is premised on the exercise of this self-control.[50]

In his study on the French "Court Society" of Louis XIV, Elias analysed this "civilizing process" paradigmatically.[51] Once physical violence had been concentrated in the monarchical ruler, the belligerent knight whose life, prestige and power had previously depended upon a disposition to aggressive behaviour and violent self-defence was transformed into the carpet-knight of court society whose battle grounds were the halls of the royal palace and the salon of the most distinguished peers. There he had to use the quill and eloquence as his weapons and his social position depended upon the suppression (or the stilted expression) of emotions and the cool calculation of the motives behind the behaviour of his competitors at court. The resultant "civilized" behaviour of the "established" aristocracy was emulated by the bourgeois middle-classes in an attempt thereby to overcome their "outsider" position. Through this process of imitation, the ideal of the disciplined and self-constrained individual spread beyond the confines of the court into society at large.

In Elias's analysis, the monopolization of physical violence by the state in the process of the formation of the modern state is thus the condition without which the formation of the self-constrained individual and the "disciplinary society" would be impossible. But Elias's emphasis on *self*-constraint makes it evident that he does not attribute causal power to the state in these processes. Michel Foucault, on the other hand, discussed the formative processes of the modern discipline in the sixteenth and seventeenth centuries through an analysis of the "secular political pastorate".[52] He showed that, when discussing the nature of the art of government, Plato in "The Statesman" denied that the ruler's art was like the shepherd's who cared for each individual sheep in his flock: "[T]he men who hold power are not to be shepherds. Their task doesn't consist in fostering the life of a group of individuals. It consists in forming and assuring the city's unity. In short, the political problem is that of the relation between the one and the many in the framework of the city and its citizens."[53] Greek politics chooses the game of citizen and laws because the ruler's knowledge and attentiveness could never extend so far as to minister to each individual. It is only in the modern state that the pastoral problem, which concerns the lives of individuals, is appropriated by the state and the two games – the city-citizen game and the shepherd-flock game – are combined.[54] The state becomes "a knowing state" (Thuau), developing a bureaucratic passion for exhaustive information in pursuit of its own autonomous power-political self-interests: "Government is only possible if the strength of the state is known; it can thus be sustained. The state's capacity, and the means to enlarge it, must be known. The strength and capacities of the other states must also be known."[55] This knowledge extends to the individual whose personal conduct and its manipulation become – as a potential resource of state strength – the concern of the pastoral state.

For Foucault, the pastoral state was implicated in the process which resulted in social order being based, not on the exercise of hierarchical, sovereign power of the "Leviathan" which externally constrained and restrained the subjects, but on the exercise of lateral, decentred *"disciplinary power"* which produced the self-managing citizen through the internalization of constraint.[56] He argued that increasingly social order was not primarily secured through overt violence and coercion but through a micro-politics of discipline targeted at particular individuals or collections of individuals whereby they were morally regulated into conformity and normality.[57] This disciplinary power, which resulted in a trans-formation of our sense and experience of "self", worked through institutions such as asylums, prisons, schools, universities, factories but also the confession and later the capitalist work organization and bureaucracies. Implicated in these disciplinary processes were the discursive formations of criminology, penology, sociology and other "social" and human sciences as the emergent new forms of knowledge which were, in turn, propelled forward in the process of exercising disciplinary power.[58] Whereas "disciplinary power" was directed towards a disciplining of individuals and their constitution as docile bodies, *"bio-power"* was directed towards the regulation and control of populations, their biological reproduction in time and their dispersal in space. This power focused on all conditions affecting the biological processes of life and thus operated through regulatory controls of reproduction and fertility, public health and hygiene, housing conditions, death, epidemics etc.[59] Behind these concerns with the body – the body of individuals and the body of populations – lay, according to Foucault, the eighteenth-century demographic upswing in Western Europe. The biological traits of a population became relevant factors for economic management, and it became necessary to organize around them an apparatus which would ensure not only their subjection but also the constant increase in their utility.[60]

Foucault was loath to identify a "subject" or agency behind the formation of the disciplinary society. Though implicated in these formative processes, the state is by no means seen as the dominant force: "the State, for all the omnipotence of its apparatuses, is far from being able to occupy the whole field of actual power relations . . . The State is superstructural in relation to a whole series of power networks that invest the body, sexuality, the family, kinship, knowledge, technology and so forth."[61] Thus, power hovers everywhere and underlies everything, but has no causal agent. But Foucault's insistence on eschewing any notion of historical causation strikes me as theoretically and empirically unwarranted.

One way of illustrating this criticism is by translating Foucault's terminology into a more familiar vocabulary. The more familiar denotation of the "secular political pastorate" is, of course, the "well-ordered police state".[62] As is well known, in the course of the sixteenth century, the term "police" came to indicate one of the major tasks of government: the ruling authorities claimed a general competence in the combating of all social disorders for which existing law and custom did not provide a remedy. In continental Europe, the police ordinances of the sixteenth and early seventeenth centuries aimed to restore the "good old order" which had been destabilized by urbanization, monetarization of the economy and religious conflicts. In the period of reconstruction after the breakdown of political, economic and religious order during the Thirty Years' War, the state's aim of achieving financial strength through economic growth gained priority over the maintenance of the old order. The state now aimed to manipulate and mobilize all sections of society in order to enhance and efficiently utilize the economic potential of the country. In order to achieve or retain "Great Power" status, and thus due to geopolitical constraints, rulers had to generate economic growth which could then be channelled into the build-up of standing armies and the conduct of military campaigns. In their efforts to increase the economic wealth of the state, governments strove to "police" their subjects. This involved the monitoring and surveillance of the population as well as mercantilistic policies. But, as Oestreich pointed out, it also became a major concern of this new type of state to educate its people "to a discipline of work and frugality and (to change) the spiritual, moral and psychological make-up of political, military and economic man".[63] This new man (or woman) was ideally conceived as a human agent capable of remaking him/herself by methodical and disciplined action, endowed, therefore, with the ability "to take an instrumental stance to one's given properties, desires, inclinations, tendencies, habits of thought and feeling, so that they can be *worked on*, doing away with some and strengthening others, until one meets the desired specification".[64]

It is thus perfectly possible to identify causal forces behind the formation of the secular political pastorate and the disciplinary society. As I presented the argument, the state as a geopolitical actor was instrumental in transforming society as well as "producing" disciplined and self-controlled individuals. Anthony Giddens has pursued this line of analysis further and shown how the regularized gathering, storage, and control of information applied to administrative ends had increased since the nineteenth century and how the nation-state achieved societal integration through surveillance.[65] State formation and the growth of the state thus manifest themselves in the expansion of the surveillance capacities of state organizations. As a matter of fact, it is only since the increase in these surveillance capacities that a legitimate monopoloy of violence within a given territory could really be achieved, rather than only claimed by the pre-modern state.

Notwithstanding the criticisms waged against Foucault, we should acknowledge that his approach sensitizes us to the fact that the state is not just to be analysed as a particular kind of organization that operates on the basis of claims to legitimate rule and which, ultimately, backs up these claims through the exercise of the means of coercion. Foucault's perspective invites us to perceive the state rather as a colonizing force, shaping our subjectivities and collective identities through its activities: the state resides within our selves. Hence, it opens up the possibility of analysing the formation of, for example, gender identities as embedded in the processes of state formation. More generally, in this perspective we would have to write the history of the formation of the modern state as the history of the "etatization of the self".

Notes

1. Most of the analyses by historical social scientists were formulated on the basis of a comparative case studies approach. This research design is possibly the biggest bone of contention between them and mainstream historians. After all, a comparison embarked upon in order to strengthen causal explanations presupposes shared properties of the compared cases; thus, despite the specific time and place setting of individual instances, they are not considered to be that "unique" or idiosyncratic as to make a comparison for explanatory purposes impossible. For an introduction to historical social science cf. P. Abrams, *Historical sociology*, New Shipton Mallet, 1982; T. Skocpol

(ed.), *Vision and method in historical sociology*, Cambridge, 1984; on comparative method cf. also R. Axtmann, "'Society', globalization and the comparative method", *History of the Human Sciences* 6, 1993.

2. M. Weber, *Economy and society*, Berkeley, 1968, vol. I, chapter 3; vol. II, chapters 10–16.

3. Weber, *Economy and society*, vol. II, p. 948.

4. M. Weber, Politics as a vocation, in H. H. Gerth and C. Wright Mills (eds), *From Max Weber. Essays in sociology*, London, 1967, p. 82; cf. Weber, *Economy and society*, vol. I, p. 54.

5. For an account of Weber's analysis of state development cf. R. Axtmann, The formation of the modern state. A reconstruction of Max Weber's arguments, *History of political thought*, 11, 1990, pp. 295–312; for a Weberian analysis of state formation cf. G. Poggi, *The development of the modern state*, Stanford, 1978, and G. Poggi, *The state: its nature, development and prospects*, Oxford, 1990.

6. R. Bendix, *Nation-building and citizenship*, Berkeley, 1977, p. 2.

7. St. Rokkan, *Citizens, elections, parties*, Oslo, 1970, p. 52.

8. R. Bendix, *Kings or people: power and the mandate to rule*, Berkeley, 1978.

9. M. Mann, *Sources of social power*, Cambridge, 1986, vol. I, p. 481.

10. Mann, *Sources*, p. 482.

11. M. Mann, The autonomous power of the state: its origins, mechanisms and results, in M. Mann, *States, war and capitalism*, Oxford, 1988, pp. 1–32.

12. Mann, Autonomous power, pp. 7–9.

13. There is, of course, a huge literature on the transition from feudalism to capitalism, mainly from within Marxist historiography. If state forms are discussed at all in this literature, then the attention focuses typically on the class character of absolutism; cf. the discussion of these debates in R. J. Holton, *The transition from feudalism to capitalism*, London, 1985.

14. See, above all, J. A. Hall, Capstones and organisms: political forms and the triumph of capitalism, *Sociology*, 19, 1985, pp. 173–92; *Powers and liberties. The causes and consequences of the rise of the West*, Harmondsworth, 1986; States and economic development: reflections on Adam Smith, in J. A. Hall (ed.), *States in history*, Oxford, 1986, pp. 154–76; War and the rise of the West, in C. Creighton and M. Shaw (eds), *The sociology of war and peace*, Macmillan, 1987, pp. 37–53; States and societies: the miracle in comparative perspective, in J. Baechler et al. (eds), *Europe and the rise of capitalism*, Oxford, 1988, pp. 20–38.

15. M. Mann, European development: approaching a historical explanation, in J. Baechler et al. (eds), *Europe and the rise of capitalism*, Oxford, 1988, pp. 12–13.

16. Mann, European development, p. 13.
17. This argument had already been advanced by Max Weber, cf. R. Collins, *Weberian sociological theory*, Cambridge, 1986, pp. 42–3.
18. Mann, *Sources*, p. 511.
19. Mann, *Sources*, p. 514.
20. Mann, European development, p. 11.
21. O. Hintze, *Staat und Verfassung. Gesammelte Abhandlungen zur allgemeinen Verfassungsgeschichte*, Göttingen, 1970, pp. 34 ff., 55, 83, 480.
22. Cf. for example, C. Tilly, War making and state making as organized crime, in P. Evans et al. (eds), *Bringing the state back in*, Cambridge, 1985, pp. 169–91.
23. C. Tilly, *Coercion, capital and European states, A.D. 990–1990*, Oxford, 1990. Tilly (*Coercion*, p. 2) defines national states as "states governing multiple contiguous regions and their cities by means of centralized, differentiated, and autonomous structures".
24. Tilly, *Coercion*, p. 15.
25. In this chapter, I do not discuss Tilly's analyses of violent collective action and its connection with state formation; cf. for example, C. Tilly, *The contentious French*, Cambridge, 1986.
26. Tilly, *Coercion*, p. 142.
27. Tilly, *Coercion*, pp. 30, 90, 150–1.
28. Tilly, *Coercion*, p. 30.
29. Tilly, *Coercion*, p. 159.
30. Tilly, *Coercion*, p. 159.
31. J. Goldstone, States making wars making states making wars, *Contemporary Sociology*, 20, 1991, pp. 177.
32. P. Anderson, *Lineages of the absolutist state*, London, 1974; cf. also C. Mooers, *The making of bourgeois Europe*, London, 1991, who applies Robert Brenner's "political accumulation" model to explain state formation and capitalism in England, France and Prussia; cf. R. Brenner, Agrarian class structure and economic development in pre-industrial Europe, in T. H. Ashton and C. H. E. Philpin (eds), *The Brenner debate*, Cambridge, 1987, pp. 10–63.
33. Anderson, *Lineages*, p. 18.
34. Anderson, *Lineages*, p. 208.
35. Anderson, *Lineages*, pp. 197–8.
36. Anderson, *Lineages*, p. 197.
37. I. Wallerstein, *The modern world system. Capitalist agriculture and the origins of the European world-economy in the sixteenth-century*, New York, 1974.
38. I. Wallerstein, The state in the vortex of the capitalist world-economy, *International Social Science Journal*, 32, 1980, pp. 743–51.

39. According to Wallerstein, a state is strong if and when it is capable of defending the interests of its "owners-producers" class: I. Wallerstein, *The modern world system: mercantilism and the consolidation of the European world-economy, 1600–1750*, New York, 1980, pp. 112–14.
40. Wallerstein, *Modern world system*, 1974, p. 354.
41. P. Gourevitch, The international system and regime formation. A critical review of Anderson and Wallerstein, *Comparative Politics* 10, 1978, pp. 423–4.
42. C. Chase-Dunn, Interstate system and capitalist world-economy. One logic or two ?, in W. Ladd Hollist and J. N. Rosenau (eds), *World system structure. Continuity and change*, Beverly Hills, 1981, pp. 30–53.
43. Wallerstein, *Modern world system*, 1974, p. 15.
44. For a sustained critique of this position from a geopolitical perspective cf. A. Zolberg, Strategic interactions and the formation of modern states, *International Social Science Journal*, 32, 1980, pp. 687–716; Origins of the modern world system, *World Politics*, 33, 1981, pp. 253–81; 'World' and 'system': a misalliance, in W. H. Thompson (ed.), *Contending approaches to world system analysis*, Beverly Hills, 1983, pp. 269–90.
45. T. Skocpol, Bringing the state back in: strategies of analysis in current research, in P. Evans et al. (eds), *Bringing the state back in*, Cambridge, 1985, p. 8. This hypothesis also informed Skocpol's study on modern revolutions: *States and social revolutions: a comparative analysis of France, Russia and China*, Cambridge, 1979. One of the most prominent sociologists who shares this position, but who has not been discussed in this chapter, is Anthony Giddens, *The nation-state and violence*, Oxford, 1985.
46. Cf. R. van Krieken, Social discipline and state formation. Weber and Oestreich on the historical sociology of subjectivity, *Amsterdams Sociologisch Tijdschrift*, 17, 1990, pp. 3–28; The organization of the soul: Elias and Foucault on discipline and the self, *Arch. europ. sociol.*, 31, 1990, pp. 354–71.
47. Weber, *Economy and society*, vol. II, p. 556.
48. Weber, *Economy and society*, vol. II, pp. 601, 975.
49. Cf. S. Breuer, Die Evolution der Disziplin, *Kölner Zeitschrift für Soziologie und Sozialpsychologie*, 30, 1978, pp. 409–37; C. Gordon, The soul of the citizen: Max Weber and Michel Foucault on rationality and government, in S. Whimster and S. Lash (eds), *Max Weber, rationality and modernity*, London, 1987, pp. 293–316.
50. N. Elias, *State formation and civilization*, Oxford, 1982, pp. 229–50.
51. N. Elias, *The court society*, Oxford, 1983.
52. M. Foucault, Omnes et Singulatim: toward a criticism of "political reason", in S. McMurrin (ed.), *The Tanner lectures on human values*

(1981), Salt Lake City, 1981, pp. 223–54.
53. Foucault, Omnes, p. 235.
54. Foucault, Omnes, p. 239.
55. Foucault, Omnes, p. 245; Thuau is quoted by: C. Gordon, Governmental rationality: an introduction, in G. Burchell et al. (eds), *The Foucault effect: studies in governmentality*, London, 1991, p. 9.
56. Krieken, Organisation, pp. 354–60.
57. M. Foucault, *The history of sexuality, Vol. I: an introduction*, London, 1979, p. 139.
58. M. Foucault, *Power/Knowledge: selected interviews and other writings, 1972–1977*, Brighton, 1980, p. 59.
59. Foucault, *Power/Knowledge*, pp. 124–5.
60. Foucault, *Power/Knowledge*, pp. 171–2; cf. also B. Smart, *Foucault, Marxism and critique*, London, 1984, pp. 90–118; Gordon, Soul, passim.
61. Foucault, *Power/Knowledge*, pp. 122, 60.
62. Cf. M. Raeff, *The well-ordered police state: social and institutional change through law in the Germanies and Russia, 1600–1800*, New Haven, 1983; G. Oestreich, *Neostoicism and the early modern state*, Cambridge, 1982; R. Axtmann, "Police" and the formation of the modern state. Legal and ideological assumptions on state capacity in the Austrian lands of the Habsburg Empire, 1500–1800, *German History*, 10, 1992, pp. 39–61.
63. Oestreich, *Neostoicism*, p. 159. As the title of Oestreich's book already indicates, he attributed great importance to the influence of Neostoicism among Europe's ruling elites when explaining the formation of this discipline and self-control.
64. C. Taylor, *Sources of the self: the making of the modern identity*, Cambridge, 1989, pp. 159–60.
65. Giddens, *Nation-state*, chapter 7; C. Dandeker, *Surveillance, power and modernity*, Oxford, 1990.

CHAPTER THREE

Elite resistance to state formation: the case of Italy[1]

Lucy Riall

I

The unification of Italy in 1860 was seen by European liberals as a great victory. Hailed by Gladstone as "the most stupendous fabric that had ever been erected on the basis of human integrity in any age or country of the world", national unification symbolized the triumph of liberty, rationality and progress over the despotism and corruption of Italy's restoration states.[2] For many, the establishment of a nation state in Italy by liberal Piedmont was the fulfilment of all the ideals and aspirations of Italy's *Risorgimento*. It emphasized the increasing legitimacy and centrality of nationalist movements within European politics. One of liberal Italy's "creators", Giuseppe Garibaldi, became an international celebrity, the inspiration for elaborate mythologies and the object of mass adulation.

Liberalism and nationalism's victorious moment in 1860 was, however, short-lived and Italian unification came to disappoint those who had celebrated it so loudly. The death in June 1861 of Italy's first prime minister Camillo Cavour, regarded as the architect of national unity, seems in retrospect to have closed definitively the "heroic" phase of the Risorgimento. By the time of his death, the fragmentation of his politically expedient but fragile liberal coalition had already begun. In April 1861, he clashed violently with Garibaldi in the Italian Parliament over the reorganization of the army and over the status within it of Garibaldi's volunteers. National unification was still incomplete in 1861: Rome and the Veneto were under the sovereignty of foreign powers, and much of Southern Italy was in a state of open civil war. In addition, the enormous problems of administrative unification prevented any normalization of political life. Finally, significant regional disparaties in economic development retarded the formation of a national market.

Attempts by the Italian government to resolve these problems after 1861 drew little praise from liberals. Ignominious military defeat marred the acquisition of the Veneto in 1866, and the seizure of Rome from the Pope in 1871 cemented rather than resolved the damaging rift between Church and State. The disastrous situation in Southern Italy was also never satisfactorily resolved. Instead the repeated use of exceptional legislation and military powers left an additional and enduring legacy of bitterness and mistrust. Slow economic growth and high taxation were the unpopular consequences of the government's attempts to balance the budget.

However, perhaps the biggest problems of all stemmed from the character and conduct of government itself. The process of administrative unification was imposed rapidly between 1861 and 1865 without consulting local or regional interests. The political structures of liberal Italy were regarded as centralized and authoritarian. Parliament was also elected on a very narrow suffrage and this reflected and contributed to the narrowness of Italy's political class. In addition, effective political change or innovation was made difficult by the use of parliamentary tactics such as *trasformismo*, whereby political rivals were bought off or "transformed" into clients. Entrenched political interests thus frustrated the development of a more open system. Italy's political class became, in this way, cut off from the rest of society. The *paese legale* was, in the Italian senator Stefano Jacini's memorable phrase, removed from the *paese reale*.[3] As a result, the diplomatic, religious, administrative and economic problems facing the Italian government after unification were accompanied and compounded by an apparently intractable crisis of legitimacy.

Nowhere was this crisis of legitimacy more acute than in Southern Italy. Garibaldi's victories over the Bourbon army in the South during the summer of 1860 had been based on, and in turn encouraged, nationalist fervour for Italian unity and popular agitation for social and economic change. At the same time, the collapse of the Bourbon government in Naples left a political and administrative vaccuum which Garibaldi and his supporters were able to take advantage of but were also unable to fill. Popular revolution and administrative crisis, combined with Garibaldi's declared intention to march on Rome at the head of a mass army, provoked an alarmed Piedmontese government to intervene against Garibaldi. Italian unification can thus be seen as, on the one hand, the product of Piedmont's intervention in the South in order to secure and safeguard its hard won domination of Northern Italy. On the other hand, however, Italian unification was also the product of an upsurge in national/popular agitation and of the collapse of an old system of government in Southern Italy. This combination of a dynastic and nationalist war directed from above, popular upheaval from below and state crisis may have produced the great liberal triumphs of 1860 but it also produced many of the disasters which followed. It is thus hardly surprising that it was in the South that the imposition of liberal government after 1860 was to meet its greatest challenge.

II

If liberal Italy disappointed its supporters by failing to live up to the ideals of the Risorgimento, this disappointment has proved an endless source of interest and debate for historians. In many ways the historiography of Italian unification is national history *par excellence*. First, it has tended to focus almost exclusively on Italian developments rather than considering the broader process of national unification and state formation elsewhere in Europe. The unique nature of Italy's experience in the nineteenth and early twentieth centuries has always been taken for granted. Categories, such as *Risorgimento* and *trasformismo*, used to describe this experience stress the "peculiarities" of Italian history and make it more difficult to develop meaningful comparisons with other countries.

In addition, the national and nationalist history of the Risorgimento has always dominated the history of nineteenth-century Italy. An implicit Whiggish emphasis within the historiography of this period has tended, at least until quite recently, to focus only on those "progressive" forces within Italian political life and to see national unification as its culminating achievement, however disappointing. Moreover, the historical controversies surrounding the Risorgimento and national unification have become inseparable from the circumstances of Italy's later development. National unification is thus assessed on the basis of Italy's subsequent political stability, its struggles to attain Great Power status or to achieve a level of economic growth comparable to its Northern European competitors. And overshadowing all assessments of Italy's liberal and national Risorgimento in the nineteenth century is the liberal state's eventual collapse into the violence and illiberalism of the fascist regime after 1922.[4]

An emphasis on the special circumstances of Italy's historical development in the nineteenth and early twentieth centuries, together with a preoccupation with the origins of the fascist regime, characterizes the Marxist approach to the Risorgimento and national unification. The essential parameters of this approach were established by the Marxist theorist and activist, Antonio Gramsci, in his *Prison Notebooks* which were published after the end of the Second World War.[5] Gramsci's notes on Italian history constitute undoubtedly the most significant and innovative contribution to post-war debates about the achievements of the Risorgimento and the nature of liberal Italy. Gramsci defined the Risorgimento as a "passive revolution", by which he meant both a revolution without mass participation and a revolution where change takes place gradually, or in what he called a "molecular" fashion.[6] Behind this experience of molecular, non-popular revolution lay, according to Gramsci, the actions of a weak and divided bourgeoisie unable to transcend its narrow "economic-corporate" interests and embody the interests and values of Italy's "subaltern classes" (and particularly the peasantry).

This failure to establish what Gramsci called a "hegemonic" alliance with the Italian popular classes meant that the Italian bourgeoisie was also unable to overthrow the existing social order and establish itself as the new ruling class. The Italian bourgeoisie, Gramsci wrote, "was incapable of uniting the people around itself, and this was the cause of its defeats and the interruptions of its development".[7] The hegemony of the Italian bourgeoisie was, in Gramsci's view, manifested only in the subordination of the radical republican or "Action" party (led by Mazzini) to the moderate liberals led by Cavour. This achievement, which Gramsci (in a direct reference to the later practice of Italian governments) calls *trasformismo*, involved the "absorption" of the most progressive section of the Italian bourgeoisie by the most conservative and feudal. This tactical defeat of the more revolutionary Mazzinians effectively neutralized the only group capable of establishing a hegemonic alliance with the mass of the population and thus of accomplishing a revolutionary transformation which was "active" rather than "passive". Instead, the Cavourian moderate liberals reached a compromise with the existing order to produce an amalgam of feudalism and capitalism, and what Gramsci called a "bastardized" political structure. In such circumstances, social revolution was feared rather than led: popular unrest was repressed rather than directed.

As a result of the class alliances entered into by the moderate liberals, or *Destra Storica* (Historic Right) as they were called after unification, bourgeois rule in Italy was characterized by "domination" (political and coercive control) rather than "hegemony" (intellectual, moral and cultural leadership). The Risorgimento could be seen as an incomplete, or even failed, bourgeois revolution, which was more authoritarian than popular. And, according to Gramsci, it was to this failure that the shortcomings of liberal Italy ("the paltry political life from 1870 to 1900, the fundamental and endemic rebelliousness of the Italian popular classes, the narrow and stunted existence of a sceptical and cowardly ruling stratum") could be attributed.[8]

Gramsci's use of a class analysis to explain united Italy's failure to live up to liberal expectations was hugely influential. During the 1950s and '60s, a new generation of Marxist historians inspired by Gramsci's writings developed a comprehensive critique of Italian liberalism.[9] The political struggle between moderates and democrats were re-examined in the light of Gramsci's analysis. Studies undertaken by historians such as Franco della Peruta and Giorgio Candeloro emphasized the tensions in the democratic movement's relationship with the peasantry and pointed out the democrats' inability to develop a coherent ideology or concrete revolutionary programme.[10] The significance of 1848–49 as a turning point in the Risorgimento, as the moment when the more revolutionary democrats lost ground to the more conservative moderates and the "passive revolution" became possible, was also stressed.

Gramsci's analysis of the process whereby both the economy and political life in Southern Italy were subordinated to the North in terms of a rural-urban divide (what he calls the "city-countryside relationship") also gave rise to significant research. National unification, specifically the union of South with the North, came to be understood as the counterpart to bourgeois rule in Italy, characterized by domination rather than hegemony. To put this in a more specific context, the *Destra Storica*'s "domination" of civil society was seen to correspond to the Piedmontese state's "domination" of Southern Italy. In this way, it could be argued that the popular revolution which took place in the South during 1860 had to be repressed by the Piedmontese army, since this popular revolution threatened a process of change (unification from above and by the North) which had hitherto been "passive".

A number of historical monographs dealing with the *Destra*'s policies in the South after unification also explored the extent of military repression and the government's repeated violation of constitutional guarantees. This repression of the Southern peasantry, and the corresponding rejection of demands for reform, was explained in terms of class relations.[11] Without any hegemony over Southern civil society, without any allies amongst the "subaltern classes", domination (or, more simply, repression) became the only option available. Moreover, it was argued, and here again Gramsci's suggestions were taken up and expanded, that the *Destra*'s repression of the Southern peasantry provided one basis for the alliance established in the 1880s between Southern landowners and Northern industrialists. This "historic bloc" provided institutional stability in liberal Italy at the expense of social and political reform.

In this way, the Southern experience of national unification was seen to be indicative of broader trends within Italian liberalism. The *Destra*'s treatment of the South could be shown to reflect the more generally authoritarian direction of policy after 1860, other symptoms of which included the rapid centralization of political institutions and the erosion of judicial independence. Indeed, it was argued that the domination of civil society by a coercive and increasingly corrupt state apparatus could be described as a liberal form of "dictatorship", a dictatorship devised to re-inforce control from the centre and prevent social change.[12]

The critique developed by Marxist historians on the basis of Gramsci's writings was part of a more general attack on the dominant position of liberal (meaning, in this context, right wing) historiography and liberal historians within the post-war Italian Republic. In his *Prison Notebooks*, Gramsci had explicitly engaged with and challenged the defence of Italian liberalism put forward by the liberal philosopher Benedetto Croce during the 1920s.[13] This dialogue was taken up by Croce's and Gramsci's successors. The post-war generation of Marxist historians challenged the liberal tendency to depict the advent of fascism as a historical accident: as an aberration produced by the emergency conditions prevailing during the First World War and, in its use of violence and one party dictatorship, as the antithesis of the parliamentary system of liberal Italy. Marxist historians argued instead that there were strong elements of continuity between the liberal and fascist periods. The repression and exceptional legislation of the liberal period clearly foreshadowed, it was argued, the fascists' systematic use of violence and coercion. On a more general level, it was also suggested that fascism could be conceptualized as an attempt by Italy's ruling class to restructure their hegemonic power, to create a new passive revolution in the aftermath of the First World War.[14] The success of the passive revolution in the nineteenth century thus created the conditions for and the necessity of a fascist "solution" in the twentieth.

The politicization of both historical debate and the historical profession in Italy reinforced the tendency for historians to talk past each other or to dismiss the arguments of the other side (a tendency not unknown elsewhere in Europe). This tendency may partially explain the neglect in Marxist accounts of the Risorgimento of the crucial role played by Great Power rivalry and by Austria's presence within the peninsula. For a focus on diplomacy, and on Italy's relations with the Great Powers, was long ago appropriated by the Right. In 1951, for example, the liberal historian Federico Chabod published a defence of liberal Italy which stressed the determining role played by foreign policy in the political decisions made by Cavour and his successors.[15] By contrast, Marxist historians always emphasized the primacy of internal, class-mediated, factors (the threat of peasant unrest in the South, the upsurge in Republicanism) in the government's decision to centralize Italy's political institutions.

Despite the historiographical and political issues which divide these two accounts of Italian unification, they both share a strongly national and particularist focus. It is thus interesting to note the similarity of these debates to debates about German liberalism. The emergence in the 1960s of a neo-Marxist modernization theory, which explained the process and outcome of German unification in terms of the bourgeoisie's weakness and the strength of old feudal structures, can also be seen in part as an attack by the Left on the entrenched power of the Right within the Federal Republic.[16] This class-based account of German unification resembles the Marxist approach to modern Italian history in significant ways. The turning point in German liberalism's fortunes is pinpointed at 1848–49, when the bourgeoisie suffered a historic defeat at the hands of the feudal aristocracy. The German bourgeoisie is blamed for this and subsequent defeats in terms which are strikingly similar to the Gramscian critique of the Italian middle classes. According to this account, the German bourgeoisie proved unable to transcend its narrow economic interests and failed to construct a coherent programme around which a revolutionary movement could be built.

German unification is thus seen as a failed bourgeois revolution: German liberals were out-manoeuvred by Bismarck and German unification, when it came, came from above. Bismarck's defeat of the liberals, and the liberals' accommodation with Bismarck, frustrated the development of parliamentary democracy in Germany. As a result, united Germany followed a "special road" ("*Sonderweg*") into the twentieth century, a road quite unlike that followed by Britain, France or other developing parliamentary democracies. The failure of German liberalism also provides the same element of continuity between the pre-war and fascist periods as it does in Italy. Although it is argued that the opposition to democracy came in Germany from pre-capitalist elements, rather than from sections of the bourgeoisie, the fundamental responsibility for fascism/Nazism in both cases is attributed to the progressive forces within the nation state. Class relations, and specifically the weakness of the bourgeoisie, account for both Italy's and Germany's deviation from the European liberal norm, and their common experience of fascism.

The Marxist account of German unification became the subject of vigorous debate in the 1980s with the publication of David Blackbourn and Geoffrey Eley's *The Peculiarities of German History*.[17] The authors identified a number of theoretical and empirical weaknesses in the *Sonderweg* thesis, some of which can also be found in the Marxist account of Italian unification. The first of these is the problem of ideal types. The model of a successful revolutionary party used by Gramsci in his scathing critique of Mazzini's Action Party is the Jacobin Party in the French Revolution. Not only, Gramsci wrote, did the Jacobins "organise a bourgeois government, i.e. make the bourgeoisie the dominant class – they did more. They created the bourgeois state, made the bourgeoisie the leading, hegemonic class of the nation, in other words, gave the new state a permanent basis and created the compact modern French nation."[18] It is thus by comparison with the French Revolution, that the Italian Risorgimento was a failure. Similarly, the bourgeois revolution in Germany is considered a failure when compared to the events in France. In many respects, however, this model of a successful bourgeois revolution is inadequate. It is now almost a historical commonplace that the French Revolution created nothing like a "compact modern nation", nor did it create a bourgeois state. It is hard to find evidence for the existence of a politically self-conscious bourgeoisie as depicted in these accounts.[19] If, as Geoffrey Eley has suggested, the successful bourgeois revolution which failed to occur in Germany (and Italy) failed to occur anywhere, then in this respect the German (and Italian) experiences did not deviate so substantially from the European liberal norm.

In identifying the Italian nation state as deviant (or at best a disappointment), Marxist historians have employed a second ideal type: that of British (or Anglo-Saxon) parliamentary democracy. Here again, the critique developed by Eley of German historiography is instructive. He suggests that the use of the British experience in the nineteenth century to measure the inadequacies of German liberalism involved a reading of the British past which is hard to sustain. He argues instead that the strength and solidarity of British liberals has been over-estimated. The success of the liberal party and liberal politics was always based on amalgam and compromise, especially in their Gladstonian heyday.[20] If this is true, then the Cavourian moderate liberals in Italy appear more typical than abnormal.

The assumption that a successful bourgeois revolution will always be liberal, and that the failure of liberalism necessarily means a failed bourgeois revolution, is also questionable. Eley suggests instead that the development of a capitalist mode of production and a bourgeois civil society can happen quite independently of a liberal parliamentary regime, and that this is precisely what did happen in Germany. Marxist accounts of the failure of a bourgeois revolution have, he argues, conflated two processes – the establishment of parliamentary democracy and the establishment of conditions for a capitalist mode of production – which are analytically and empirically quite distinct.

One of the bases of Blackbourn and Eley's critique of the *Sonderweg* thesis is thus a disagreement about the nature of historical causation. In much Marxist historiography of the Risorgimento, however, such a reductionist view of politics and ideology is less evident, perhaps because of Gramsci's own emphasis on political and cultural change. Nevertheless, an insistence that the structure of the Italian state reflected weaknesses in bourgeois civil society remains fundamental. Indeed, one area that has always been neglected in the Marxist approach to the Risorgimento is the Italian state. Since class relations and, specifically, the relationship between the Northern ruling class and the Southern peasantry are assigned a determining role in the troubled process of national unification, the existence of the state is taken for granted. The state, in this account, is seen as the political expression of bourgeois power, as the unproblematic vehicle of the Northern ruling class. Implicitly, therefore, an instrumentalist view of the state is adopted, where the ruling class controls the state and the state reflects the weakness of the ruling class.

It is precisely this view of a fundamental, unmediated link between the economic base and political superstructure which non-Marxist historians take issue with. The proliferation, during the last decade, of studies focusing on regional and local experiences of national government in Italy has in fact drastically altered historians' views of the Italian state. It now seems inaccurate to treat the Italian state in this period as a centralizing, monolithic entity, which expressed the interests of the ruling class. Rather, it is more helpful to see the process of state formation itself as problematic, undermined by institutional weaknesses, political conflicts and economic constraints. The capacity of the state to control or to "penetrate" society can be questioned too. Certainly there is now an abundance of evidence to suggest that this capacity was limited by the resistance of local elites, who were willing and able to frustrate the dictates of the central power.[21]

An instrumentalist view of the relationship between the ruling class and the Italian state after 1860 thus seem very hard to sustain. The relationship between the Italian ruling class and the Italian state was immensely complex. No simple state-society dichotomy can take account of this complexity, or of the blurring of boundaries between base and superstructure. Far from being the unproblematic political expression of Italy's ruling class, the new state actually had to struggle to assert its particular authority over a ruling class which was itself far from cohesive. In this process, as much recent research has indicated, political change and social change were inextricably intertwined. The next section of this chapter will attempt to examine these points in more detail.

III

The use of concepts of class (the rise of the bourgeoisie) or ideology (the triumph of liberalism over absolutism) to explain the unification of Italy has tended to obscure many political aspects of this process. Without discounting the role played by class tensions or ideological convictions, it is also helpful to look at national unification in Italy as part of a much longer process of state formation. In this way, it is possible to observe some of the striking continuities in the problems which Italy's rulers faced during the nineteenth century.

One of the challenges confronting the Italian restoration states after 1815 was the need to modernize their administrative structures and control all of their territories. It was a challenge which few of these states responded to effectively, hampered as they were by a resolute opposition to constitutionalism and other forms of political "modernization". The vulnerability of these states to pressure from the Great Powers further constrained their political development. Efforts made by the Bourbon government in Naples, for example, to attract internal support and stability by promoting economic development were frustrated by British merchants and by the British government, whose commercial interests were directly involved.[22] In retrospect, it can be argued that the restoration states' dependency on Austrian support for their internal political stability was also damaging. The presence of Austria in the peninsula may have prevented popular revolution but it did little to promote long-term stability. The ability of the restoration governments to rely on Austrian protection allowed them to ignore the impact of broader administrative, political and social changes which, elsewhere in Europe at this time, forced governments to modernize. Thus, no organic solution to the problems of restoration Italy ever developed.

The failure of restoration states in Italy to undergo a process of modernization and adaptation to changing circumstances had two important consequences. First, the administrative structures of these regimes became "fossilized", unable to respond to the deepening political and financial crises which affected them after 1849. Second, this institutional collapse was accompanied by a growing crisis of legitimacy. The economic policies pursued by the restoration states after 1849 were viewed as, at best, timid and, at worst, downright reactionary. Speaking very generally, the refusal to consider new forms of representation, together with the maintenance of an authoritarian line against expressions of dissent, also made the governments far more enemies than friends. Newly enriched members of the bourgeoisie were frustrated by their exclusion from decision-making in matters of economic policy, while many enlightened nobles were disturbed by the extent of political repression.[23]

The maintenance of absolutist systems of governments, unaltered for the most part since the 1830s, into the 1850s was fraught with difficulties. Moreover, in the absence of any effective form of representation or consultation, efforts at administrative reform or modernization often proved counter-productive. Administrative centralization encountered resistance and increased the government's unpopularity, particularly in regions such as Lucca, Genoa, Sicily and Lombardy where existing particularist (or nationalist) sentiment was very strong. Resentment of the centre fuelled the liberal/nationalist opposition movements intensifying political instability. The internal isolation of Italy's restoration states by the 1850s was mirrored by their growing international isolation. On the one hand, an increasingly liberal public opinion, most notably in Britain, denounced the governments of the Papal States, the Two Sicilies and Central Italy as obscurantist and reactionary. On the other, the declining influence of Austria between 1854 and 1859 deprived the restoration states of their one source of international support and of domestic stability.

The great liberal triumph of Piedmont in 1859–60 was due in part to the skill of its leaders in transcending the same crisis which destroyed the old regimes. Arguably one of the most unstable (and certainly one of the more reactionary) of the restoration states before the 1830s, thereafter Piedmont developed along different lines. The attractiveness of the Piedmontese "solution" to this crisis, first attempted half-heartedly during the reign of Carlo Alberto (1830–49) and brought off with energy and daring by Cavour in the 1850s, is obvious. The Piedmontese "solution", as Gramsci pointed out, represented an effective amalgam of old and new, a compromise between liberal demands and an absolutist administration. This compromise produced a form of conservative modernization which had eluded the other restoration states. By the mid-1850s, Piedmont possessed a liberal constitution with an independent parliament. It also possessed an efficient and centralized administration and a modern legal system, both based on the Napoleonic model. Cavour's government pursued a programme of state intervention to encourage economic growth through free trade and to build up a modern infrastructure. Finally, Cavour tirelessly promoted Piedmont's standing among the Great Powers. As a result, Piedmont was able to resist the combination of political opposition, international pressure and administrative collapse which proved so devastating elsewhere in Italy.

Piedmontese success thus rested on the twin tenets of a successful foreign policy and a programme of economic and political modernization. That the legitimacy of the Piedmontese "solution" within Italy (for instance, the ability of its leaders to attract the support of former democrats and republicans) rested on these achievements is, of course, well known. However, in order to explain the extraordinary events of 1859–60 it is necessary also to recognize that these achievements were inherently unstable. Thus, Cavour's notorious ruthlessness, and his reported near hysteria, during the crucial events of these two years were not simply the expression of a volatile personality but were also an indication of just how fragile were his and Piedmont's control over events. The alliance with France, and all the various concessions to Napoleon III, showed how vulnerable Piedmont still was to foreign pressure. The behaviour of the Piedmontese monarch during the war against Austria, and the Treaty of Villafranca itself, also showed how vulnerable Cavour's position was. And, at least from Cavour's point of view, the resurgence of republicanism in the South led by Garibaldi threatened to destroy the liberal-authoritarian compromise which had hitherto brought him such success.

After unification, as the introduction to this paper has already indicated, the domestic and foreign policy achievements of the Cavourian era proved almost impossible to sustain. Unlike Bismarckian Germany, for example, liberal Italy's foreign policy undermined rather than strengthened the new state's legitimacy. Added to this, the refusal of the Church even to recognize the

Kingdom of Italy was both a humiliation and a source of political weakness. Most of all, however, the political compromises which had produced such spectacular results in Piedmont were simply not adequate in the broader confines of the Italian nation state. One problem was that the new Italian government inherited in 1860 the administrative and political problems which had destabilized its predecessors. In many parts of Italy, most obviously in the South, it had actually to rebuild the now defunct administrations and establish new bases of legitimacy.

The administrative and political chaos in the South, and to a lesser extent elsewhere, was a major factor in Cavour's decision, (later confirmed by his successors), to complete national unification rapidly and on a very centralized basis. In this way, the need to extend the Piedmontese "solution" to the rest of Italy: to extend territorial control on the one hand, and the benefits of modern, liberal government on the other, was expressed through administrative "normalization". State formation was thus both the problem and the solution in completing the process of national unification. However, this decision created as many problems as it solved. A modern, centralized bureaucracy, and administrative "normality", requires substantial and constant economic resources. The new government of Italy in 1860 lacked anything like this level of economic resources. The cost of rapid economic growth in Piedmont, of the wars of independence and of amalgamating the national debts of all the restoration states, imposed enormous financial constraints. Put simply, for a long time after 1860 the government could not afford to implement either the kind of bureaucratic control of territory or the forms of liberal modernization which had proved so successful in Piedmont.

The ability of the government to extend bureaucratic control or "surveillance" throughout Italy was severely constrained in other ways too.[24] One administrative advantage enjoyed by the rulers of Piedmont, Tuscany and Lombardy since the late eighteenth century, but absent in the rest of Italy, was a modern network of roads. Equally, the rapid construction of railway lines and telegraph installations in Piedmont during the 1850s, a programme entirely lacking elsewhere in Italy, facilitated the growth of administrative power. Not only did these transport and communications networks promote economic modernization through access to foreign markets but they also made possible the systematic penetration of rural areas by the central power. The absence of modern communications in the Southern Papal States and the Kingdom of the Two Sicilies imposed significant limitations on the power of the central government, as a number of recent studies have indicated. After unification, lack of roads or railways were a major problem in controlling the spread of popular disorder (banditry, land occupations) in the South.[25] It was a major handicap in organizing the movement of security forces in rural areas and in bringing criminals to justice. It was also a significant problem in gathering information about local conditions, reinforcing an already high level of ignorance in the central government about the South. Infrastructural problems thus directly undermined the centralizing initiatives of the liberal government and allowed, in practice, a substantial amount of autonomy to emerge in local areas.

The lack of economic resources and of an adequate infrastructure might have been less important obstacles to state formation had there been a significant base of support for the liberal government in peripheral areas. Particularly important in this respect was the support of local power holders, those who dominated the economic, social and political life of a community and who constituted a vital mediating link in the administrative chain of command. In many areas of Italy, however, the sort of political loyalty necessary to maintain this link did not exist. Although the process of national unification had involved the formation of a national political elite (most notably through the work of the National Society), few members of this elite had any kind of insititutional control over local areas.[26] Since so much of the Risorgimento had been driven by various forms of conspiracy, with the state as the main focus of activity, democrats and moderates alike had become almost cosmopolitan, cut off from any grass roots support. The lack of much systematic research on this issue makes it difficult to reach definite conclusions. It does seem clear, however, that the absence of political organizations with substantial links in local communities, a problem sustained by the maintenance of a narrow suffrage, increased the "distance" between centre and periphery. Arguably, this distance was also greatly increased by the refusal of the Church, immensely powerful in many local rural areas, to recognize the new state.

In order to understand the problems of national unification in Italy, state formation must be seen as the product of an interaction between centre and periphery, even as a struggle between central and local power holders, which can produce diverse results. It is clear that in many areas, the benefits of national unification or liberal government offered little incentive for the local elites to co-operate with the central authority. The response of local communities to the impact of national unification has been examined in a number of recent studies. Maria Malatesta has described, for example, how landowners in the Lombardy plain resisted government attempts to restructure their agrarian associations.[27] This restructuring, which involved the creation of assemblies under the prefect's control and was conceived as a means of imposing greater uniformity and control by the centre over local elites, was not a success. In areas where there was a great deal of internal cohesion amongst the elite, such as Milan, the agrarian association simply took over and controlled the local assembly. Even where resistance was less successful than this, parallel organizations continued to function alongside the assemblies and the assemblies were often unpopular. Resistance to the centre was also manifested within local government, particularly in the control of finances where in practice there was a great deal of "space" for local initiative.[28]

As the above example suggests, resistance to state formation by local elites could subvert the operation of local government. This subversion was, paradoxically, facilitated by the way in which local government was controlled by the central power. Within a given province, the prefect and the mayors were nominated by the central government (officially by the king). All the other key positions in the commune were elective, and based on a wider suffrage than for parliamentary elections. Members of the provincial assemblies which oversaw the administration of the communes were also elected, with the exception of the prefect who was a permanent member. This system actually gave considerable power to local bodies, as a recent study by Raffaele Romanelli has shown. The responses to a government circular in 1869, proposing greater provincial and communal autonomy and inviting the opinions of Italy's prefect, offer an interesting view of the relations between centre and periphery in this period.[29] Prefects throughout Italy opposed greater decentralization, insisting almost unanimously that local administrations already enjoyed enough, if not more than enough, autonomy. Mayors, according to many prefects, although nominally controlled by the centre, were in reality strongly influenced by the local community.[30]

As Romanelli suggests, this particular source is useful since it indicates that for those working inside government administration the state did not seem centralized at all. Another problem, referred to also in his source, was the difficulty in finding reliable or competent government employees. In Western Sicily, for example, there were immense problems connected with all levels of the bureaucracy.[31] However, the apparent weakness of bureaucratic mechanisms of control does not necessarily mean that the new state had no effect on local government. Rather, the introduction of new administrative structures after 1860 changed dramatically the way power was exercised in local communities, but it did this by offering new possibilities for the subversion of central power. The control of taxation, electoral lists, policing and public works by the local councils gave their members the opportunity to build up substantial personal power bases which could then be used to resist the "penetration" of central government. The powers delegated by the centre could be used to bolster the power of local elites in ways that were not always favourable to the central power. This problem became particularly acute in regions of the "far periphery", such as Western Sicily, where it was reinforced by existing practices and physical distance.[32]

The extent to which local government offered possibilities for personal aggrandizement is indicated by the behaviour of new social groups within local communities. After unification, local government increasingly became a means of making a social and political fortune. One historian of Pisa's social structure in this period has argued that local government was used as a "channel of upward mobility", whereby the new class of professionals and merchants replaced the old land-owning class.[33] In the South too, the local administration came increasingly to be seen as the key to controlling political and economic activity within a given community.[34] However, perhaps the strongest indication of the importance of local administration to the structure of power within local communities is the high level of conflict over the key administrative positions. The prevalence of personal rivalry within communal administrations was a complaint frequently voiced in the 1869 inquiry studied by Romanelli. Political (or more accurately party political) differences usually had little to do with these conflicts which were more often connected to local issues and schisms.[35] Control of local government was frequently the object of the explosive conflicts which erupted in the Sicilian communes during the 1860s, where the police forces as well as local bandits were used to defeat rival factions.[36]

In situations such as this, the behaviour of central government representatives also tended to be rather different from how the central government had conceived it. For example, the prefects, the crucial mediating link between centre and periphery, were often unable to fulfil the bureaucratic function expected of them. Romanelli indicates that in local communities their function was usually limited to intervening in local conflicts, to mediating and keeping the peace between rival groups.[37] Beyond this function, they had little control over local affairs. The prefects seem, in general, to have been more useful as a symbol of the central government's new authority, an authority they were not able invariably to execute in practice. They could, for example, act to organize national elections but could not always, as the example of Western Sicily again indicates, enforce the national conscription law.[38] Energetic prefects could also be a vital source of information about conditions in the more peripheral provinces.[39] Most of all, however, the prefect's presence was crucial in emergencies, at moments of popular disorder or political conspiracy. In other words, although the prefects did fulfil a vital role, they were rarely an effective instrument of bureaucratic surveillance.

IV

Reflecting on the huge economic, diplomatic and political problems faced by liberal Italy after 1860, it is tempting to conclude that the achievement of national unification was not that much of a failure. Clearly the decision to centralize the political and administrative structures was a mistake but it is difficult to see what alternatives existed, given the collapse of government in the South and its association elsewhere with the intractable enemies of Italian liberalism. The Italian experience of national unification was far from unique; this experience resembles in many ways the experience of Germany ten years later. However, the extent of administrative collapse and popular upheaval in Italy meant that a process of unification which relied, as in Germany, on the power of the state was inherently problematic. The weakness of Italy's political institutions thus reflected weaknesses in the process of national unification which could never be overcome.

The interaction between centre and periphery, and between state and civil society, produced results quite different from those expected by the centre. Centralization had an effect, but not the intended effect. Political and administrative "modernization" did occur in Italy after 1860, but it failed to "penetrate" civil society. Romanelli makes a distinction between a "controlling centralization", which never existed in Italy in this period, and what he calls an "impulsive centralization" (*"un centralismo d'impulso"*), which did.[40] The government could affect the situation in peripheral areas without ever controlling it. Romanelli's distinction can be linked to Michael Mann's distinction between "despotic" and "infrastructural" control, an infrastuctural control which was lacking in liberal Italy.[41] What is most interesting about the Italian case is that the failure of infrastructural control caused the government to fall back on more "despotic" mechanisms. It was precisely the failure of centralization, of political and administrative modernization, to create a united nation state that led to the use of military repression and exceptional legislation. In this way, the Italian state's despotic, dictatorial face masked a weak and unstable reality.

However, to many outside the state (the *paese legale*) the reality which they experienced was that of a coercive, repressive structure. One problem with current approaches to state formation in liberal Italy is that they focus overwhelmingly on the relationship between local elites and central government. But there is a missing dimension in this exploration which is the relationship between local elites and popular classes. Thus the neglect and political exclusion of the popular classes by liberal Italy's leaders is now reflected in the work of its historians as well. Yet the experience which the Sicilian peasantry or the Milanese proletariat (the *paese reale*) had of the new political structures was of course very different from the one outlined in this paper. Repression may not have produced the results desired by the central power, but it did exist all the same. Class relations, and specifically the threat of popular upheaval from below, were also a major source of political instability which dogged liberal Italy from 1860 up until 1922. Moreover, the inability of local elites to control popular upheaval is one reason why resistance to state formation remained just that. Liberal Italy survived at least partly because, in the final analysis, many local elites needed the coercive power of the state as much as the state needed them.

As a final reflection on the history and historiography of Italian unification, it is interesting to note how well Gramsci's notion of passive revolution holds up to critical analysis. However, unlike in Germany where the historiographical traditions of the 1960s have been subject to a critical and sometimes hostile analysis, historians in Italy have tended tacitly to abandon Gramscian categories which have become unfashionable. The absence of a critique of Gramsci's historiography is problematic since the categories established by him continue to infiltrate and affect historical debate. John Davis has remarked recently upon the extent to which distinctions and terminology borrowed from Weber are adapted to fit questions about Italian history which remain essentially Gramscian.[42] It is obvious from recent research, the results of which have been described here, that Gramsci's view of the state, and the state-civil society dichotomy, was far too rigid and deterministic. But his attempt to analyze Italian unification as an inherently unstable and incomplete process of change, imposed from above to avoid mass upheaval, is still as vital today as it was forty years ago.

Notes

1. I would like to thank Mary Fulbrook and John Breuilly for their comments on an earlier draft of this chapter.
2. Quoted in M. Urban, *British opinion and policy on the unification of Italy, 1856–1861*, Scottsdale, Pa. 1938, p. 604.
3. S. Jacini, *Sulle condizioni della cosa pubblica in Italia dopo il '66*, Florence, 1870.
4. My focus here is on the Italian rather than the Anglo-Saxon historiography of Italian unification, although similar comments apply. For a (perhaps extreme) example of an Anglo-Saxon approach to Italian unification dominated by the fascist experience, see the contributions to A. W. Salomone (ed.), *Italy from the Risorgimento to fascism: an inquiry into the origins of the totalitarian state*, New York, 1970.
5. Gramsci's notes on Italian history were first published as *Il Risorgimento*, Turin, 1949. Translated extracts were published in Britain in *Selections from the Prison Notebooks of Antonio Gramsci*, Q. Hoare and G. Nowell Smith (eds & trans), London, 1971. .

6. For a discussion of "passive revolution", see John Davis's introduction to J. Davis (ed.), *Gramsci and Italy's passive revolution*, London, 1979.

7. *Selections from Prison Notebooks*, p. 53.

8. *Selections from Prison Notebooks*, p. 90.

9. I use the term "Marxist historian" as a shorthand to describe a variety of left-wing historians, not all of whom were communists but who were all influenced by Gramsci's Marxist analysis. For a recent survey of Marxist historiography in Italy, see F. de Giorgi, *La storiografia di tendenza marxista e la storia locale in Italia del dopoguerra. Cronache*, Milan, 1989.

10. G. Candeloro, *Storia dell'Italia moderna*, vols. II–V, Milan, 1958–68, F. della Peruta, *I democratici e la rivoluzione italiana*, Milan, 1958, *Mazzini e i rivoluzionari italiani*, Milan, 1974, *Democrazia e socialismo nel Risorgimento*, Rome, 1977, *Conservatori, liberali e democratici nel Risorgimento*, Milan, 1989.

11. The best examples of this kind of work are P. Alatri, *Lotte politiche in Sicilia sotto il governo della Destra (1866–1876)*, Turin, 1956 and F. Molfese, *Storia del brigantaggio dopo l'unità*, Milan, 1964.

12. A. Caracciolo, *Stato e società civile. Problemi dell'unificazione italiana*, Turin, 1959, C. Pavone, *Amministrazione centrale e amministrazione periferica da Rattazzi a Ricasoli, 1859–1866*, Milan, 1964, E. Ragionieri, *Politica e amministrazione nella storia dell'Italia unità*, Bari, 1967.

13. B. Croce, *History of Italy from 1871 to 1915*, trans C. M. Ady, Oxford, 1929.

14. Gramsci's own references to fascism in the *Prison notebooks* are fairly rare. In one passage, he does explicitly raise the possibility of drawing analogies between nineteenth-century passive revolutions and twentieth-century fascism: "does the conception of 'passive revolution' have a present significance? Are we in a period of 'restoration-revolution' . . . In present conditions, is it not precisely the fascist movement which in fact corresponds to the movement of moderate and conservative liberalism in the last century?" *Selections from Prison Notebooks*, pp. 118–19.

15. F. Chabod, *Storia della politica estera italiana dal 1870 al 1896. vol. I. Le premesse*, Bari, 1951.

16. For a survey of this literature, see R. J. Evans, The myth of Germany's missing revolution, in R. J. Evans, *Rethinking German history*, London, 1987.

17. First published in Germany in 1980 and published in a revised version in Britain in 1984.

18. *Selections from Prison Notebooks*, p. 79.

19. For a critical examination of Gramsci's use of Jacobinism see P.

Ginsborg, Gramsci and the era of bourgeois revolution in Italy, in Davis (ed.), *Gramsci and Italy's passive revolution.*

20. G. Eley, Liberalism, Europe and the bourgeoisie 1860–1914 in D. Blackbourn and R. J. Evans, *The German bourgeoisie*, London, 1991, pp. 296–7, 301–9.

21. A useful general discussion of the way in which a nominally central-ized system can in practice be extremely decentralized and susceptible to local influence is P. Aimo, Stato e autonomie locali: il ruolo dei prefetti in età liberale, *Passato e Presente*, 14–15, 1987, especially pp. 220–1.

22. John Davis has discussed this incident in: Palmerston and the Sicilian sulphur crisis of 1840. An episode in the imperialism of free trade, *Risorgimento*, 1/2, 1982, pp. 5–24.

23. Marco Meriggi also argues that a major source of dissatisfaction with the Austrian administration in Lombardy and the Veneto was the failure to employ members of the middle class in the bureaucracies. *Il regno Lombardo-Veneto*, Turin, 1988, pp. 80–105.

24. The concept of "bureaucratic surveillance" is used in the recent work of historical sociologists such as Anthony Giddens and Chris Dandeker. See A. Giddens, *The nation state and violence*, Oxford, 1985; C. Dandeker, *Surveillance, power and modernity*, Oxford, 1990.

25. Thus the Neapolitican journalist Ruggiero Bonghi wrote to Cavour from Naples in 1860 that "the railway question here is above all a question of politics. We need to show that the liberals know how, in two months, to put their hands on those who the Bourbons neither knew, wanted or were able to do in twenty years". in *La liberazione del mezzogiorno e la formazione del Regno d'Italia. Carteggi di Camillo Cavour con Villamarina, Scialoja, Cordova, Farini ecc*, Bologna, 1949–54, vol. III, p. 414.

26. On the formation of this new political elite, see R. Grew, *A sterner plan for Italian unity: the Italian national society in the Risorgimento*, Princeton N.J. 1963.

27. M. Malatesta, *I signori della terra. L'organizzazione degli interessi agrari padana (1860–1914)*, Milan, 1989, pp. 40–50.

28. A. Polsi, Le amministrazione locali post-unitarie fra accentramento e autonomia: il caso del comune di Pisa (1860–1885), *Società e Storia*, 22, 1983, pp. 829–67, R. Romanelli, Il problema del potere locale dopo il 1865 in *Il comando impossibile: stato e società nell'Italia liberale*, Bologna, 1988, A. Alaimo, *L'Organizzazione della Città: amministrazione Urbana a Bologna dopo l'Unità (1859–1889)*, Bologna, 1990.

29. R. Romanelli, Tra autonomia e ingerenza: un'indagine del 1869 in *Il comando impossibile.*

30. *Ibid.*, pp. 116–20.

31. L. Riall, Liberal policy and the control of public order in Western Sicily, 1860–1862, *The Historical Journal*, 35, 2, 1992, pp. 358, 361–2.

32. *Ibid.*, pp. 356–8. On resistance to the centre within communal administration in Sicily prior to unification, see P. Pezzino, Autonomia e accentramento nell'ottocento siciliano: il caso di Naro, in C. Pavone and M. Salvati (eds), *Suffragio, rappresentanza, interessi: istituzioni e società fra '800 e '900*, Milan, 1989.

33. A. Polsi, Possidente e nuovi ceti urbani: l'elite politica di Pisa nel ventennio postunitario, *Quaderni Storici*, 56, 1984, pp. 493–4. On the way in which local government and social mobility interacted see also A. M. Banti, *Terra e denaro: una borghesia padana dell'ottocento*, Venice, 1989.

34. A. Recupero, Ceti medi e "homines novi". Alle origini della mafia, *Polis* I, 2, 1987, p. 320, and La Sicilia all'opposizione (1848–74) in M. Aymard and G. Giarrizzo, *La Sicilia*, Turin, 1987, p. 65. For a more general discussion of these processes in the Southern mainland, see G. Civile, *Il comune rustico. Storia sociale di un paese del mezzogiorno nell'ottocento*, Bologna, 1990 and G. Gribaudi, *A Eboli: il mondo meridionale in cento anni di trasformazione*, Venice, 1990.

35. Romanelli, Tra autonomia e ingerenza, pp. 122–6.

36. Riall, Liberal policy, pp. 359–61. On similar conflicts before unification see G. Fiume, Bandits, violence and the organisation of power in Sicily in the early nineteenth century, in J. A. Davis and P. Ginsborg (eds), *Society and politics in the age of the Risorgimento*, Cambridge, 1991, pp. 81–91.

37. Romanelli, Tra autonomia e ingerenza, p. 125.

38. L. Riall, Social disintegration and liberal authority: the Sicilian experience of national government, 1860–1866 (Unpublished Ph.D. thesis), Cambridge, 1988, pp. 267–94.

39. The most famous of these information gathering prefects was the former garibaldian Giacinto Scelsi. See L. Gambi, Le "statistiche" di un prefetto del regno, *Quaderni Storici*, 45, 1980, pp. 823–66.

40. Il problema del potere locale, p. 72.

41. M. Mann, *A history of power: from the beginning to AD 1760*, Cambridge, 1986. See also the chapter by Roland Axtmann, above.

42. J. Davis, Remapping Italy's path to the twentieth century, *Journal of Modern History* (forthcoming).

CHAPTER FOUR
Peasants, gendarmes and state formation[1]

Clive Emsley

The last two decades have witnessed considerable historical research into the origins and development of national police forces. Allan Silver's essay on "The Demand for Order in Civil Society" has been a starting point for much of this work; yet as Silver stressed in his title his focus was on the perception of urban problems in the origin of police, moreover his orientation was purely Anglo-Saxon.[2] David Bayley's comparative study of police development in Great Britain, France, Germany and Italy offered a broad brush, comparative treatment relating police to the political process in the formation of nation states but it has been little explored by subsequent historians. Bayley linked urban and rural police, civilian patrolman and para-military gendarme, in his definition of police. Yet while, as will be argued below, he was right to link the development of gendarmeries in particular to the process of state formation in Europe, his definition of a police force as "an organization authorized by a collectivity to regulate social relations within itself by utilizing, if need be, physical force"[3] gives a legitimacy to much gendarmerie-style policing which is open to question.

Gendarmes were different from the Anglo-Saxon police which, as rightly described by Silver, were essentially an urban and ostensibly civilian phenomenon. Gendarmes often patrolled on horseback and were generally to be found in rural districts. They were commonly recruited directly from the army, uniformed and equipped like soldiers, but often better paid, and treated as an elite corps. For organization, finance, equipment and discipline they were usually responsible to the ministry of war, not to a civilian ministry of the interior or of justice, and not to representatives of civilian local government. Yet apart from these differences, gendarmerie corps appeared at roughly the same time as the new civilian, urban police. The French *gendarmerie nationale* was created in December 1790, but it had a long pedigree being largely a reorganization of the old regime's *maréchaussée*. The Bavarian and the Prussian Gendarmeries were both created in 1812. Two years later the antecedent of the united Italy's *Carabinieri* was organized in Piedmont; at the same time, the government in Vienna established a gendarmerie regiment for its provinces of Lombardy and South Tyrol, and, over the next few years, other gendarmeries were established on the peninsular notably in the Papal States in 1816 and even the reactionary Bourbon regime in the Kingdom of the Two Sicilies followed the French model creating its *Gendarmeria Reale* in 1837. In 1814, with the collapse of Napoleon's empire, the French *gendarmerie* was replaced in the new Kingdom of the Netherlands by the *Koninklijke Marechaussee*; and when, sixteen years later, Belgium achieved independence her Dutch *Marechaussee* was replaced by a *gendarmerie nationale*. Legislation in the British parliament in 1822 provided for a constabulary in every county in Ireland; it built on Robert Peel's act of 1814 creating the Peace Preservation Force, and formed the basis of what was to become the Royal Irish Constabulary.

Russia's Corps of Gendarmes technically came into existence in 1826 when a group of military and para-military units, formed a dozen or so years earlier, were put under the command of Count A. K. Benckendorff. The Marquess of Amarillas proposed a gendarmerie-style corps for Spain in 1820, though the *Guardia Civil* was not established until 1844. Five years later, in 1849, the government in Vienna built on its Italian and Tyrolian experiment creating a gendarmerie for the whole Habsburg Empire.[4]

Since gendarmeries were established in roughly the same period as the Anglo-Saxon, urban police it would be foolish to deny that there was not a shared underlying motive in their creation. The fears of crime and disorder, together with the desire to establish a new threshhold of order maintenance which contributed to the development of the new urban police contributed also to the development of gendarmeries. In France, as the eighteenth century progressed, the propertied members of the population seemed prepared, more and more, to let the state take over the management of public concerns, notably security and law enforcement. The state was fully prepared to extend its authority in this direction, and many of the new burdens were shouldered by the *maréchaussée*.[5] The Revolutionary and Napoleonic wars convulsed Europe for a quarter of a century: principalities and states tottered, some fell, others were restructured and/or enlarged; economies were brought into the Napoleonic system under *le blocus continental* which was constructed on the principle of *la France avant tout* – some did well, but many suffered especially as the British blockade bit, then, with the fall of Napoleon, they were again forced to restructure; armies were recruited, marched and counter-marched leaving in their wake refractory conscripts, deserters and camp followers, and at the end of the wars hundreds of thousands of soldiers and sailors were sent back to their homes as their national economies sought to come to terms with the new economic realities of peace. All of these elements coalesced with fears of revolution to generate among many persons of property and among many men of power and influence beliefs in the need for control and surveillance by strong government. At the same time the wars had fostered notions of the nation state and even conservative powers like Prussia and Austria had taken steps towards creating national armies in which all adult males served at some stage of their lives. National armies were to fight a nation's international wars; they could, of course, be used to defend the nation's monarch or government, but the logic of the emergent idea of the nation-state was that there needed to be something to deploy against threats to domestic peace before the use of the nation's line regiments.

There were also changes in patterns of authority and control in the countryside and new perceptions concerning the role and enforcement of law. The emancipation of the serfs and the withering away of the vestiges of the feudal system loosened the traditional means of supervising and controlling the majority in the countryside; developing nation states were more than ready to assume this burden. Conservatives like the Prussian Junkers insisted that the good landowner acted paternally in the interest of his local community; but, while the Junkers clung to their authority, most such conservatives were giving way before the encroachment of the state. The good state, according to its apologists, acted in the interest of what was best for the nation; the actions of its functionaries were uniform and subject to the law. This law claimed not to be arbitrary, in the sense of depending on the discretion of the courts and their perception of the offender; it was more certain, applied automatically, impartially and uniformly across the state. The gendarme was central to the spread of the state into the countryside; he was the impersonal authority of its abstract law and, like other functionaries, also subject to that law. He was there to protect the people; he was also there to supervise and act as a first line of control.

I

The model, and the name for most of these particular police institutions, came from the French gendarmerie, itself a development of the old regime's *maréchaussée* – the men of the military marshals (*maréchaux*) of France. The old force had been developed in the middle ages to control the king's soldiers which were generally reckoned to be as much a danger to the king's subjects by their disorderly behaviour as they were to the king's enemies by their military prowess. By the early eighteenth century there was a motley collection of companies of *maréchaussée* scattered across France, commanded by officers with a variety of different titles and often overlapping with each other's areas of operation. In 1720 the companies were reorganized into a single national force under the minister of war; each company was tied to a *généralité* and financed from the state coffers. Already its duties had been extended from the supervision of the king's soldiers to the supervision of a variety of offenders and offences, notably by the ordonnance of 1670. During the eighteenth century the force developed many of the recruitment policies, the deployment and organization which were to become typical of gendarmerie corps. The system had its critics. There were some who suggested that regular troops might perform the policing tasks of the *maréchaussée* with a greater efficiency; yet the consensus, at least among persons of property, was that the force needed to be augmented and that it would thus provide better protection against brigands, highway robbers and vagrants. When the revolutionaries carried out the reform which transformed the *maréchaussée* into the *gendarmerie nationale* they more than doubled the numbers of rural policemen from about 3300 to 7420.[6] They also stressed the impartial nature of the new force and how it was to stand above traditional community divisions which might lead to the local justice of the peace being a relation, ally, or enemy of one party in a dispute or offence.[7]

The wars of the Revolution and of Napoleon gave other states of Europe the opportunity of seeing the system function at first hand as gendarmes were deployed to keep the French armies in order, but also as French administrative and legal systems were imposed on different nationalities under the Napoleonic hegemony so too were gendarmeries: Italy, the Rhineland and Hanover all had their first experience of gendarmes while part of the French empire.[8]

As with the urban, Anglo-Saxon police the occasions which gave rise to the establishment of a gendarmerie varied, though underlying the individual occasions there is detectable a heightened perception of the need to impose a new level of order and uniformity in the countryside. The *gendarmerie nationale* was created as part and parcel of the legal reforms at the beginning of the Revolution, though these reforms had been preceded by concerns over brigands and vagrants and demands for an improved, or at least enlarged, system of police in the provinces. The creation of the gendarmeries in Prussia and the new states of southern Germany also coincided with more general reform, both constitutional and fiscal, and with a strengthening of central government possessed of a clearer, more positive idea of the state. Brigands and vagrants were perceived as a problem in the southern German states both during and at the close of the Napoleonic wars; the problem was made worse by the fact that, since these states were now so much bigger than their eighteenth-century predecessors, the old expedient of deporting offenders across one of the multitude of frontiers into a neighbouring territory was not as readily available.[9] Italian states and rulers were faced with the problems of reconstituting themselves in the midst of ferment at the end of the Napoleonic wars. In the Italian departments of Napoleon's empire the organizers of the gendarmerie had stressed the need for a force above local faction; it was present not only to enforce the will of the state, but to keep the local factions apart and to provide an impartial form of policing which, they believed, would be otherwise impossible. These attitudes were less marked after 1814 when the House of Savoy returned. But while much of the imperial structure and many of the imperial improvements were destroyed, a gendarmerie, the *Carabinieri Reale*, was established with a much greater emphasis on making the state highly visible, in propaganda terms, than it had been under the Empire. In the

Papal States Cardinal Consalvi, ever a critic of Napoleon, drew nevertheless on his perception of the French imperial example to create the new Papal *Carabinieri* in 1816. He publicly expressed his intention of providing an honest service to which people could appeal instead of the loathed and corrupt *Sbirri*. His new force was to win public support by acting as the "moral force" of a moral, and all-powerful-regime.[10] In Ireland it was fear of serious disorder among the peasantry which had brought about the creation of the Peel's Peace Preservation Force in 1814. The problem was still present in 1822 when Henry Goulburn prepared his Constabulary Act; but this act was largely an attempt to rationalize the system of policing which had developed out of earlier legislation and place it under a single command. The *Guardia Civil* was a deliberate attempt by the *Moderados* (conservative liberals) to establish a national and military organization, above party, which could be used to bring order to a country wracked by civil war and *pronunciamentos*, and within which the exisiting system of regional militias was dissolving in a welter of local influence and corruption; there were, in addition, problems with banditry, especially in the south, and Carlism.

Gendarmes could be very thin on the ground. While the original 7420-man establishment of the *gendarmerie nationale* was more than twice the size of the old *maréchaussée*, yet when the size of France is taken into consideration, together with the estimated population of about 28 million on the outbreak of the Revolution, of which rather more than four-fifths were rural dwellers, the scale of the gendarmes' tasks appears daunting. The situation improved over the middle years of the next century as gendarme numbers gradually increased, but even if the ratio of gendarmes to population was not greatly different from the ratio of police to population in the main provincial towns (see tables 1 and 2), the men still had large tracts of land to patrol. Elsewhere gendarmes could find themselves spread even more thinly. In Prussia the original establishment had been 9000 men, but in 1820 the force was reduced to just over 1300 excluding officers. Initially, for example, in the department of Rhein-Mosel there had been 130 gendarmes for a population of about 280,000; the reform of 1820 left only 63 for a population which had grown to some 400,000.[11] In Russia the Corps of Gendarmes has been calculated as containing 4000 men in 1836 spread across the whole empire in six Gendarme Districts;[12] the Russian population then stood at something in the region of 60 million. In the other great

Table 1 Gendames, gardes and the population of rural France

	(a) Total Population Dwellers	(b) No. of Rural Brigades	(c) No. of Gendarmerie	(d) No. of Gendames	Ratio (d) to (b)	No. of gardes champêtres	No. of gardes particuliers assermentes[2]	No. of gardes forestier	No. of gardes-pêche[3]
1846	35.4m	26.7m	2695[1]	14671[1]	1:1824	34,742	29,017	9985	
1851	35.8m	26.6m	3121	17041	1:1564	35,025	29,276	9865	
1861	37.4m	26.6m	3500	18979	1:1401	34,818	31,179	9723	
1866	38.0m	26.5m	3526	18997	1:1393	35,003	33,710	9135	4997
1872	36.1m	24.9m	3508	16712	1:1488	31,923	32,067	7997	4787

1 Excludes the Corsican equivalent of the gendermerie, the Voltigeurs Corses.
2 Gardes sworn in to protect a specific property and paid for by the proprietor.
3 Until 1862 when they were put under the management of the department of Bridges and Roads, the gardes-pêche were included with the gardes-forestiers.

Table 2　　Urban Police in France, 1855[1]

(a) City/Town	(b) Population	(c) Police (all ranks)	Ratio (c) to (b)
Amiens	42,000	36	1:1167
Angers	33,000	25	1:1320
Besancon	30,000	21	1:1428
Bordeaux	90,900	154	1:590
Caen	30,900	20	1:1545
Lille	54,000	52	1:1038
Limoges	24,500	30	1:816
Marseille	195,000	103	1:1893
Metz	32,100	31	1:1035
Montpellier	33,900	28	1:1211
Nancy	29,700	24	1:1237
Nantes	73,800	142	1:520
Nimes	38,800	32	1:1212
Orleans	36,100	26	1:1388
Rouen	87,000	96	1:906
Strasbourg	49,000	52	1:942
Toulouse	50,000	96	1:521

1　Excluding Paris and Lyon where the police were determined by central government.

multi-national empire, that of the Habsburgs, the new gendarmerie created in 1849 was rather more numerous: initially there were to be sixteen regiments of 1000 men each for a population approaching 41 million. The country where gendarmes were thickest on the ground was Ireland (see table 3); and the density of policing in Ireland was much greater than in rural England.[13] Even after the famine of the 1840s the Irish Constabulary continued to increase in numbers; when France lost territory and population to Germany in 1871, in contrast, the *gendarmerie* was reduced in size proportionately.

The size and significance of the gendarmeries was circumscribed by the strength of both local elites and national organizations in relation to the developing central state. If policing depends on legitimacy it is, above all, the legitimacy acknowledged by those with some power and authority within the state. During the nineteenth century peasants had little, if any, such power, even when, as in France following the Revolution of 1848, they were enfranchised. Across rural Europe the old elites wielded power and enjoyed independence and authority in varying degrees; this, in turn, influenced the growth

Table 3   The Irish Constabulary and the Irish Population

	(a) Total Population	(b) Number of RIC Policemen	Ratio (b) to (a)
1824	6.8m	4792	1:1419
1831	7.8m	5940	1:1307
1841	8.1m	8606	1:950
1851	6.5m	11286	1:580

and authority of the gendarmeries. In France the nobility gave up many of its police powers in criminal cases during the eighteenth century because of the expense and inconvenience.[14] The Revolution swept away the last vestiges of feudal privilege and thus, in the nineteenth century, the centralized state in France had little need to negotiate with provincial notables over the power and authority of its gendarmes. In direct contrast, the Junkers of East Prussia were loyal to their king, but equally they were jealous of the encroachments of the government bureaucracy in Berlin and their strength enabled them to impede its advances and hang on to much of their authority, including their police powers. They perceived the gendarmerie, as it had been established in 1812, as one aspect of the central administration's threat to their authority. In 1820, in league with the army which itself resented the gendarmerie's independent claims on state finance, the Junkers were instrumental in bringing about the reduction in the size of the force. This extended the Junkers' lease on their personal power and independence. At the same time the army had also profited since the gendarmerie was brought much more directly under the control of the generals.[15] The traditional elite and the newly enriched agrarian middle class in the Kingdom of Sicily, as well as feuding with each other, both sought to resist the centralization attempts of the Bourbon monarchy which included the deployment of a gendarmerie. The Sicilian elites not only constantly criticized and gave little support to the gendarme brigades, they also acted as patrons to many of the larger brigand bands. This lack of legitimacy among the provincial elites, together with the myriad of administrative and protection tasks imposed on the gendarme brigades, seriously impeded their effectiveness; and the *Carabinieri* of the new Italian nation state faced similar difficulties after unification.[16] The Ascendancy Irish disliked the loss of their authority which came about with the creation of the Peace Preservation Force. Yet as they had proved so ineffective in coping with peasant disorder at the end of the eighteenth and beginning of the nineteenth centuries, it was possible for the government to marginalize them. More importantly the troubles of 1848 and 1867 showed the value of a para-military constabulary and the extent of the Ascendancy's isolation in a sea of Catholic peasantry.[17]

The sparseness of the gendarmes on the ground had an obvious effect on their efficiency. As an elite military body the men had a strong *esprit de corps*. Their brigades of about four or five men were strategically stationed in small barracks and, in addition to their regular patrols, they were expected, and prepared, to confront, courageously, bodies of armed and angry peasants. Often they were successful in such confrontations and they were preferred by many local authorities to the varieties of local police that were sometimes available, and even to larger squads of soldiers.[18] The contingent of *Guardia Civil* deployed in Madrid during the July Revolution of 1854 was noted for their discipline and for the fact that they were the last to surrender; equally noteworthy, the revolutionary crowds singled them out as the men who had to be disarmed.[19] But generally in times of major disorder in the countryside the small brigades could be neutralized relatively quickly and easily. The turbulence in peasant France towards the close of the Second Republic provides a good example: some gendarme brigades, finding discretion the better part of valour, went to ground; some were disarmed; those that resisted disarming, but without using their weapons, might simply be ignored or by-passed; the few that resisted with force, especially where they had a reputation for enforcing unpopular laws, were annihilated.[20]

The difficulties created by their lack of numbers could be exacerbated in those peasant areas where the "national" language was not spoken, or where the local patois was thick. There is a traditional image of the gendarme as a stranger to the region which he policed, and deliberately selected as such by the authorities. This was manifestly a problem for the *carabiniere*, mostly recruited on the mainland, who were stationed in Sicily. As one contemporary noted in the 1870s: "They live isolated amidst the population as if in a desert. They see and hear, but do not understand."[21] Elsewhere, however, the evidence suggests that the situation was rather more complex; men were appointed to their province of origin, though probably not to their home town or village. Following the practice of the old regime with the *maréchaussée*, the Napoleonic regime often appointed men to gendarmerie brigades in their province of birth. In the middle of the nineteenth century nearly half of the recruits to the gendarmerie requested, and got, an appointment to the department of their birth. Such a posting was probably seen by some soldiers as a way of returning to their *pays natal*.[22] The decree of 13 May 1844 outlining the organization of the *Guardia Civil* also specifically allowed volunteers from the army to serve in their province of origin.[23] Later regulations forbade the guardias from associating familiarly with the locals and marrying their women; and given the particular problems of nineteenth-century Spain with the *caciques* (local bosses, generally drawn from the large landowners or their surrogates) appointing mayors, controlling judges, in league with bandits, backed by their own gangs of toughs, and delivering the election results which governments wanted, the *gardias* became especially isolated from the communities in which they were stationed – they became known as *la Pareja* (the pair) since for safety's sake they patrolled in twos.[24] Of course, a man who had spent several years in the national army, and who had transferred to an elite military corps, was probably sufficiently removed from his peasant and local origins not to be a liability even if stationed in his province of birth, while his ability to understand the local language or dialect was a positive asset.

Gendarmes were the representatives of central governments which increasingly had developed their own laws based on the jurists' conception of justice as order defined, imposed and maintained from above by the state. They were the executive arm of the law and, in accordance with the law, they were expected to apprehend bandits, illicit distillers, runaways, smugglers, thieves, and vagrants. They were to maintain order and a measure of decorum at fairs, feasts, fires, markets, public ceremonies and parades. They were also to suppress illegal assemblies, to ensure that conscripts reached their regiments, and to carry out a degree of political surveillance. These tasks were given different degrees of stress at different times and in different national contexts. In its early years the *gendarmerie nationale* was heavily involved in enforcing the military recruitment policies of first the Revolution and then Napoleon's empire.[25] In the aftermath of the Napoleonic wars in Piedmont and southern Germany the gendarmeries were particularly ordered to act against vagrants who were commonly equated with "criminals".[26] In Ireland the fear of peasant disorder was the main concern of the gendarmes in their early years and this was recurrent throughout the nineteenth century; the ratios of police to population were greatest in the turbulent counties of the centre and south, notably Westmeath and Tipperary which, in 1871, had one gendarme for every 194 inhabitants. The role of political surveillance and intelligence was most apparent in Russia where the Corps of Gendarmes was closely linked to the Third Department, or Section, of His Majesty's Private Imperial Chancery. This department was responsible for political policing throughout the empire and the gendarmerie's links with it have led one historian to conclude that, in consequence, there was no similarity between the Russian and French gendarmeries other than that they were both para-military.[27] In fact, however, the *gendarmerie nationale* also played a political role and while some senior officers objected to their men taking on undercover political work, and while in 1852–53 the corps won formal exemption from such tasks, gendarmes continued to do such work throughout the Second Empire.[28]

Although they were the executive arm of the state's law, and generally feted and favoured as such, the gendarmes were not the only policemen to be found in the rural districts of many states. Other police were recruited by and among the population, or at least by the landowners or principal inhabitants of the rural communities. There were some 11,500 men in the *Guardia Civil* in the early 1860s, and about 17,200 *Guardas rurales*; a decade later the numbers had increased respectively to 13,000 and 18,850. Moreover the provinces, spearheaded by the Valencian Society of Agriculture, remained keen to preserve their own rural police.[29] In France the *gendarmerie* functioned alongside even greater numbers of *gardes champêtres*, *gardes-pêche* and *gardes forestiers* (see table 1). Being local men, probably only doing their policing tasks part-time, these *gardes* were naturally subject to pressures from their fellow villagers or from the local mayor or principal landowners who appointed them. They shared their community's view of order, rather than that of the jurist; and they lacked the discipline and *esprit* of the gendarmes. At the end of the Directory and beginning of the Consulate, and again during the Second Republic and the Second Empire there was talk of brigading the *gardes champêtres* like the *gendarmerie*. The idea would have required significant reorganization and could have created a potential rival to the *gendarmerie*. It would also have been very expensive and, probably for this reason above all, it came to nothing. At both the beginning and the end of the nineteenth century in France the rural guards were universally condemned for inefficiency; the gendarmes, in spite of the fact that they had enormous areas to patrol, and in spite of growing concerns that the insistence that they always patrol in uniform advertised their presence to offenders and prevented some arrests, had much better arrest records than either the rural guards or the municipal police.[30]

Alternative views of order created problems for the gendarmes. Often they found themselves having to function in an environment where other forms of justice were recognized by the population, and sometimes even by the state itself. The *Rittergut* (Knight's Estate) in East Prussia defined the boundaries of the local community, and its owners had police and judicial powers over all those within it. While this power was greatly circumscribed by Bismarck in 1872, the landowner of East Prussia retained disciplinary powers over unmarried workers living on his premises (*Gesindeordnung*) until the end of the First World War. In Russia the elders of the commune (*mir*) were authorized to settle the lesser offences; they decided upon physical or financial punishments (though the former were supposed to be supervised by the lord's bailiff), and they were known to send persistent troublemakers into the army or to seek to have them exiled to Siberia.[31] There were also the unofficial forms of community justice ranging from the different forms of charivari, generally a form of shaming punishment, to forms of lynching which, no matter how brutal, generally followed an identifiable code recognizable within the peasant community. While the jurist would have objected and have insisted on the maintenance of his concept of order, gendarme brigades sometimes used their discretion and stood aside during a charivari;[32] the sensible brigade commander recognized that his intervention could make a situation far worse, especially where no physical violence to the victim of the demonstration was likely, and on occasions he may well have shared the community's attitude towards the victim.[33] An eviscerated or impaled corpse resulting from a Russian peasant community's implementation of *samosud* (literally judging by oneself) did call for action,[34] though in Russia the gendarme might have left such an investigation to the local police on the grounds that his principal concern was with offences which threatened the political or social order, such as the murder of a landowner, or brutal repression by a landowner which might, in turn, prompt peasant disorder.[35] However when any gendarme, anywhere, decided to act, penetrating the silent solidarity of the peasant commune could prove impossible. Writing in the early 1880s to correct 'the confident ignorance of some English papers' about the Royal Irish Constabulary, Henry Blake admitted that getting information and evidence was one of the force's main problems.[36] In his unfinished autobiographical novel *Kaspar Lorinser*, intended as a tribute to his *Heimat*, Ludwig Thoma explained how poaching offences were dealt with by the gendarmerie in Upper Bavaria. "Only newcomers to the *gendarmerie* who came from outside took the trouble to conduct investigations. The older ones knew with what ease our people lied to the authorities."[37]

The lack of criminal offences in the occurrence book of a gendarmerie brigade might reflect the peasant community's decision to investigate and to settle offences, as far as possible, in its own, traditional ways rather than have recourse to outsiders. Franz von Haxthausen-Abbenburg, travelling in Russia in the early 1840s, witnessed an investigation into a petty theft conducted by an old woman, reputedly a witch, and traditional healers were commonly consulted to help find lost or stolen goods.[38] This preference for the "cunning man" or "cunning woman" (*znakhar'* and *znakharka* in Russian) rather than a local policemen could also be found in nineteenth-century England,[39] and probably elsewhere.

In Spain the *caciques'* control and manipulation of the courts and the peasants' general suspicion and hostility towards the *Guardia Civil* probably ensured that few opted for the state's system of criminal justice when they were the victim of an offence.[40] Though, of course, it is also true that a paucity of offences listed in an occurrence book might also reflect the desire for a quiet life on the part of the commander of a gendarmerie brigade stationed in a remote area.[41]

Peasants in France prayed to be delivered from evil and from "justice", and these peasants' definition of "justice" invariably made some reference to gendarmes.[42] Yet there were times when gendarmes took the part of peasants against landowners, and while they suppressed peasant tumults they might, at the same time, remind landowners and their agents of their own responsibility for the maintenance of the public peace. Shortly after Italian unification the commander of the *Carabinieri* in the province of Verona responded indignantly to landowners' appeals for more effective policing following an increase in the statistics of rural theft; he suggested that the landowners had brought the problem on themselves by not providing sufficient work during a severe winter and by not digging deeply enough in their pockets to provide guards for their fields.[43] In Russia Nicholas I intended that his subjects should be able to approach his gendarmes with any complaint about local abuses of power or corruption; they were to be the link between the good autocrat and his people, and to emphasize this the flag of the Moscow gendarmes bore the motto *Le bien-être générale en Russe*. One Russian wit translated this as "It is good to be a general in Russia" and hostility to the gendarmes went even higher up the social scale in Nicholas's empire. When the governor of Simbirsk, about 700 miles east of St. Petersburg, heard that some individuals had petitioned the local gendarme commander about abuses, he summoned them to a meeting: "Gentlemen, we've had a little disagreement – that's our affair. Why call in the gendarmes?"[44]

II

Gendarmeries then were thin on the ground, and while they might be popular with authorities in time of trouble, they were easily overwhelmed in times of revolutionary disorder. They could pick up vagrants and beggars with relative ease, and several brigades might unite for a brief campaign against brigands and bandits; activities such as these could bring forth popular approval. But even in heavily policed rural districts like Ireland the gendarmes' numbers were insufficient for the realistic prevention and detection of crime over the whole of a brigade's district. In some instances they sought to enforce the jurist's conception of order; but at times they were expected to function alongside other law enforcement agencies and other courts which had, albeit reluctantly, state sanction. The succession of negative elements here leads, inevitably, to the question: Was there a positive common denominator at least implicit in gendarmerie-style policing?

On transferring from the army to the *gendarmerie* in 1838 Major A.I. Lomachevsky had an interview with Benckendorff in which his new duties were explained to him:

[Benckendorff] added that this post required not only an honest, noble and wholly irreproachable kind of conduct but also the caution of a diplomat because, as he expressed it, our Sovereign, in appointing a Gendarme staff-officer to every province, desires to see in him the same kind of emissary, the same kind of honest and useful government representative as he has in London, Vienna, Berlin and Paris.[45]

But it is not only the staff officers who can be seen in such a light. The small brigades of gendarmes either patrolling in their smart military uniforms, or just resting in their barracks with the national flag flying over the top, were a demonstration to rural communities that the *pays natal* of the members of those communities was not simply a village and its immediate environs but a developing nation state. If this was not articulated elsewhere as clearly as in Benckendorff's statement, it was nevertheless implicit in the way that the gendarmeries developed and increasingly were expected to enforce a reciprocity of responsibilities. The rural dweller was to fulfil his obligations to the nation state by paying his taxes and yielding conscripts; and the gendarme was to ensure that these obligations were fulfilled, by force if necessary. The state was, in turn, to protect the rural dweller by acting against the vagrant and the brigand, and by rooting out corruption among local officials; the gendarme was, in theory at least, available to the peasant to ensure the state's part of the bargain.

The articulation of this role of internal colonization and, for want of a better word, the domestication of the peasant may not always have been clearly stated, though perhaps it should be stressed again that, to date, the origins and development of the European gendarmeries has been little explored by historians. Yet even if not clearly articulated, this role fitted well with other policies of state formation and centralization on lines which governments and reformers insisted were both rational and fair. The creation of the *gendarmerie nationale* came at the height of the initial liberal, reforming phase of the French Revolution as the Constituent Assembly sought to establish a well-organized, rational, and enlightened state. Twenty years later the Prussian Gendarmerie Edict coincided with a string of other reforms which further battered the old order, already weakened by the defeat of 1806, and sought to develop a better organized state; the better-off among the newly enfranchised peasants were allowed to become free proprietors of two-thirds of their holdings, individuals who wished to practice a particular trade no longer had to acquire membership of a guild, but had to pay a tax (*Gewerbesteuer*), other new kinds of taxes were introduced payable by the heads of households, and all young men were liable for conscription. The new *gendarmerie* was not specifically seen as having a role to play in the collection of taxes or recruiting, though neither was the *gendarmerie nationale* in 1791. Nevertheless the different acts can be seen as parts of the same project rather than one as the instrument of the other. The newly expanded states of southern Germany offer similar examples in the same period. The Bavarian state also established its gendarmerie in 1812, at the same time as it embarked on a massive administrative reorganization. It issued constitutions designed to create a common all-Bavarian identity in its conglomerate of territories, many newly acquired following treaties with Napoleon, and it seriously concerned itself with questions of identity-building.

Comparison with those countries, and those districts, where the Anglo-Saxon, urban style of policing developed also underlines the implicit colonising role of the gendarmeries. Peasants of the kind, and in the numbers, known across most of continental Europe, were unknown in eighteenth- and nineteenth-century England. The perception of belonging to an English state linked with notions of "Englishness" seems to have been apparent in ways unknown on the Continent. The English policeman was a hybrid: the office of constable was, in origin, one of local responsibility; he was the man being appointed and responsible locally for presenting offenders to local courts. His duty to maintain "the king's peace" was something grafted on to the office, probably with the name constable itself, by court lawyers in the twelfth or thirteenth centuries. This process was drawn attention to a century ago,[46] but a detailed analysis has never been attempted. As professional police forces both of the Anglo-Saxon and the gendarmerie models developed during the late eighteenth and early nineteenth centuries, the government at Westminister boasted a much greater reluctance to interfere with English institutions and to "govern" in the manner of its continental neighbours. Disorder on the English periphery or in the British Empire, where peasant societies existed with some similarities to those in Europe, could lead to paramilitary policing; the obvious example, of course, is Ireland with its gendarmerie-style Royal Irish Constabulary.[47] But the dispatch of Metropolitan Policemen to south-west Wales, and their deployment alongside regular troops during the Rebecca disorders of the 1830s and 1840s, provides a similar example. It might be argued that the subsidence of trouble in the peasant districts of Wales, as much as any perception of a civilian, English model of police prevented the development of a Welsh gendarmerie.[48]

However the unique nature of the English state should not be pressed too far and the government at Westminster was not averse to centralizing in its own ways. The creation of Her Majesty's Inspectors of Constabulary in 1856, and the government's decision to pay a quarter, and later a half, of the costs towards police forces deemed efficient by these Inspectors, established a much greater degree of uniformity, and perhaps efficiency (though this word is notoriously difficult to define in policing terms), over the locally-run forces of England and Wales. The annual inspections of the English provincial police, with the prize of a certificate of efficiency and government funding, possibly contributed to these forces being in some ways rather closer to gendarmeries in smartness, drill, and book-keeping, than the rural guards or even the locally-recruited and locally-run police of many continental municipalities.

The federal government in the United States was even less inclined to govern than its national counterpart in Westminster; indeed given the constitutional structure and states' rights it was less able to govern. The democratic nature of American politics and society led to a plethora of police forces, each one responsible to the leaders of the local community in which it served. The colonization of the indigenous peoples was generally achieved by direct military force rather than gendarmerie-style police; the possible exception is Texas where what might be construed as a "democratic gendarmerie" developed from the 1840s in the form of the companies of Texas Rangers.[49] Many permanent immigrants to the eastern cities had some idea of "Americanness" or an "American dream", but they might also require a degree of colonization and domestication involving the local city police. William McAdoo, a former commissioner of the New York City Police, comparing his former command with the Metropolitan Police of London, noted that the latter did not have the cosmopolitan problems of New York since most Londoners were English born and English by tradition.

One of our greatest police problems on the East Side especially is to make the new-comer understand that the word "police" does not carry with it here, as in Europe and Asiatic countries, the sense of outrage, injustice, cruelty, deadly menace, and even death, and that our laws, when honestly enforced, mean impartial justice, fair dealing, protection, security, and equity. The New York police, unlike their London contemporaries, are teachers and drillers for the nation of these vast divisions . . . [50]

McAdoo's pride in his old force and his country probably led to too rosy an image of the New York Police and American law. Nevertheless to the extent that they acted as "teachers and drillers" of a nation the New York Police were fulfilling the same kind of task as European gendarmes patrolling and enforcing state regulations upon European peasants in their native lands.

Rural communities existing within emerging nation states had their own organizations for regulating social relations, sometimes with physical force. In England, from the twelfth century, these organizations had begun to acquire royal as well as local authority in a process not yet fully analyzed. Elsewhere, into the nineteenth and even into the twentieth century, these community organizations continued to function outside the formal structure of the state. Sometimes they might be peasant dominated, as in Russia; sometimes they might be neo-feudal, as in East Prussia. Nobles, like the East Prussian Junkers, might owe allegiance to their king but resent the emerging nation state and insist on the maintenance of their traditional courts and system of control. Peasants were often notorious for their stubborn inability, or refusal, to recognize the existence of a polity beyond their *pays natal*. It is in this context that the development of gendarmerie-style policing should be understood. Gendarmerie-style policing fulfilled a role largely different from that of the kind of policing which developed in states, or parts of states, where the population acknowledged some sort of national identity. Members of the *gendarmerie nationale*, the *Carabinieri*, the *Guardia Civil*, the Third Section were as much involved in turning peasants into Frenchmen, Italians, Spaniards and Russians and marking out "national" territory, as members of the Northwest Mounted Police or the Royal Irish Constabulary were involved in turning indigenous peoples into loyal subjects of the British Crown and marking out imperial territory. Of course they were only one element in the process of the state's expansion and colonization of its rural peripheries; and they functioned alongside a variety of other modernizing elements – roads, railways, schools and schooling, conscription into national armies, political activists – which helped to transform peasant Europe.

Urban police regularly complained about their lack of numbers, but gendarmes were much thinner on the ground and far less likely to be able to prevent crime – the key public aim of the new bureaucratic police in the nineteenth century. National, and imperial, governments justified the gendarmes' presence by their role in order maintenance, especially their repression of bandits and vagrants, and such activity could bring the gendarmes a degree of community acceptance. But there was a hidden agenda to the creation and continuing development of the European gendarmeries; gendarmes were deployed to show the flag, to demonstrate to rural communities that they were part of a bigger entity – a state, be it a nation or an empire – and that they had obligations to that entity in the form of taxes and sometimes military recruits.

Notes

1. My thanks to Richard Bessel, John Breuilly, Michael Broers, and Mary Fulbrook for their comments on an earlier draft of this paper.
2. Allan Silver, The demand for order in civil society: a review of some themes in the history of urban crime, police, and riot, in David J. Bordua (ed.), *The police: six sociological essays*, New York, 1967.
3. David H. Bayley, The police and political development in Europe, in Charles Tilly (ed.), *The formation of national states in Western Europe*, Princeton, 1975, p. 328.
4. Few of these forces have been the subject of recent detailed historical enquiry, though there are some official histories. For the *gendarmerie nationale* see L. Larrieu, *Histoire de la Gendarmerie depuis les origines de la Maréchaussée jusqu'au nos jours*, 2 vols, Paris, 1927–33; Howard C. Payne, *The police state of Louis Napoleon Bonaparte, 1851–1860*, Seattle, 1966, especially pp. 232–44; Pierre Miquel, *Les Gendarmes*, Paris, 1990. For the Prussian Gendarmerie, see Reinhart Koselleck, *Preussen zwischen Reform und Revolution; Allgemeines Landrecht, Verwaltung und soziale Bewegung von 1791 bis 1848*, Stuttgart, 1965, esp. pp. 195–204 and 460–3. For the gendarmeries in the states of southern Germany, see Bernd Wirsing, 'Gleichsam mit Soldatenstrenge': Neue Polizei in süddeutschen Städten. Zu Polizeiverhalten und Bürger-Widersetzlichkeit im Vormärz, in Alf Lüdtke (ed.), *Sicherheit und*

Wohlfart: Polizei, Gesellschaft und Herrschaft im 19. und 20. Jahrhundert, Frankfurt am Main, 1992. For the *Carabinieri,* see John A. Davis, *Conflict and control: law and order in nineteenth-century Italy,* London, 1988, pp. 232–4. For Belgium see Lode Van Outrive, Yves Cartuyvels and Paul Ponsaers, *Les Polices en Belgique: Historie socio-politique du système policier de 1794 à nos jours,* Brussels, 1991. For the origins of the Royal Irish Constabulary, see Stanley H. Palmer, *Police and protest in England and Ireland 1780–1850,* Cambridge, 1988. For the Russian Corps of Gendarmes, see P. S. Squire, *The third department: the establishment and practices of the political police in the Russia of Nicholas I,* Cambridge, 1968, chapter 3. For the *Guardia Civil,* see Enrique Martinez Ruiz, *Creación de la Guardia Civil,* Madrid, 1976, and Diego López Garrido, *La Guardia Civil y los orígnes del Estado centralista,* Barcelona, 1982. For the Austrian Gendarmerie see Franz Neubauer, *Die Gendarmerie in Österreich,* Vienna, 1925.

5. Robert M. Schwartz, *Policing the poor in eighteenth-century France,* Chapel Hill, 1988. The suggestion that, during the eighteenth century, the French became more and more reliant on the state in this way, was initially put forward by de Tocqueville; Schwartz develops it with reference to the treatment of the poor in the *généralité* of Caen.

6. For the development of the *maréchaussée* during the eighteenth century see Iain A. Cameron, *Crime and repression in the Auvergne and the Guyenne, 1720–1790,* Cambridge, 1981; Claude C. Sturgill, *L'oganisation et l'administration de la maréchaussée et de la justice prévotale dans la France des Bourbons (1720–1730),* Vincennes, 1981.

7. Citoyen Guichard, *Manuel de la Gendarmerie Nationale,* Paris, 1791, pp. 137–39.

8. Stuart Woolf, *Napoleon's integration of Europe,* London, 1991, pp. 62 and 90–2.

9. For this treatment of beggars and vagrants in eighteenth-century southern Germany see Ernst Schubert, *Arme Leute, Bettler und Gauner im Franken des 18. Jahrhunderts,* Neustadt an der Aisch, Kommissionverlag Degener, 1983; for war-time banditry see Wolfgang Seidenspinner, Wirtschaftliche Krisensituation und Bandenkriminalität. Das Beispiel der Spessart-Odenwald-Bande (1802–1811), in Gherardo Ortalli (ed.), *Bande Armate, Banditi, Banditismo e repressione di giustizia negli stati europei di antico regime,* Rome, 1986, and Norbert Finzsch, Räuber und Gendarme im Rheinland: Das Bandenwesen in den vier rheinischen Départements vor und während der Zeit der französischen Verwaltung (1794–1814), *Francia,* 15, 1987, pp. 435–71; and for the southern German gendarmeries, see Wirsing, 'Gleichsam mit Soldatenstrenge'.

10. Steven C. Hughes, Police, public order, and the Risorgimento in Bologna, Ph.D., Michigan, 1984, pp. 51–5.

11. Koselleck, *Preussen zwischen Reform und Revolution*, p. 461.
12. Squire, *The third department*, p. 95, n. 2; see also the maps between pp. 90 and 91.
13. Palmer, *Police and protest*, table III.3, pp. 560–1.
14. J. Q. C. Mackrell, *The attack on feudalism in eighteenth-century France*, London, 1973, pp. 67–71; Steven G. Reinhardt, *Justice in the Sarladais 1770–1790*, Baton Rouge, 1991, p. 61.
15. Koselleck, *Preussen zwischen Reform und Revolution*, p. 460; Albrecht Funk, *Polizei und Rechtsstaat: Die Entwicklung des staatlichen Gewaltmonopols in Preussen 1848–1914*, Frankfurt, 1986, pp. 41–3.
16. Giovanna Fiume, Bandits, violence and the organisation of power in Sicily in the early nineteenth century, in John A. Davis and Paul Ginsborg (eds), *Society and politics in the age of the Risorgimento*, Cambridge, 1991; L. J. Riall, Liberal policy and the control of public order in Western Sicily 1860–1862, *Historical Journal*, 35, 1992, pp. 345–68.
17. Palmer, *Police and protest*.
18. Roger Price, Techniques of repression: the control of popular protest in mid-nineteenth-century France, *Historical Journal*, 25, 1982, pp. 859–87, at pp. 866–7; Alf Lüdtke, *Police and state in Prussia, 1815–1850*, Cambridge, 1989, pp. 76–7, and 156.
19. V. G. Kiernan, *The revolution of 1854 in Spanish History*, Oxford, 1966, pp. 63 and 65–6.
20. Ted W. Margadant, *French peasants in revolt: the insurrection of 1851*, Princeton University Press, 1979, pp. 38 and 273–85.
21. Quoted in Christopher Duffy, *Fascism and the mafia*, New Haven, 1989, p. 60.
22. Clive Emsley, *Policing and its context, 1750–1870*, London, 1983, p. 41; Terry W. Streiter, Drinking on the job: *Ivresse* among the French gendarmerie in the nineteenth century, *Proceedings of the Annual Meeting of the Western Society for French History*, 16, 1989, pp. 173–81: at p. 174.
23. Ruiz, *Creación de la Guardia Civil*, p. 395. Raymond Carr, *Spain 1808–1975*, 2nd edn., Oxford, 1982, states (p. 233) in discussing the origins of the *Guardia Civil* that officers and men could not be natives of the districts in which they served.
24. Gerald Brennan, *The Spanish labyrinth: an account of the social and political background of the civil war*, Cambridge, 2nd edn., 1950, p. 157. The people of the Asturias disliked Galicians and in a song from the miners' uprising of October 1934 they equated Galicians with *guardias*:

> Inside the bullring
> The Galicians in three-cornered hats

Used us to play bullfighter.
Some used sabres
And others whips,
And the policemen from Galicia
Kicked us as well.

Quoted in Adrian Schubert, *The road to revolution in Spain: the coal miners of the Asturias 1860–1934*, Urbana, 1987, p. 72. It is not clear whether this dislike originated from the belief that the *guardias* were "foreign" Galicians, or simply whether the two were lumped together as equally unpopular.

25. Alan Forrest, *Conscripts and deserters: the army and French society during the Revolution and Empire*, Oxford, 1989, pp. 220–2 and 228–35.
26. Davis, *Conflict and control*, p. 71; Wirsing, 'Gleichsam mit Soldatenstrenge', pp. 67 and 90–2.
27. Squire, *Third department*, pp. 236–7.
28. Payne, *Police state*, pp. 90–1 and 236–39.
29. López Garrido, *La Guardia Civil . . .* , pp. 151 and 159–60.
30. Jean-Marc Berlière, L'Institution policière en France sous la troisième république 1875–1914, Thèse pour le doctorat, Université de Bourgogne, 3 vols, 1991, ii, 774–80 and 799–805; Octave Festy, *Les délits ruraux et leur répression sous la Révolution et le Consulate*, Paris, 1956, p. 174. These rural police have been even less studied than the gendarmeries; for the *gardes champêtres* see, in addition to Festy, Emsley, *Policing and its context*, pp. 90, 94 and 141, and Marie-Renée Santucci, *Délinquence et répression au XIXe siècle: l'exemple de l'Hérault*, Paris, 1986, pp. 22–3.
31. Rodney D. Bohac, The mir and the military draft, *Slavic Review*, 47, 1988, pp. 652–66, at p. 655; Steven H. Hoch, *Serfdom and social control in Russia: Petrovskoe, a village in Tambov*, Chicago, 1986, pp. 149–53.
32. Christian Desplat, *Charivaris en Gascogne: La "morale des peuples" du XVIe au XXe siècle*, Paris, 1982, pp. 132–57.
33. Carolyn A. Conley, *The unwritten law: criminal justice in Victorian Kent*, Oxford, 1991, pp. 23–8, has shown how rough-musicking could be tacitly condoned by magistrates and police in rural Englnd when, regardless of statute law, it conformed to generally-accepted norms.
34. Stephen P. Frank, Popular justice, community and culture among the Russian peasantry, 1870–1900, *Russian Review*, 46, 1987, pp. 239–65; Cathy Frierson, Crime and punishment in the Russian village: rural concepts of criminality at the end of the nineteenth century, *Slavic Review*, 46, 1987, pp. 55–69.
35. John P. Ledonne, Criminal investigation before the great reforms,

Russian History, I, 1974, pp. 101–18; at p. 104 and n. 8. Ledonne stresses that we have very little information as yet on how the Russians gendarmes did act on the ground in matters of investigation.

36. Henry A. Blake, The Irish police, *The Nineteenth Century*, IX, 1881, pp. 385–96; at pp. 391–2.
37. Ludwig Thoma, *Kaspar Lorinser*, in *Gesammelte Werke*, Munich, R. Piper, 1956, 8 vols, v, pp. 11–12.
38. Franz von Haxthausen-Abbenburg, *The Russian Empire: its people, institutions, and resources*, trans, Robert Faire, 2 vols, London, 1968, i, pp. 228–29. Samuel C. Ramer, Traditional healers and peasant culture in Russia, 1861–1917, in Esther Kingston-Mann and Timothy Mixter (eds), *Peasant economy, culture, and politics of European Russia 1800–1921*, Princeton University Press, 1991, p. 223.
39. Clive Emsley, *Crime and society in England 1750–1900*, London, 1987, p. 82.
40. For the caciques and the peasants' attitude to the *Guardia Civil* see Gerald Brennan, *The Spanish labyrinth*, 1950, pp. 7–8 and 156–7, and Murray Bookchin, *The Spanish anarchists: the heroic years 1868–1936*, New York, 1977, pp. 94–5.
41. Ian Bridgeman, "Is that dog licenced?" Policing rural Ireland in the late nineteenth-century, unpublished paper (this forms the basis of a chapter in his forthcoming dissertation for the Open University on crime and the Royal Irish Constabulary); Lüdtke, *Police and state in Prussia*, p. 88 notes a *gendarmerie* brigadier supplying an annual arrest report in which "each of the five entries was identical to the previous year's submission".
42. Eugen Weber, *Peasants into Frenchmen: the modernization of rural France, 1870–1914*, Stanford, 1976, p. 50.
43. Davis, *Conflict and control*, p. 284, and see also p. 140. This, of course, was by no means always the case, especially where gendarme officers conceived of the peasantry as a race apart, or persons not fully evolved, and where they shared the values and interests of the landowners. See Frank M. Snowden, *Violence and the great estates in the south of Italy: Apulia 1900–1922*, Cambridge, 1986, p. 141.
44. Monas, *The third section*, pp. 286 and 109.
45. Quoted in Squire, *The third department*, p. 86.
46. H. B. Simpson, The office of Constable, *English Historical Review*, XL, 1895, pp. 625–41.
47. Probably, however, there was never a distinct, identifiable "Irish model" developed for the policing of the British Empire; see Richard Hawkins, The "Irish Model" and the empire: a case for reassessment, in David M. Anderson and David Killingray (eds), *Policing the Empire: government, authority and control, 1830–1940*, Manchester, 1991.

48. Clive Emsley, *The English police: a political and social history*, Hemel Hempstead, 1991, pp. 52, 55 and 236.
49. Frank Richard Prassel, *The Western peace officer: a legacy of law and order*, Norman, 1972, pp. 151–8.
50. William McAdoo, The London police from a New York point of view, *The Century Magazine*, LXXVIII, 1909, pp. 649–70; at pp. 667–8.

CHAPTER FIVE

Sovereignty and boundaries: modern state formation and national identity in Germany[1]

John Breuilly

I Introduction

National identity can be regarded as primarily cause or consequence of nation-state formation. The first view stresses the way in which various processes created, intensified and diffused a sense of nationality and how this in turn contributed to the formation of the nation-state. There are many possibilities within this general approach. Some historians stress cultural history – e.g., the work of intellectuals who standardize and popularize a version of the "national" language and use this language to project images of the nation through poetry, folklore and music collections, etc. The literary history of Gervinus, for example, portrayed late eighteenth and early nineteenth century German history in this way. Luther had constructed a national religion; Goethe and Schiller a national literature; it now remained for statesmen of comparable stature to complete the historic journey by constructing a national state.[2]

More recently, the fashion for structures rather than individuals has given this culturalist approach a new twist. The development of new patterns of communication is seen as the necessary base upon which intellectuals can project their "imagined community" to a wider audience.[3] More profoundly, the nature of those communications are seen directly to press such imaginations into a national shape and to make a "standard culture" a key component of any successful modern society.[4] Following on from this historians have looked at how different patterns of communication developed a sense of national identity more in some parts of Germany than others;[5] and also at how different kinds of social communication, for example, in the form of voluntary associations and the development of a periodical and newspaper readership, could promote a sense of national consciousness, at least at certain elite levels.[6]

Clearly these structural-cultural accounts can be linked to approaches which stress social and economic change. Intensified networks of communication are related to the extension of market relations, increased geographical mobility, urban growth, higher rates of literacy, etc.[7] In this context nation-state formation, when it takes the particular form of *unification*, can be seen as functional for such economic development. Functional accounts describe rather than explain. To explain one must pinpoint either a deliberate intent to carry out the function (e.g. German businessmen use their influence to promote unification because they know it will help their businesses) or some mechanism which "selects" the particular function (e.g. economic development strengthens those agents which pursue unification policies, in particular by tipping the balance of power from Austria to Prussia).[8]

There are problems with these approaches. First, they tend to overstate the degree to which there actually *is* a sense of national identity on a cultural or economic plane. There is a temptation to read back from unification as a politico-military process to these "underlying" conditions. Second, they find it difficult to move from such a sense of identity to an account of the specific political and military changes which more narrowly define what nation-state formation actually was.

The other approach takes its departure point from these weaknesses and exaggerates them. One cannot demonstrate a widespread sense of national identity on an economic or cultural base – therefore there was *no* such sense to any significant degree. One cannot demonstrate direct connections between cultural and economic achievements on the one hand, and the process of diplomacy and success at war which actually created the nation-state on the other hand – therefore there were no such connections.[9]

The problem then is to account for why we describe those politico-military events as "nation"-state formation. The answer to this (unless one wishes to argue that the concept of the nation-state obscures rather than illuminates the nature of what had been achieved) is to focus upon the way in which the new state itself sets in train policies which shape a sense of national identity. Partly one can go over the same ground that I have already covered, claiming only that the major cultural and economic changes which produce national identity *followed* rather than *preceded* nation-state formation. Partly one can argue that for some reason the new state is particularly committed to promoting such a sense of national identity. It is then possible to look at political as well as cultural and economic history – for example, at the importance of new institutions such as elected parliaments, state schools and welfare bureaucracies.[10]

If compelled to choose between one or other of these accounts, I would, at least so far as the German case is concerned (and, incidentally, even more for the case of Italy), opt for the second. I think it contains a good deal more of the truth than the first approach. However, it does not explain why the language of nationality played an important role before and during the crises which ended in the formation of the German Second Empire in 1871; nor why that state should, at the political level, whether deliberately or inadvertently, promote "national identity".

To understand that we need to turn back to the period before nation-state formation. Here one is immediately struck by an asymmetry between the two broad approaches. The focus on national identity as contributor to nation-state formation tends to leave out political processes, whereas the focus on national identity as consequence of nation-state formation tends to give pride of place to political processes.

In this essay I intend to correct that asymmetry. I will argue two main points. First, political processes play as vital a role in shaping a sense of identity which precedes and contributes to nation-state formation as it does after nation-state formation. Second, it is a mistake to look only for *direct* relationships (i.e. that the sense of identity must be that of being *German* in order to contribute to the formation of a *German* state). Instead, what matters is the *form* rather than the *content* of that sense of identity. It is in this respect that the development of new attitudes towards two aspects of the state – its sovereignty and its boundaries – is of importance. In sketching how the (very closely related) issues of sovereignty and boundaries relate to the process of German nation-state formation I will focus on two broad periods – 1800–1847 and 1848/49–1871 with an excursus on the post-1871 period.

II *Sovereignty, the state and the citizen, 1800–47*

Pre-Napoleonic Germany was a complex and fragmented collection of patrimonial polities. At one extreme were the states of Austria and Prussia and at the other were about 540 families of imperial counts and knights ruling some 1600 distinct territories. Altogether there were some 1800 rulerships immediately subject to imperial authority.

A patrimonial polity is one in which government is identified with a dynasty or corporation, such as the cathedral chapter in ecclesiastical states. In the case of the Holy Roman Empire, these bodies exercised power under the authoritiy of the imperial institutions. These institutions could be and were used to protect liberties, and furthermore, in many individual territories humane and intelligent rulers exercised their powers on behalf of their subjects and frequently initiated beneficial and rational reforms. In that sense, to call the polities of the Holy Roman Empire "archaic" or "pre-modern" is not to call them ineffective or unenlightened. Nevertheless, there were severe limits on the degree to which modern developments could take place in such a fragmented and patrimonial structure overseen by the empire, and this applied to *all* German states.[11] Only some drastic crisis would provide the opportunity for making the modern territorial and constitutional state the political norm in the German lands.[12]

What did sovereignty mean in such a situation? In the legal reasoning of the time sovereignty resided with the Empire. A key distinction was between those "immediately" and those "mediately" subject to imperial authority. In both cases the imperial authority was the sovereign authority, but in one case one had to approach that authority through intermediate authorities and in the other case one did not.

Historians have often assumed that, as the Empire was virtually a political nullity, therefore "real" sovereignty resided with those "intermediate" authorities, in particular the territorial states. However, this assumption is flawed in two ways. First, even where the intermediate authority was a powerful one, the idea that there was a higher authority to which appeal could be made remained an important component of the political culture of the period.[13]

Second, even the most powerful and concentrated intermediate authority, that is the Prussian state, did not possess or even claim sovereignty in the manner that nation-states do. There was little in the way of a uniform legal system; indeed, when Frederick II seized Silesia he undertook to observe all its laws and customs and administered the area through a separate ministry. This was typical of pre-modern ideas of sovereignty: to be sovereign was to interpret and enforce the law which was based on religion and tradition.[14]

This understanding can be seen even in the very "modern" legal codification of 1794, the Allgemeines Landrecht [ALR].[15] This claimed in its very title to be the code for the Prussian States. Many sections – relating to the rights and obligations of peasants, urban artisans and shopkeepers, and nobles – have very little content because they could not produce any meaningful synthesis of the provincial and even sub-provincial variations. Only with respect to the monarchy, to the nobility as a political service class (rather than as a local landed elite), and to the educated bourgeoisie (the *eximirte Bürgertum* – meaning exempt from local urban law) could more detailed state-wide rules be stated.

One should also note that the ALR divides people according to social estate or order – that is, according to particular categories of privilege. When I used the word "rights" above, I should have used the word "privilege" instead. There was not, and could not be, a meaningful account of the "rights" of men or citizens as people standing outside all social estates in the ALR. But equally there could be no meaningful account of the state as sovereign in the modern sense of all subjects standing in the same legal relationship to that state. The ALR was "modern" only in a certain rhetorical sense, which was that it was a systematic codification and that it claimed to ground privilege upon function (above all, service to the state) rather than regarding it as a matter of tradition and property.

These were not merely matters of legal theory. What is striking about even the Prussian state(s) on the eve of defeat at the hands of Napoleon is the lack of institutionalized sovereignty as we understand it. The monarch was immensely powerful, but that power was expressed through a range of very varied, often ad hoc agencies. There was no central bureaucracy with a clear hierarchy and division of labour. The ministers of the

General Directory had no "responsibility" for the work of their ministries, no collective organization, no first minister, and no control over some provinces and some key operations such as customs collection.[16] Even the army had no unified system of control below the personal command of the king.[17] If this was true of Prussia, it was much more true of every other part of the German lands.

One component of a modern sense of national identity before the construction of a nation-state is finding a putative nation-state with which to identify and/or a state which does not represent one's own national identity against which to act. The nature of sovereignty in the late Holy Roman Empire and its constituent parts prevented such a sense of identity developing. There were imperial "patriots" who, as Germans, counselled reform of the Empire. But they could not even dream of transforming the Empire into a sovereign state on modern lines – that would have actually destroyed much of what they cherished in imperial institutions.[18]

On the other hand there were those – princes and their officials – who wished to strengthen the particular intermediate authority they controlled. However, they were divided by a gulf of privilege from the bulk of their subjects, and noble officials in particular stood in a tense relationship to the majority of the members of their social estate whose nature as landowners was tied up with regional particularism. "Patriotism" in this context (and the term was applied in the same way in countries like England and France as well as in German or Italian lands) simply meant commitment to reforms designed to create a state with a more effective and modern kind of sovereignty.[19] However, in the particular German case such "patriotism" was in a way *anti-German*, because such reforms would undercut imperial authority and claims to sovereignty. This imperial authority in turn acted to preserve the structures of privilege at and below the level of the intermediate authorities which blocked the construction of modern sovereign institutions. The point is put well by Vann in his study of the Duchy of Württemberg:

> . . . the secondary sovereign powers in Germany simply lacked the capacity to develop fully as long as they were held in check by an imperial organising force whose principal thrust was the preservation of traditional corporate interests.[20]

The force of this was made clear in the Napoleonic period. The "secondary sovereign powers" were emancipated from imperial authority. One must remember that, although the Holy Roman Empire was destroyed only through the military defeat (Austria) or neutralization (Prussia) of the two major powers, it was precisely those states and some others (notably Baden, Bavaria, Württemberg) which collaborated in 1803 (the *Reichsdeputationshauptschluß*) effectively to destroy a large number of the "traditional corporate interests". In compensation for annexations made by France on the left bank of the Rhine, these states claimed territories on the right bank. All this was done at the expense of the many small ecclesiastical states and imperial counts and knights who were concentrated into the southern and western parts of the Empire. The official end of the Holy Roman Empire in 1806 was, after this, merely a formality.

Now the "patriots" had their chance. In the cases of the two major powers this opportunity only came with the crisis of war, either its preparation or defeat. The project of creating a sovereign state had been pursued most consistently in Austria during the reign of Joseph II (1780–90). Partly he was responding to particularly acute problems of diversity and maintaining great power status, partly he was assisted by the fact that much of his territory fell outside the Holy Roman Empire and so did not run into problems about imperial sovereignty, and even within the Empire he was helped by holding the imperial title himself. However, obstacles and resistance to his reforms had already led to retreat in the 1790s, and there was little time to pursue reforms in the period of near-continual war against France between 1792 and 1805. Some attempts at further reform, especially in the military sphere, were pursued by the "war party" under Stadion's leadership in 1808–9, including an appeal to "German" patriotism, but the defeat of 1809 killed off much of this reform impulse and brought to power Metternich who remained suspicious of all such appeals to patriotism for the rest of his long political career.[21]

In Prussia reforms before 1806 were made within the existing structure of privilege and provincial variation. Even a "radical patriot" like Stein did not go much further than this until 1806, and even then his major demands in the immediate aftermath of Jena were confined to the reform of the central administration in order to give it more independence from the monarch, embodied for example in the famous "Nassau Memorandum". It was only after the war was effectively finished in 1807 with Russia coming to terms with France at Tilsit that Prussian patriotic reformers were able to pursue more radical goals.[22]

In the case of the "collaborator" states of Baden, Bavaria and Württemberg that influence was already being exercised from at least 1803 as the problems of integrating new territories in the absence of an overarching imperial framework and the destruction of many corporate institutions had to be confronted. Arguably the lack of institutional continuity, the dependence upon France which meant little energy had to be committed to foreign and military affairs, and the dangers these vastly expanded states faced of being swamped by their new acquisitions all meant that institutional reform in these states was more thoroughly carried through than in Prussia. It is not possible to recount the details of the subsequent reform process.[23] I will just focus on the major features.

A modern ministerial system based on functions (usually police, finance, and justice were the most important), with the ministers meeting as a group and with a first minister, perhaps complemented by a Council of State, was normally established. The state was divided into regions and localities. It usually proved impossible to impose this system down to the locality, or even the province. At the one extreme little reform at all was attempted, as in Saxony, perhaps because there the power of local nobles had already been attenuated and explicit reform from above was unnecessary. Dalberg, as Grand Duke of Frankfurt, introduced the nomenclature of French-style government but simply grafted that upon existing regions and institutions. Most thorough-going were the reforms in Baden, Bavaria and Württemberg. Administrative reform extended at least down to regional level. In Bavaria the bureaucracy was granted fixed pay scales and superannuation arrangements, a clear hierarchy and systematic discipline; uniforms to help create an ethos; and an ennoblement policy to give leading officials prestige.[24]

Yet the ennoblement policy showed the continuing hold of the aristocratic ideal, and the use of uniforms and privileges that of the idea of officialdom as a privileged caste. At the local level, reform stalled both for lack of resources and in face of local resistance. Justice could not be separated from administration at this level in Bavaria. In Prussia Hardenberg's 1812 Police Edict failed, and the key rural local government office of Landrat fell into the hands of the nobility. In Bavaria, as in Prussia, it was not possible to abolish the judicial powers of noble estate owners until 1848. In Prussia, even at the key level of government above the locality – the Regierungen – the functional, bureaucratic pattern could not formally replace the collegial one, although in practice the role of experts did increase. The Oberpräsident of each province, although a deliberately limited and in many ways ornamental office, tended after 1815 to turn into a representative of provincial interests against the central government.

It was not possible therefore simply to import a French-style modern bureaucracy. Government had to work with the social grain, the more so the lower down one went. This led reformers to engage in various constitutional experiments to try to overcome resistance to change. In the Confederation of the Rhine (and later in the German Confederation) an additional motive was to forestall the imposition of a confederal constitution. Having freed themselves from the sovereignty of the Holy Roman Empire, these rulers had no wish to see this reimposed in some modernized form. Certainly this was one reason for Bavaria enacting a constitution in 1808.[25]

Prussia more modestly convened an Assembly of Notables in 1811 and an interim national representation in 1812 and again in 1814. Convening such assemblies and issuing constitutions was closely bound up with a claim to a new kind of sovereignty. What is significant is that this claim could only be made also by paying at least lip service to the modern notion of citizenship. The claim to sovereignty implied the construction of a new political identity centred on the state-citizen relationship.

In practice these representative assemblies had rather more limited functions, namely consultation in order to improve the credit of the government and to provide some support for its policies.[26] This led to the constitutional doctrine known as "dualism", in which executive power rested with the prince and consultative rights only were vested in representative institutions. Later in some aspects of German liberal constitutional thought this would be expressed in terms of an ideal relationship between state (prince) and society (assemblies) and justified on the grounds that society was pluralistic and factional whereas sovereignty only made sense in terms of a concentrated and unitary focus of state power.[27] This also justified an attempt, both in the Napoleonic and Vormärz periods, to organize "society" as represented through consultative assemblies in terms of social estates, although this became increasingly difficult both as influential bourgeois groups resented their treatment and as rapid social change made estate divisions and related notions of "social honour" difficult to sustain.[28]

One problem encountered in these early constitutional experiments was that the people who came to dominate such assemblies were opposed to many of the reforms planned by the government, precisely because these reforms would threaten the position of the predominant social elites. Koselleck has argued that this entailed a contradiction between administrative and constitutional reform. Other historians have put the contradiction or tension in different terms – economic versus political liberalism, or in terms of contrasting regional patterns of reform – more economic in some areas, more constitutional in others.[29]

One should also note that this attempt to move towards citizenship encountered resistance not merely from those members of corporate and privileged bodies whose status was undermined (e.g. guildsmen and urban burghers). There was also reluctance on the part of putative citizens to shoulder the burdens of freedom, something Stein observed with disgust in relation to his law of 1808 on the government of towns.

One vital aspect of administrative and constitutional reform was financial. Some historians have gone so far as to see financial motives as the most basic cause of reform.[30] In Prussia the granting of autonomy to towns in the 1808 edict can be seen as a means of transferring the cost of urban administration to the inhabitants of the town. This might explain some of the reluctance to assume the rights of citizens which evoked Stein's contempt. The introduction of the freedom to practice a trade (*Gewerbefreiheit*) also served as a means of introducing a new tax (*Gewerbesteuer*). This "fiscal" interpretation has been effectively challenged for Prussia,[31] but governments certainly were in desperate financial straits.

Nevertheless, this narrow financial theme can itself be related back to the broad issue of modernization. The most thorough study of financial reform, focused upon Napoleonic Baden and Bavaria, has demonstrated its close connections to modernization, especially the construction of a modern sovereign state. Debt was unified, centralized and brought under the public laws of the state. On that basis it was possible to construct funds to service such debt and for the state to make commercial contracts with creditors.[32]

Compared to the character of "public" debt in pre-1803 German states, one now confronted the state as a clear and distinct idea, vested with sovereignty, and dependent upon citizen consent if it wished to increase taxation or borrow on a large scale.

This relationship expressed itself in a range of other spheres. Corporations were abolished not merely because they were regarded as politically obstructive but also because they were seen as economically retrograde. The penetration of the ideas of "political economy" into the "common sense" of rulers and their officials led to a wholesale attack on the connections between privilege and property.[33] Supported by the French, guilds were abolished; land was transformed into a commodity like any other; town-country distinctions with their implications for different kinds of fiscal and administrative practices and privileges were eroded, if not removed; individuals rather than holders of statuses such as guild masters or heads of households were subject to taxation.

To understand these "political" changes, it is clear that we have to see this in the context of a broader set of changes which I will call modernization. It is not merely a question of the state becoming "more" powerful, sovereignty becoming more clearly centred upon the territorial state, and state boundaries becoming sharper and more effectively policed. Rather it is that the very meaning of state, and with it of sovereignty and boundaries was transformed. To grasp this it is necessary to make some theoretical points about modernization.

Modernization involved a *double transformation*. This has to be seen in terms of understanding modernization as a transition from a corporate to a functional division of labour. By a corporate division of labour I refer to a society with a very complex range of functions but where bundles of different functions are carried out by particular institutions, usually on behalf of some distinct group. For example, the ideal-typical guild performs economic functions (regulating production and distribution of particular goods and services); cultural functions (taking care of the general as well as vocational education of apprentices, organizing the major recreational and ceremonial activities of members of the guild, even enforcing religious observance); and political functions (running courts which impose and enforce penalties upon members, having automatic membership of town governments). Churches, lordships, peasant communes and even the monarch in his capacity as privileged landowner also exhibit such multi-functional characteristics. One should not portray such a division of labour as in any way consensual or "organic". There are many points of conflict. In some functions particular institutions claim universal or at least over-arching powers (churches and religious doctrines; monarchs and the law) although they usually depend upon other institutions actually to enforce these powers at lower levels. There are also disputes over the boundaries of competence to be drawn between different institutions and there are internal conflicts within various institutions. This notion of a corporate division of labour is an ideal-type. In reality there are many deviations from that type. Certainly by the late eighteenth century such a division of labour was subject both to incisive intellectual critiques and, in many parts of western and central Europe, was crumbling in the face of commercial and demographic pressures.

The critiques – especially those associated with rationalist creeds such as the Enlightenment, physiocracy and classical political economy – envisaged a different division of labour, one where each of the major social functions was concentrated into particular institutions. Thus economic functions would be disentangled from other functions and concentrated into individuals and firms operating in a free market. Churches would become free associations of believers. Power would be exercised by specialized bureaucracies under the control of elected parliaments or enlightened despots. There were great variations in the critiques which sometimes might raise up one of these functions above the others (classical political economy and the market; Jacobins and the polity) but they all pointed to this basic transformation.

In practice such a transformation did not proceed smoothly. Furthermore, the different elements of the transformation developed at different speeds and times and in different ways. In the German case, however, the key moment of breakthrough at a political level came during the Napoleonic period. This was, however, only the departure point because that change had implications for the general social division of labour.

The development of the modern state in the German lands involved a concentration of "public" powers into specialized state institutions (assemblies, bureaucracies), while leaving many "private" powers under the control of non-political institutions (free markets, private firms, families, etc.). That involved the double transformation of government I have referred to: institutions such as the monarchy lost "private" powers (e.g. the principal source of revenue from royal lands and the granting or possession of monopolies); other institutions such as churches, guilds, and lordships lost their "public" powers to government. In this way a clear and distinct idea of the state as "public" and "civil society" as "private" was elaborated and seemed to have some hold upon reality.

The clock was not put back in 1814–15. The Catholic church did not regain its temporal powers, nor its lands which had been secularized. The imperial knights and counts were largely ignored, though some did receive significant powers as *Standesherren* (mediatised nobility) – the very terminology is redolent of the older conceptions of sovereignty as something diffused through the structure of privilege.[34] The myriad of small states that had been abolished between 1803 and 1806 in western Germany were not restored. The German Confederation, although its articles implied some kind of sovereign status (e.g. laying down the general and rather archaic constitutional principles on which all member states should organize themselves) was never vested with the legal rights of intervention that had been held under the Holy Roman Empire. Where guilds and communal autonomy were restored, this tended to be more in terms of helping impose social discipline rather than as institutions with any effective political control.

As a consequence the territorial state was a much clearer and more public entity after 1815 than it had been before 1800. This meant that the lack of constitutional advance – notably the limited powers granted to representative assemblies – was glaringly obvious. The emergence of political liberalism as the most important intellectual and political opposition to the states of Vormärz was predicated upon the prior acceptance of the state as a distinct public realm, governing on behalf of its subjects, with its ruler and his officials bound by fundamental laws. These states were regarded as reactionary because they had by their very nature created expectations of progress which they failed to live up to. In fact the Confederation did intervene more effectively into the affairs of individual states than the Holy Roman Empire had ever been able to do. However, the intervention was in terms of the Austro-Prussian dualism – that is, it expressed the dominance of two particular territorial states within the Confederation – rather than in terms of the sovereign powers of the Confederation.

Political liberalism contributed to the formation of a new kind of political identity at elite level. Representatives of these elites could meet in state-wide or provincial assemblies and there could develop a public critique of the deficiencies of the state as non-accountable. At the same time, many state officials sought to develop the other aspect of the double transformation, continuing to concentrate the public powers of the state by removing the residual privileges of different groups. "Political" and "administrative" liberalism could often conflict with each other, but both were based upon a shared understanding of sovereignty as something public and concentrated.

Where does "national" identity come into this? At first the relationship between political identity based on citizenship and cultural identity based on nationality seemed tenuous. One can see this in two different areas.

The construction of a German national culture, focused on such ideas as a national language and national theatre, was highly elitist. It was associated, especially in the case of Schiller, with a very strenuous and elevated notion of culture as a quasi-religious experience. Up to 1815 this current of thinking was largely unrelated to any populist theme such as that associated with gymnastic and choral societies. It was not until the 1830s that Goethe and Schiller were recruited to a more widespread, though still largely bourgeois conception of national culture.[35]

More populist projections of "Germandom" were usually somewhat detached from the political world (perhaps the major execption being Jahn's gymnastic movements of 1813–15). It is interesting that in 1808 it was the Bavarian government which asked Goethe to produce a *Volksbuch* to express and project notions of German culture; and it was the Austrian court which dressed up in "traditional German peasant costume" in the early nineteenth century, while the Frederician court in Berlin remained strongly Francophile in its culture. In Vormärz it was the Bavarian government again which was the most assiduous builder of national monuments. Yet *politically* these were the two states which stood to lose most from the formation of a German nation-state. At an apparently unrelated level, for example, the Bavarian state had been trying to create a new political identity, that of the "Bavarian".[36] Clearly the cultivation of German cultural identity was seen to be important but in a way which buttressed rather than challenged the construction of modern sovereignty at the level of the territorial state.

The development of liberal opposition movements also contained a national implication. The repression of liberalism was carried out not just at state but also at a Confederal level, as was made abundantly clear in 1819 and in the early 1830s. The Confederation developed significant political policing power, though this was the product of more effective coordination between states which themselves were developing more modern policing techniques.[37] Liberal oppositions were compelled to take up supra-state connections with one another. At first this had a largely negative purpose – to remove the repressive power of the Confederation so that liberal reforms could proceed in the individual states. However, political movements create their own momentum and develop objectives based on the direction in which they are moving rather than the purpose for which they were first established. Thus the liberal movement shifted from the idea of removing to that of reforming and finally to that of replacing the Confederation.[38]

At this point the issue of nationality made its entry. With the construction of new institutions such as the Zollverein it was possible for the images of what would replace the Confederation to be given varying and increasingly concrete forms.[39] By 1848, therefore, the dominant ideas of national political reform were expressed by liberal movements which, however, had a rather attenuated notion of national culture to which they could relate such reform ideas.

III   Boundaries, territoriality and political identity, 1800–47

The development of modern sovereignty also required much clearer definition than hitherto of the boundaries of the state, particularly as the process of modern state formation in Europe was something which went on in the context of competition between a number of states. It is interesting, for example, that one of the issues at dispute when the war between France and ancien regime states broke out in 1792 was the source of power over enclaves within France which owed some allegiances to the Holy Roman Empire. The modern conception of France as a tightly bounded space within which the French state was sovereign was opposed to an older conception of power as varying bundles of privileges related to different groups and territories. Clear and distinct ideas of the state as sole source of sovereignty and as a bounded territory are hallmarks of the modern state.[40]

One can see this directly in relation to the German lands. In the Napoleonic period there were frequent and extensive changes of state boundaries. At the same time they were associated with the overthrow of many "legitimate" forms of rule and with the project of creating legal uniformity within particular states. This made it impossible to use the language of tradition and legitimacy to justify the particular boundaries.

Instead rulers were forced to one of two possible justifications: nature or reason. Both were hostile to ideas of "enclaves" or "mixed territories". As we have seen, the enclave idea was challenged by France in the early 1790s. At the same time the French revived the notion of the Rhine as a national frontier and used it to justify the direct annexation of left-bank territory. Internally, however, the construction of departements was deliberately designed to undermine traditional, legitimate orderings of space (just as the revolutionary calendar attacked such orderings of time). Yet reason and nature were claimed to be in alliance (again just as the revolutionary calendar claimed to relate to the natural annual cycle) as one sought to base boundaries upon criteria such as the catchment area of a river.

Similar problems and solutions obtained in the German case. So long as rulers respected varying laws and customs in a corporate order a state did not require a single and continuous boundary, although of course most powerful states had a core territory on which their power was founded. As a consequence, the boundary changes of the Napoleonic period, not rooted in any traditional-legal continuities, created confusions. What should be the boundaries of particular states?

One answer was to look for underlying continuity. Some German geographers of the time, confronted with the "artificiality" of political boundaries, claimed to identify more enduring physical criteria which underlay those fragile and man-made constructs. Partly this was a purely practical concern – political boundaries were changing too fast to be able to produce valid atlases for much of Europe which were not quickly rendered obsolete. The geographer Zeune, for example, tried to identify essential boundaries based on man–land relationships, and in this way claimed to have discerned an essential France and an essential Germany. For a time he saw Napoleon as the "executor" of geography, though he was both changing his mind by 1813–14 and also expanding the boundaries of the "essential" Germany.[41]

Clearly the boundaries of the individual German states created by Napoleon made little sense, even if a construct such as the Confederation of the Rhine, as its very name implies, claimed some kind of geographical basis (although some of the states incorporated into the Confederation were a long way from the Rhine). Breaking from tradition and lacking any physical geographical sense, the new collaborator states made a virtue of · reason as something imposed by man upon nature. The construction of sovereignty made it imperative that the "artificial" boundaries of the state be stringently controlled. One of the functions of the new gendarmeries established at this time was to improve boundary controls. Banditry and vagrancy decreased dramatically, especially with the ending of endemic warfare in 1815, as a consequence of such controls.[42] Indeed, one of the major arguments of economic liberals in Vormärz for national unification was the perceived effectiveness of such controls, allowing more movement within the new states but tightening up on movement between those states. Popular cartoons in favour of the Zollverein, for example, portrayed Germany as a series of tightly controlled spaces which inhibited movement. What is interesting is that, although railway lines and trains figured prominently in these cartoons, they also included horse-drawn transport. People were, through both the enlarged territorial state and the Zollverein, becoming aware of both the inhibiting and the positive role of boundaries.

There is an apparent paradox here. The construction of larger territorial states which broke down internal spatial restrictions based on province or town/country was associated with a critique of these states as constricting, enemies of movement. There were two reasons for this. First, the larger states raised expectations. The existence of enclaves or separate physical regions for one state was now seen as unnatural, a problem requiring solution. Second, the boundary controls of the older German state system were very ineffective – because there were much longer boundaries in toto, because those boundaries were often based upon something much less clearcut than state citizenship (e.g. guild membership or propertied status), and because those boundaries were much less efficiently patrolled. Now movements could be more effectively controlled, yet the larger territorial states also encouraged more internal movements. There was also an expectation of movement across state boundaries. The Confederation actually institutionalized this expectation as one of its articles declared there should be freedom of movement between the member states.[43] This development first made more urgent the legal standardization of state citizenship or at least membership within individual states in order to settle disputes between different localities about the rights and obligations of people who had moved within the state.[44] With movement across state boundaries the same problem presented itself at a Confederal level.[45]

The example of many artisans can flesh out some of these points. Artisans, especially journeymen, had long been a problem of control in the Holy Roman Empire. However, such controls as were attempted were very inadequate.[46] The real destruction of journeymen organizations came at the turn of the century as part of the Napoleonic state-transformation.[47] The Confederal constitution promised freedom of movement but then frustrated it at two levels. First, there were many state border controls imposed for a variety of reasons – political, financial, and hygienic.[48] Second, in some states, especially in southern Germany, towns were allowed to introduce various communal controls on population movement. These contradicted state modernization programmes as well as artisan expectations, and later Prussia would lead the way in removing such archaic controls after the German National Assembly had failed to do so in 1848–9.

At the same time it is interesting to note that effective border controls were closely linked to improvements in internal policing.[49] Because states were able to enforce the requirement upon journeymen to keep up-to-date work records (the *Wanderbuch*), journeymen knew there was little point in trying to evade border controls. Finally, co-ordination between police across state boundaries also made it increasingly clear to these artisans that the frustrations they suffered were related to a notion of Germany. In these various, often contradictory ways, changes in internal policing and boundary controls contributed to a (negative) sense of national identity.

The further extension of boundaries was associated with the same tensions and internal contradictions. The Zollverein was accepted by many smaller states in part because it enabled a much more effective and lucrative control of the movements of goods. This could weaken the pressure for constitutional concessions (pointing again to the tension between economic and political liberalism). Just as the Zollverein could be vaunted as a triumph of economic liberalism internally, so could it be conceived of as an instrument of very effective economic protectionism (and economic nationalism) externally. The idea of the state as a zone of internal freedom radically separated from the rest of the world could clearly be formulated in this context.[50]

At the same time it was very difficult for the states of Vormärz to create a strong sense of territorial identity. The construction of sovereignty involved an assault upon traditional regional identity. Historians of twentieth-century colonialism have often claimed that there is a trade-off to be made between accepting existing power structures in the colonial territory and imposing innovations designed to secure real control from the centre.[51] The newly expanded states of Napoleonic and Vormärz Germany faced a similar situation. Dalberg represented the most extreme case of administrative conservatism, even if he had to use the new language of French reason to disguise this strategy. However, for most of the new Napoleonic states the major policy was to impose innovations (including deliberately redrawing internal political boundaries), if only because their states would have had no institutional shape or stability without that. The problem was that this could alienate the very different populations they now controlled.

A particular problem was the confessional one. The fragmented political map of the Holy Roman Empire avoided many confessional problems which had been frozen into a particular kind of tolerance, at least for the Calvinist, Lutheran and Catholic faiths, by the settlement of 1648. The construction of larger territorial states made such problems acute. Bavaria acquired a "Protestant" problem with the acquisition of the Palatinate and Franconia. Württemberg had been a largely Protestant state but now acquired many Catholic subjects. Prussia in 1814 acquired many new Catholic subjects in the province of the Rhinelands. What is more, these confessionally distinct areas also had a legal, social, and economic character of their own. The imposition of state-wide uniformity could be perceived as the trampling of religious sensitivities. There soon developed a sense of "regionalism" which was invested with an oppositional political character, even if this was to be de-politicized under the Second Empire.[52]

Such regional opposition was another political basis, along with the momentum of the liberal movement, for the cultivation of a national case. Unable to envisage a breakaway to a smaller political unit as practicable anymore, dissidents in such areas could see a national state as one way of freeing themselves from the interventions of a distant state capital – be it Munich, Karlsruhe, or Berlin.

Finally, it should be noted that the boundaries of the Confederation were hardly designed as "national". Rather they arose out of the complex negotiations of 1814–15, European rather than German negotiations, and were determined more by the territorial settlements made upon individual states rather than any overarching national conception. Boundaries were a matter of "souls" and military strategy and monarchical prestige, as much, if not more, than of nationality.[53]

Between 1800 and 1848 Germany had changed dramatically from being a cluster of many political units with diffused sovereignty and porous and ill-defined boundaries to being a stronger (but less legitimate) political system made up of fewer, larger territorial states with clear developing distinctions between public sovereignty and civil society, as well as clear and effectively patrolled boundaries. However, the lack of constitutional progress (it was bureaucracies rather than parliaments which embodied the sovereign state) and the efficient control of state boundaries made liberal and regional minorities perceive much of this achievement as incomplete, indeed as so incomplete as to be reactionary. The idea of building political reform on supra-state institutions (whether the Confederation or the Zollverein or newly created) appeared increasingly attractive. When that point was reached it was possible to use the rather separate currents of thought associated with German nationality and culture to build a case that was based on ideas such as natural frontiers and language. In this, rather indirect and unintended way, changes in the nature of sovereignty and boundaries helped create a sense (or rather senses) of national identity.

IV Sovereignty and national identity, 1848/49–1871

The German revolution of 1848 raised the issue of sovereignty in a stark way.[54] At the level of the individual states the argument could only be put in a "pure" constitutional fashion. There was little sense of a Prussian or Bavarian or Austrian state identity precisely because there had not been constructed any state-wide participatory institutions which could have furnished such a sense. In the cases of Austria and Prussia there had been no such institutions at all (discounting the brief convening of the United Diet in Berlin in 1847); in other cases they had had too little influence and had been too restricted in participation.

Moreover, many of those who came to prominence in the liberal ministries and state parliaments of 1848 never really concerned themselves with the problem of legitimacy in the sense of a commitment to the doctrine of popular sovereignty and the building of effective political movements to realize that doctrine. For example, the Rhenish liberals Camphausen and Hansemann, who headed successive Prussian ministries in the spring and summer of 1848, saw their tasks in the very practical terms of restoring economic and political security and using constitutionalism to pursue economic liberal goals which in fact were rather unpopular.[55] Only the radicals were prepared to speak out and organize for the clear principle of popular sovereignty, sometimes adding a republican credo in order to make it clear how different this was from the old monarchical order. However, they were soon marginalized and then repressed. Partly this was because they could only tap popular support by appealing to local interests and exploiting local cultural practices.[56] They were difficult to suppress at a local level but also found it difficult to organize at a national, or even state-wide level. The liberal opposition colluded with the monarchy to blur the question of sovereignty – insisting that there had not been a revolution, that parliaments were legitimate because the monarchs had freely summoned them, and that a new constitutional order would be based upon amicable agreements between parliaments and monarchs, not the victory of one over the other.

On the other hand, monarchists did have a clear idea of legitimacy and, at least in the core territories of the major states, this was a widely shared idea. So long as the monarchy conceded the most pressing popular demands, especially peasant demands for the completion, on satisfactory terms, of the emancipation programme, it could then confront the revolution with renewed strength. Monarchical legitimacy could then come to co-opt rather than confront ideas of grounding power upon a popular appeal.

Different questions were raised at the national level. The demand to replace rather than reform the Confederation had, by early 1848, become the major concern of the diverse national movement made up of various liberal and regional minorities. That had led on to national elections and the convening of the German National Assembly (GNA) in Frankfurt in May 1848.

Once the assembly got down to business the issue of sovereignty posed itself in a number of different ways. There was the immediate question of the authority of the GNA over the member states. It was clear to most deputies that they could not challenge state sovereignty, especially at a time when this was a major cause of contention in the individual states. State parliaments and liberal ministries would oppose "outside" interference as energetically as the princes. The GNA fudged the issue by establishing a Provisional Authority that it hoped would be generally acceptable, and then delaying making politically contentious decisions until the dust had settled at state level and it could see what kinds of political negotiations might be managed.

That in part accounts for the long debates which took place through the summer of 1848 on "Basic Rights". If the modern concept of state sovereignty limits this to the "public" sphere, then the GNA decided to approach this issue not by defining the boundaries and political structure of that sovereign state first, but rather by defining the character of the "private" sphere, that is what lay *outside* the state, as well as the rights which the state should protect and promote.

Indirectly this procedure did address the issue of sovereignty. First, it continued with the modern project of dismantling, at least in constitutional theory, corporate controls. Churches, guilds, urban communes, remaining noble privileges – all these were rhetorically put to the sword in the Basic Rights of the GNA. The obstacles between the state and the individual citizen were removed. Organizations outside the state were defined as private and voluntary. At the same time the state was bound to respect and protect the private and voluntary character of these associations.[57]

These were implicitly highly political decisions. First, they gave a real meaning to the idea of unification as being something more than the construction of a government. To be a German, that is a citizen of the German state, was to possess a whole range of freedoms in every part of Germany. Second, this was a very divisive meaning – one which many Germans, e.g. as Catholics and guildsmen, noble landowners and privileged burghers, would vehemently oppose.

The political section of the constitution was more conventional, expressing one variant on the (hopefully) consensual doctrine of constitutional monarchy. However, whereas the only matter at issue in each state was the nature and division of authority between parliament and prince, in the case of the GNA there was also the issue of which monarchy.

I do not want to consider the well-known contrast between *kleindeutsch* and *großdeutsch*, the choice between Prussia or Austria. The main point I want to make is how innocent, in retrospect, the GNA appears to have been. On the one hand, its constitutional endeavours outlined a consistent picture of a national society formed on liberal principles with a single sovereign power. On the other hand, many of its most realistic deputies were trying to work out ways in which the stark political question – where does power lie, in Berlin, Vienna or somewhere else? – could be evaded. Particularly given the logic of the "national" solution, which would involve the division of Austria into a German and a non-German part conjoined only by personal monarchical union, there was no feasible solution.

I would not explain this failure in "realism" in terms of the triumph of hope over experience, or the innocence of a parliament of impractical professors. Rather I would stress that the idea that sovereignty was grounded, in however a disguised way, upon the will of the people, had not yet been tried in Germany, and therefore most people did not yet understand what it ruled out. The Confederation, continuing in part the tradition of the Holy Roman Empire, considered that a loose union of legitimate states (that is, monarchical states which consulted with the major social estates of their realms) did not need to have sharp boundaries or sharply defined sovereignty. Austria and Prussia could "share" influence over the whole of Germany (rather than over different territorial parts of Germany) within such an arrangement. The challenge to monarchical legitimacy and the construction, through the Basic Rights, of a society of citizens, undermined that type of arrangement. Yet the GNA sought to graft these new principles on to a structure not unlike the Confederation. Most deputies still did not inhabit a political culture in which sovereignty and territoriality were inseparable, but rather had only a partial understanding of the implications of the modern notion of sovereignty for the nature of territory in state power.

When hard choices finally had to be made, then coalitions were formed which were based less on some firm sense of national identity than on pre-existing loyalties. Catholics opposed any solutions which would exclude Austria; Protestants looked more to Prussia. Radicals combined with pro-Prussian liberals in order to achieve democratic elements in the Imperial Constitution. State loyalty had an important bearing upon the choices finally made.

Once the GNA had clearly failed, what is interesting is that the new solutions that were immediately brought forward broke with any continuities with the Confederation. The *Unionpolitik* of Prussia aimed at establishing a zone of influence in north and central Germany, a precursor of the establishment of the North German Confederation in 1867. The idea of a huge central European customs union pressed by Austria envisaged the merging of the German lands into a larger entity. The two policies cancelled one another out and the Confederation was restored.[58] It did actually develop even more effective political policing powers than it had exercised in Vormärz, but few now believed that it had any legitimacy. What this policing power, as well as various quite effective economic agreements demonstrated, was not so much the power of the Confederation as the need increasingly to coordinate affairs between more and more sharply defined territorial states.[59] The problem then remained – given that the smaller states lacked real independence, on what basis were Austria and Prussia to "share" influence in the German lands? And could any solution be given a national character?

At this point enter Bismarck. He brought two highly unusual qualities to Prussian politics.[60] First, he had been catapulted into public life through the emergence of popular and constitutional politics in 1847 and 1848. His was not a career based on service at court or as an official. He was at home in the public politics of the day and fully realized that monarchical legitimacy was based no longer upon traditional and religious foundations but upon a consensus established through some kind of political recognition of broad social classes and the securing of their material interests.

Second, he was appointed as Prussian ambassador to the restored Confederation without any previous diplomatic experience. He confronted what he quickly took to be the nonsense of "shared" sovereignty which had no clear territorial expression. His consistent concern from 1851 until 1866 was how to move towards two territorial spheres of influence – a Prussian and an Austrian one.

Given the diplomatic and military strength of Austria in relation to Prussia through the 1850s, as well as the attitude of the Prussian government that what Bismarck preached broke with monarchical legitimism and exposed the Prussian monarchy itself to challenge, and one can understand why Bismarck's advice to Berlin to challenge Austria and to destroy the Confederation was rejected.

The story of how Bismarck took power in Berlin and then put into practice his policy of "dividing" Germany between Prussia and Austria is well known and I will not repeat it here. I simply want to focus on certain features which relate to the issue of sovereignty and national identity.

First, one can note that there are implicitly points of convergence between Bismarck and the liberal opposition in Prussia. Neither wished to defend monarchical legitimacy in its present form but recognized that it must be put on to a popular and constitutional basis. Both realized that sovereignty must be given clear territorial expression. Both realized that Prussia must take the leading role in bringing about these changes. Obviously the differences are also significant. Liberals believed that the popular and constitutional reshaping of Prussia must precede an active policy in Germany and wished to bind the monarchy more within such a constitutional order. For Bismarck an expanded Prussian sphere of influence rather than the liberal vision of a German nation-state (*großpreußisch* rather than *kleindeutsch*) was central.[61] What I find especially interesting is that the events of 1866–67 revealed the degree of convergence and the realistic nature of the assumptions made by both Bismarck and the liberals. By contrast, the events of 1870–71 pointed to tensions and also challenged the understandings of both. I will explore this briefly by considering the issue of sovereignty and the constitutions of the North German Confederation and of the Second Empire.

Even before 1866 Prussia had gone some way to giving a constitutional expression to her statehood. The first official document to refer to the Prussian state in the singular was the "imposed" constitution of December 1848. More than any other measure this provided an institutional expression of Prussian state identity which extended beyond servants of the monarchy. Deputies from the different provinces could now meet regularly in Berlin. A Prussian political class based on modern principles of representation could slowly form. The anti-democratic changes introduced to the original constitution, above all the replacement of equal, direct and universal manhood suffrage by the three-class system of indirect voting, if anything helped that process by confining representation to certain elites. It was indeed a propertied, oligarchic franchise, modelled on that of the Rhenish cities and opposed by some principled conservatives. On this basis it was possible for a *großpreußisch* position to be formed outside the ranks of officialdom.[62]

Bismarck directly challenged that political class between 1862 and 1866. At home he ruled without a constitution; abroad his diplomacy up to 1866 paid no heed to national opinions, whether expressed through the Confederation or liberal organizations. Nevertheless, one should note the implicitly conciliatory nature of his justification for unconstitutional rule. The view of the "ultras" was that the constitution was a gift from the king which could be revoked at any time. Bismarck instead argued a theory of the "constitutional gap", i.e. if parliament and monarchy could not agree, then there had to be provision for carrying on the work of the government. The constitution did not make allowance for this (hence the "gap") and this justified the executive in filling the gap by continuing to collect taxes and carry out administrative duties. The theory conceded that sovereignty should be organized constitutionally under "normal" conditions.

The steps Bismarck took immediately following upon the defeat of Austria showed how seriously he took this argument. The Indemnity Bill of September 1866 sought to return to the principle that monarchical sovereignty was expressed only through the constitution in which parliament had a key role. The theoretical issue of sovereignty, therefore, became the key to forming an alliance with liberalism.

The nature of the Prussian state, both how it was theoretically understood and actually operated, was vital in 1866–67 because Bismarck then pursued a greater-Prussian and not a little-German solution. Most of the new sphere of influence established by Bismarck in north and central Germany was swallowed up through direct annexation.

However, there were important features to these annexations which made them different from any previous alteration of Prussian territory. The restored Prussian constitutional order was extended to these new provinces, and this order gave a much more central role to a bourgeois dominated parliament than had the political arrangements of the states which were abolished. Simultaneously the princely houses of these states were abolished, not merely reduced in size and influence. That was a hammer-blow to the "pure" principle of monarchical sovereignty. Prussia could not hope to gain support by a transfer of monarchical loyalty. Apart from brute power and material opportunities, the creation of legitimate authority in the expanded Prussian state would have to be achieved through the creation of acceptable state institutions organized under the principles of rule of law and a written constitution.

Bismarck was well aware of this. He quickly brought the period of direct military government to an end in the annexed provinces. He resisted the exportation of Prussian bureaucrats as a kind of colonial governing class to these provinces. He respected the traditional boundaries of the annexed states in drawing the boundaries of the new provinces. Given also that the system of Prussian administration was extended in a sensitive way which drew attention to its efficiency and cheapness, then one can understand why annexation was not seen by many of the inhabitants of those states as conquest. Indeed, where some of the annexed states had more appropriate administrative structures, these actually fed back into all-Prussian arrangements.[63] In other words, it was the liberal character of annexation which made it effective. Not surprisingly, these annexed provinces provided the bastions of the National Liberal movement which was to form a partnership with Bismarck in the period 1867–73 and laid the foundations for a modern liberal state and free market economy.[64]

The establishment of the North German Confederation also provided a mechanism for establishing common laws for the other states of north and central Germany which had been brought within the Prussian sphere of influence but not actually annexed to Prussia.

Bismarck's new partnership with liberals meant that these common laws emphasized the liberalizing and integrating features of the new state system. For example, a vague reference in the constitution of the North German Confederation to a kind of confederal citizenship – the "Indigenat" – was used by Berlin to impose freedom of movement and settlement within the Confederation.[65] Typically what had been hinted at as desirable but not practiced in the Articles of Confederation of 1814, and proclaimed as a basic right in the Imperial Constitution of 1849 but never converted into reality, was now negotiated, under pressure from Berlin, through the Bundesrat of the North German Confederation. Finance and banking, the liberal *Gewerbeordnung* of 1869, and much other legislative and administrative reform also pushed things in this direction. Finally the Reichstag, elected on the basis of universal, equal, and direct manhood suffrage exercised through the secret ballot, paid some lip-service to the idea of popular sovereignty, though hedged about by the limited competence both of the Reichstag within the Confederation and of Confederal institutions relative to member states.

The problem was that the North German Confederation could hardly be defended as a national solution. At most it could only be regarded as a stage towards such a solution. For many liberals it was this "instalment" view of the Confederation, reinforced by its liberalizing character and the key role of liberals in the reforming politics of the period which made the Confederation acceptable. As the National Liberal leader Bennigsen put it:

> If there is success . . . in organising all north and central Germany with the help of parliament militarily and economically, and in these areas some emergency bridges are built to south Germany, a very firm basis for further development will have been achieved. The nation cannot ask for more at this time.[66]

Yet as liberals worked to concentrate sovereignty in Berlin, both on a Prussian and Confederal level, this process also emphasized more strongly how "Germany" was now divided into three zones – north of the river Main, south of the Main and north of Austria, and Austria.

Of course, after 1871 the North German Confederation did appear as just a stage on the national road (though one which excluded Austria). However, apart from the unwillingness of many south Germans to join a unified Germany dominated by Prussia, one needs to stress that what appeared as "progress" in national terms (that is in terms of bringing the boundaries of the state closer to one or other geographic conception of the nation) was also apparently "regress" understood in terms of modern sovereignty. South German states were treated very differently in 1871 from north German states in 1867. They retained their own and varying constitutions. Monarchical legitimacy was respected. The preamble to the constitution expressed the view of the document as a treaty between independent states which were giving up a portion of their power to establish an imperial state. State rights were much more sensitively protected compared to 1867. In many ways this appears as a regression to eighteenth-century principles whereby the conquering ruler agreed to respect the laws and traditions of the newly conquered province.[67]

This sits uneasily with the understanding of the German Empire as a nation-state. It was not liked by many of Bismarck's liberal collaborators who found state-rights, the language of empire, and the failure to make government accountable to parliament deeply disturbing. (Just one small step towards this was taken, namely the requirement for the Chancellor to counter-sign imperial measures. Yet this could also serve to increase the power of the office of Chancellor.) Even before the problems created by the economic downturn from 1873–74, possible moves away from the modern liberal conception of a sovereign, constitutional and "public" state regulating the affairs of a civil society structured on the basis of a free and national citizenry (which required certain economic and cultural conditions) was hinted at in the constitution of 1871. The problems of sovereignty and national-identity in the new state will be addressed in Section VI.

V   Boundaries, territory and national identity, 1848/49–1871

The GNA and the Imperial Constitution of 1849 appear to be quite clear as to *where* Germany is: it is the territory of the German Confederation. How this came to be the dominant assumption by mid-century is worth some consideration.

The creation of a system of modernizing territorial states which were wholly members of the Confederation made the boundary of the Confederation much clearer than in the period of the Holy Roman Empire. In this sense a modern Bavaria or Baden or Württemberg, although presenting some of the main resistance to the construction of German sovereignty helped make much clearer the idea of a German territory.

However, this statist definition of German boundaries confronted, even in its own terms, the problem of what happened when a particular state was territorially divided, with part of it being in the Confederation and part of it outside. On the one hand there were states in which the core territory was outside the Confederation –

for example, Denmark, whose king ruled, in personal union, the duchies of Schleswig and Holstein, the latter being within the Confederation. On the other hand, there were the two "German" states of Austria and Prussia, part of whose territory was outside the Confederation.

It is worth noting that *every* national boundary dispute during the 1848–49 revolution was related to these specific areas, at least so far as Germans were concerned.[68] No significant claim was made to territory beyond the present boundaries of the Confederation except in the cases of the two provinces of East and West Prussia and the territory of Schleswig. Conversely, no significant concession was made to non-German speaking populations who were concentrated into certain regions within the Confederation – notably the Danish speaking region of north Schleswig (once claimed for Germany) and the Czech speaking regions of Bohemia and Moravia.

Partly one can explain this on pragmatic terms. To raise issues which called into question the international boundaries settled in 1814–15 would arouse the hostility of the other major European powers. Partly, however, it also can be explained by the way in which the modernizing states had fixed boundaries much more precisely than before.

Seen from the political centres of Germany this arrangement appeared stable. Political elites in western Germany, for example, had come to terms with the destruction of the Holy Roman Empire, even with the removal from French control in 1814–15. Here boundaries were fixed with political-administrative precision, above all because German states touched upon the boundaries of France, the most modern, boundary-conscious European state. Boundary issues here could only be raised in the context of war or the threat of war with France.

The southern border also presented no particular problem. However, this was not because it was well-defined either politically or culturally. It was not. The "southern boundary" of Germany (i.e. the German Confederation) was simply a line drawn on the map of Austria. There were differences in the ways in which the "German" parts of Austria were governed compared to the Italian and Hungarian parts, but these were more in terms of administrative and fiscal arrangements, and not in terms of strict border controls. The reason this boundary was never a problem was because it was subsumed within the broader question of Austrian sovereignty. Only if the division of Austria-Hungary into a German and a non-German part, whether completely separate or joined by purely personal union had come close to realization would this have been seen as a problem. On the other hand, the "solution" of 1866/1870–71 established the boundary simply by means of the expulsion of all of Austria from Germany: the actual southern boundary had no "national" content whatsoever.

The national issue did, however, arise with regard to the northern boundary. From a legal point of view the "German" position was clear – the duchies of Schleswig and Holstein were indivisible. Holstein belonged to the Confederation. That was fine in Confederal terms because sovereignty rested with the member states rather than the Confederal authority. Membership of Confederation and subjection to the authority of a state largely outside the Confederation were compatible. However, the GNA wished to shift sovereignty to the central, the "national" state. That generated two responses. First, on a purely political level, the Danish monarchy resisted the threatened diminution of its power in the duchies. In fact, it riposted with the claim to create a more uniform and modern form of state sovereignty which would incorporate the duchies into Denmark. On the other hand, the Germans argued that the shift of sovereignty to a central state, combined with the membership of Holstein in Germany and the indivisibility of the two duchies, meant that the Schleswig also should be incorporated into Germany. The "boundary" dispute arose via the issue of "national sovereignty".

These conflicting moves from Frankfurt (aided briefly by Berlin) and Copenhagen therefore reinforced the idea of the nation-state as a territorially sovereign state. Boundaries come to matter more in this political conception. This problem then interacted with local conditions. In part the political events of 1848–49 made Danish and German speakers more aware of their nationality, and the need to look to their core territory for support. There were also local economic and cultural changes which underlay this shift towards national attitudes.[69] However, it is worth noting that at no time in this period did the other logical method of devising national boundaries, namely by consulting the local population (whether in terms of plebiscites – the "subjective" method, or by cultural categorizing – the "objective" method) ever prevail over the state-centred approach.

Because the GNA had not invoked cultural criteria for national boundaries in the north, west and south, it could consistently deal with the objections of "non-Germans" as a cultural, not a political matter. A German was a citizen of the German state: state territory and citizen rights defined nationality. There was a problem, the Imperial Constitution acknowledged this, of non-German speaking minorities, but that would be dealt with through educational and other cultural means.[70]

The only boundary where the cultural criterion of nationality was invoked to draw a boundary in 1848–49 was in the east. There were a number of reasons for this. First, the Polish question presented a problem to liberal nationalists who thought of the nation-state in historic-legal terms. There had existed, until the late eighteenth century, a Polish kingdom which had been progressively destroyed and distributed between the three states of Russia, Austria and Prussia. The Polish nationalist argument by mid-nineteenth century was mainly presented in terms of the restoration of this kingdom. The Prussian state had implicitly recognized at least the case for some political distinction in the way a "Polish" territory should be treated by according the Grand Duchy of Posen (excluded from Confederation along with West and East Prussia) a different legal status from the rest of its territories.

What is more, for most German (including Prussian) liberals, support for the Polish cause was closely linked to hostility to Russia. Russia controlled most of the territory of historic Poland, and much of that in a constitutionally separate kingdom ("Congress Poland") joined to the rest of the monarchy by personal union. The Polish possessions of Austria were largely separated from the rest of the dynasty in the kingdom of Galicia, also outside the German Confederation. Therefore, to give up the Grand Duchy of Posen in support of historically grounded Polish nationalism seemed reasonable to Prussian liberals in the spring of 1848. On the other hand, they also wished to include Western and Eastern Prussia into the elections for the GNA as well as the Prussian national assembly.

This contained within it two "nationalizing" implications. First, German-speaking inhabitants of Posen objected to being handed over to Polish control. Now a "periphery"-based nationality movement could come to influence the politics of the centre, especially when traditional Prussian power began to reassert itself. The move towards partitioning Posen along nationality lines has, in this context, to be seen as a compromise between this "border

German"-cum-loyalist Prussian tendency and the liberal national-cum-pro-Polish tendency. What is more, it was in the first instance a Prussian affair which was only subsequently brought to the GNA for approval. This, I would argue, is the exception that proves the rule. In 1848–49 ethnic or linguistic conceptions of nationality, although increasingly present in certain peripheral regions in the south, east and north, were less important in determining national boundary claims and disputes than were historic-legal conceptions which prevailed in the political centres of Germany.

The second implication took much longer to manifest itself. That was the Polish response to an increasingly German national rather than Prussian dynastic approach to those Polish-speaking areas which were in the Prussian state. In 1870–71 Polish deputies to the Reichstag convened to debate the constitution of the Second Empire made it clear that the definition of the new state as national called into question their allegiance in a way in which the Prussian dynastic principle had not. Yet this should be seen as putting down a marker for the subsequent development of nationalist tensions in eastern Germany rather than expressing significant conflict at the time. It was in turn associated with the shift of Polish nationalism away from historic to ethnic principles.

All other boundary disputes up to 1871 were purely to do with power and sovereignty, not any claim as to "where" Germany was. The major one, of course, was between Austria and Prussia. The *kleindeutsch* conception of the German nation-state was not less ambitious or nationalist than the *großdeutsch*. Rather it looked to Prussia rather than Austria for leadership. The proponents of *Kleindeutschland*, like the supporters of the North German Confederation, looked at it as worthwhile if it was also a liberal achievement and if it provided the basis for the later territorial completion of the nation-state. For the liberal nationalist of mid-century this would come about with the division of Austria-Hungary. This division would happen because of internal weakness rather than being compelled by Prussia through war. A redrawn "national" map of central and southern Europe would consist of states controlled by the "historic" nations of Germany, Italy, Hungary and Poland.[71] *Kleindeutschland* was a first step. Nevertheless, there was one very important cultural consequence for how such liberals conceived of German nationality. It was linked to the dominating Protestant-secularist tendencies in north and central Germany. *Kleindeutschland* was a state with a Catholic minority, unlike *Großdeutschland* which would have had a Catholic majority. This was to have a major impact upon the development of a sense of nationality in the Second Empire.

This was not Bismarck's vision. As a Prussian conservative he deplored any encouragement of Polish nationality feelings and his first major foreign policy move as Minister-President was to signal his solidarity with Russia in its repression of the Polish rising of 1863. He cooperated with Italian nationalists in 1866 and 1870, and threatened to support Hungarian insurgency in 1866, but only to put the necessary pressure upon Austria to concede a territorial sphere of influence to Prussia in north and central Germany. Otherwise he was concerned to prevent the break-up of Austria-Hungary. *Großpreußen* (rather than *Kleindeutschland*) was to be the last step. Germans outside its boundaries were to be encouraged in their loyalty to their different rulers. Indeed Bismarck believed that the presence of a significant German cultural and political presence in neighbouring states, especially Austria and Russia, would make a major contribution to peaceful international relations.[72]

The extension of Germany to the south German states was arguably undertaken to secure the achievements of 1866–67 rather than out of a national motivation.[73] Again the boundary issue was a matter of state boundaries and power, not based on any national identity argument. Bismarck's lack of commitment to these boundaries is revealed by the fact that in 1878 he was even prepared to consider further extension of Prussian boundaries (e.g. the annexation of Saxony) along with the reduction in the boundaries of Germany by partitioning Bavaria with Austria.[74] How seriously one should take such talk, which was part of Bismarck's efforts to bludgeon National Liberals into a major change of political direction, is one matter. But the very fact that Bismarck could talk in this way shows just how unformed the idea of the nation-state as a particular territorial entity was in his mind.

This mode of thinking is difficult for us to grasp. More importantly, it was increasingly difficult for many of Bismarck's contemporaries to grasp as well. Although, as I have already argued, the unification of 1871 was a regression on the North German Confederation in terms of linking national identity to a clearly defined centre of sovereignty, in boundary terms it advanced the national idea far more. First, the Franco-Prussian war was a national war, unlike the

Austro-Prussian war. Bismarck could not avoid invoking the cause of Germany. Second, the annexation of Alsace-Lorraine transformed the way in which national boundaries were understood.

Here, for the first time, a boundary claim was legitimized not on grounds of tradition or law or an appeal to popular sovereignty (by allowing the inhabitants of the region to choose) but upon the principle of ethnic nationality. (There was the additional argument of the strategic necessity of the area, but that is an argument based on power, not legitimacy.) Von Treitschke's ominous assertion that the inhabitants of Alsace were "German" even if they had forgotten that they were points to a conception of nationality which ran counter to the way Bismarck understood the nature of statehood and political identity.

Finally, the failure to extend Prussian institutions into south Germany meant that anyone wishing to continue the process of national integration and the cultivation of a sense of national identity based on shared citizenship and laws now had to look to imperial institutions as the principal vehicle of progress.

By 1848–49 the repressive nature of the Confederation, combined with the sharper definition of sovereignty and boundaries which had been developed in the various German states, had helped to form a cluster of elites which looked to some kind of national state as a way of realizing their liberal values or regional identity in opposition to the state in which they found themselves. The boundaries of that state were taken unproblematically to be those of the Confederation and there was initially little appreciation of the contradiction between the liberal project of a civil society matched by a sovereign constitutional state and the Austro-Prussian dualism. The failure of 1848 made that contradiction clear. To achieve clear sovereignty meant focusing on the boundaries of *Kleindeutschland*.

Constitutionalism after 1849 also cultivated a greater sense of Prussian identity. The idea of a constitutional *Großpreußen* provided a possible point of compromise between *kleindeutsch* national liberals and Bismarck. This compromise was expressed in the expanded Prussia of 1867 where the issues of constitutionality and sovereignty could be addressed, but which emphatically was not a nation-state in boundary terms.

The final unification of 1871 moved closer to the idea of the nation-state in boundary terms and established nationality as the basis of the state in a new and irreversible way. At the same time it reversed some of the momentum established between 1867–71 towards creating a single constitional order with a clear focus of sovereignty.

VI Excursus: the problem of national identity in the Second Empire

For Bismarck the "Reich" would become its own justification; create its own identity. That turned out to be true, but in ways he had not expected.

The boundary of the new state came to mean more than ever before. The customs union came to be coterminous with the political boundaries, and the shift to protectionism in 1879 invested that boundary with an increased economic significance. Integrating measures, even when along lines which involved the further elaboration of a free civil society, made it clear that these applied only to the territory bounded by the national state.

Policy initiative to start with lay with liberal nationalists. They were concerned to continue the economic and cultural policies which would deepen their conception of the nation as secular, free, and civilized.[75] The "struggle for culture" (*Kulturkampf*) as the anti-Catholic campaign was revealingly entitled was as significant in this project as was legal codification or the construction of a national railway network.

Yet states controlled many of the institutions which affected everyday life such as the churches and schools. A uniformity of development, along with increased geographical mobility within the national "cultural zone" created by the Second Empire,[76] was essential to state policy helping shape a more homogeneous and nationally conscious society.

The other development which was vital, and equally "unintended", was the development of a more powerful set of imperial institutions. Such a process created more common experiences, encouraging people to look increasingly to Berlin and to organize themselves accordingly.

This process was mainly a consequence of modernization. To start with, the imperial government was confined only to what might be called "boundary maintenance" functions – diplomacy, defence and tariffs – and even the first two of those was largely organized by

Prussian institutions. However, new tasks were taken in hand in such fields as welfare, navy building, communications and transport, and legal codification. New imperial institutions were established to carry out these tasks. Departments for justice, statistics, postal services, railways, internal affairs and the navy were all created. These functions needed, in a constitutional state, a legal mandate and also funding. The first increased the significance of the imperial legislature – Bundesrat and Reichstag. The second made it necessary to search out new sources of finance.

All these processes meant that more and more people were aware of the need to influence imperial institutions in order to promote their interests. Pressure groups and political parties with a purely localist or even state orientation declined in the face of a trend towards national organization and a focus upon Berlin. In terms of mass participation this received its strongest expression in elections for the Reichstag.[77]

In these ways a process of national integration took place. It made the boundaries of the Second Empire appear increasingly national and stable, except where non-German groups (in Polish Prussia, Danish Schleswig, and in Alsace-Lorraine) objected to the process of "nationalization".

Yet at the same time the issue of sovereignty became more contentious. It was seen that imperial institutions were increasing in importance relative to individual states. But that only drew sharp attention to the unsettled nature of the constitutional order. Bismarck by the 1870s was beginning to back away from a liberal view of nation-state development. His concern to bind the "propertied elements", the "producing classes", to the state increasingly took on a corporate rather than individualist form. Yet this ran against the trends of the day. For example, in 1889 Bismarck advocated that minors be paid via their parents, in order to bring family control to bear upon Ruhr miners. It was pointed out that the level of migration from east to west Germany by young workers made this quite impracticable. This was but one example of how out of touch Bismarck was with current trends.

Above all, the division of sovereignty between state and empire, monarch and parliament was unsatisfactory in a modernizing society such as that of Germany. Without proper accountability under the constitution and proper funding, the imperial institutions found it increasingly difficult to formulate policies acceptable to most people or to pay for those policies it did pursue.

Apart from that the sheer power of the Second Empire and the increasingly common experiences furnished by schools, elections, a mass press which both moulded and expressed an increasingly vociferous public opinion, as well as much else all helped shape a sense of national identity. This did not extend to a national consensus on how the imperial state should be organized; indeed if anything the rise of national parties polarized conflicts on this matter. But underlying that there was a common sense of national identity forming in terms of overcoming regionalism and increasing participation in national institutions. If anything that also created new problems, for this emergent national identity was not adequately reflected in the official political symbolism as well as institutional structure of the state, because at the time the state had been formed it had been hostile to much of what existed of a national political tradition.[78]

VII Conclusion

The construction of the modern state has involved two kinds of conquest. First, there is the internal conquest of intermediate bodies and internal boundaries. At a political level, so far as the German lands are concerned, the crucial steps were taken during the Napoleonic period. However, this was largely the achievement of the individual states, not a German achievement. It did, however, establish the idea of statehood as bound up with a constitution and clear boundaries. Opposition to the Confederation moved that idea up to a national level by 1848. A sense of being German was thought about not in ethnic terms but in historic-legal terms based on the Confederation, although also increasingly bound up with the culture of secular or Protestant liberalism. Nation-state building was seen as a process of negotiation in which changes in the focus of sovereignty could be agreed. The creation of a sovereign nation-state was part of a larger process of creating a society of citizens, of the process of civilization. This meant it often had to take a strong and authoritarian form, especially where corporate ties and opposition to the individualizing society of citizens were encountered. The state as an overarching order, bound by constitutionality and the rule of law, was the key to achieving these goals.

National unification then was about the construction of this kind of state.

However, this could not be achieved through negotiation. It was not just a question of constructing a state which then carried through the various internal conquests I have mentioned. It was also a question of forcibly concentrating sovereignty into one centre for a particular territory. That could only be achieved through war. The role of the strong state was even further accentuated here. "Germany" was largely taken for granted territorially. The actual boundaries created were a function of power, not nationality, and only in exceptional cases were justified in nationalist terms.

In boundary terms, therefore, the Second Empire increasingly came to be identified as "Germany". The territorial idea of Germany as co-terminous with the Second Empire has continued into the twentieth century. In cultural and economic terms the Second Empire witnessed a process of nation-building. In political terms sub-national institutions diminished in importance relative to national institutions. However, the failure to achieve parliamentary sovereignty meant that much of that national feeling expressed itself in opposition to the actual state and that that state found it difficult to exploit many of the symbols associated with the idea of a nation-state based on the principle of popular sovereignty.

Only with the establishment of Weimar was there created a state based on the principle of parliamentary sovereignty with common constitutional principles applying to the whole country and which could adopt many national symbols such as a constitution which proclaimed the rights of citizens as well as the powers of government, a flag, and an official national anthem. The tragedy was that this state was also the product of defeat – its boundaries were seen as artificial and its constitution as imposed. The nationalism that would eventually destroy and succeed it abandoned clear principles of national boundaries and constitutionally defined sovereignty and replaced these with a destructive doctrine of a leader state based on race and committed to endless imperial expansion. Only with the destruction of that state and that creed has it been possible to return to a historic-constitutional notion of Germany.

Notes

1. This essay began life as a paper delivered to a conference on "European Frontiers and Boundaries in the Nineteenth and Twentieth Centuries" held at Oxford in June 1992. I am grateful to the organizers of that conference, David Blackbourn and Ruth Harris, and to participants for criticisms and comments on my paper.

2. See P. Hohendahl's essay, Literary criticism in the epoch of liberalism 1820–1870, in P. Hohendahl et al., (eds), *A history of German literary criticism, 1730–1980*, Lincoln, 1988, pp. 179–276, as well as idem., Bürgerliche Literaturgeschichte und nationale Identität. Bilder vom deutschen Sonderweg, in *Bürgertum im 19. Jahrhundert: Deutschland im europäischen Vergleich*, edited by Jürgen Kocka, Munich, 1988, vol. 3, pp. 200–31.

3. See Benedict Anderson, *Imagined communities: reflections on the origins and spread of nationalism*, London, 1983.

4. See Ernest Gellner, *Nations and nationalism*, Oxford, 1983.

5. See the approach, utilizing Karl Deutsch's theory of social communication, in P. Katzenstein, *Disjoined partners: Austria and Prussia since 1815*, Berkeley, 1976.

6. See O. Dann (ed.), *Vereinswesen und bürgerliche Gesellschaft in Deutschland*, Munich, 1984; D. Düding, *Organisierter gesellschaftlicher Nationalismus in Deutschland (1808–1847). Bedeutung und Funktion der Turner und Sängervereine für die Nationalbewegung*, Munich, 1984. An English summary is in idem, The nineteenth-century German nationalist movement as a movement of societies, in H. Schulze (ed.), *Nation-building in central Europe*, Leamington Spa, 1987.

7. For a general and comparative approach which relates these elements to nationalism see M. Hroch, *Die Vorkämpfer der nationalen Bewegung bei den kleinen Völkern Europas: eine vergleichende Analyse zur gesellschaftlichen Schichtung der patriotischen Gruppen*, Prague, 1969. A shorter English language version of Hroch's case is to be found in idem, *Social preconditions of national revival in Europe: a comparative analysis of the social composition of patriotic groups among the smaller European nations*, Cambridge, 1985.

8. On functional explanations see S. Rigby, *Marxism and history*, Manchester, 1987, chapter 6.

9. I have myself been guilty of this approach to some extent in the way I treated nationalism in the unification of Germany and Italy in the original edition of my book *Nationalism and the state*, Manchester, 1982, chapter 2.

10. I review some of this work in: Nations and nationalism in modern German history, *The Historical Journal*, 33/3, 1990, pp. 659–75. On

the use of the "nation" building approach see Werner Conze, Staatsnationale Entwicklung und Modernisierung im Deutschen Reich 1871–1914, in idem, et al., (eds), *Modernisierung und nationale Gesellschaft im ausgehenden 18. und im 19. Jahrhundert*, Berlin, 1979.

11. For a general history of this period see H. Möller, *Fürstenstaat oder Bürgernation. Deutschland 1763–1815*. In English see James Sheehan, *German history 1770–1866*, Oxford, 1990; and Michael Hughes, *Early modern Germany, 1477–1806*, London, 1992.

12. I argue this case at greater length in: State-building, modernization and liberalism from the late eighteenth century to unification: German peculiarities, *European History Quarterly*, 22, 1992, pp. 257–84. For a detailed argument about the transformation of the revolutionary and Napoleonic period see Hans-Ulrich Wehler, *Deutsche Gesellschaftsgeschichte: vol. 1, 1700–1815*, Munich, 1987.

13. This was a central theme in Leonard Krieger, *The German idea of freedom: history of a political tradition*, Chicago, 1957. See especially section 1: The tradition, liberty and sovereignty in the German old regime. The theme has been taken up, only now as one aspect of a political culture rather than as an intellectual doctrine, in Michael Hughes, Fiat justitia, pereat Germania? The imperial supreme jurisdiction and imperial reform in the later Holy Roman Empire, in J. Breuilly (ed.), *The State of Germany: the national idea in the making, unmaking and remaking of a nation-state*, London, 1992, pp. 29–46.

14. See the chapter by Roland Axtmann, The emergence of the modern state: the debate in the social sciences.

15. I consider this at greater length in: State-building. The most important modern analysis of the ALR is by Reinhard Koselleck, *Preußen zwischen Reform und Revolution: Allgemeines Landrecht, Verwaltung und soziale Bewegung von 1791 bis 1848*, 3rd edn., Stuttgart, 1981.

16. See H. Johnson, *Frederick the Great and his officials*, New Haven and London, 1975.

17. For example, on its regionalized recruitment system and how that related to a highly decentralized, agrarian and noble-dominated society, see Otto Büsch, *Militärsystem und Socialleben im alten Preußen 1713–1807*, 2nd edn., Frankfurt, 1981.

18. Hughes, Fiat justitia.

19. See the essays in *Nationalism in the age of the French Revolution*, edited by O. Dann and J. Dinwiddy, London, 1988.

20. J. A. Vann, *The making of a state: Württemberg, 1593–1793*, Ithaca, 1984, p. 20.

21. On German patriotism in Austria in 1808–9 see W. Langsam, *The Napoleonic wars and German nationalism in Austria*, New York, 1930.

22. There is a general overview of these reforms in Barbara Vogel (ed.),

Preußische Reformen, Königstein im Taunus, 1981.

23. In English see Sheehan, *German history*, and Breuilly, State-building. For a good overview in German see H. Berding and H.-P. Ullmann (eds), *Deutschland zwischen Revolution und Restauration*, Königstein im Taunus, 1981.

24. For a general survey see L. Knemeyer, *Regierungs- und Verwaltungsreformen in Deutschland zu Beginn des 19. Jahrhunderts*, Cologne & Berlin, 1970. On reform of the bureaucracy see especially H. Wunder, *Privilegierung und Disziplinierung. Die Entstehung des Berufsbeamtentum in Bayern und Württemberg 1780–1825*, Munich, 1978.

25. K. Möckl, Die bayrische Konstitution von 1808, in E. Weis (ed.), *Reformen im rheinbündischen Deutschland*, Munich, 1984, pp. 151–68.

26. The financial motive behind Prussian constitutional experiments, as well as other reforms, is stressed in E. Klein, *Von der Reform zur Restauration. Finanzpolitik und Reformsgesetzgebung der preußischen Staatskanzlers von Hardenberg*, Berlin [W], 1975.

27. On German constitutional thought see Dieter Grimm, *Deutsche Verfassungsgeschichte*, Vol. 1, Frankfurt, 1988.

28. For example, attempts in Prussia to maintain the idea of different punishments for members of different social estates could not be embodied in law and was left to the courts to try to work out on a pragmatic basis. The whole approach was quietly dropped in the revised criminal code of 1851. See Dirk Blasius, *Bürgerliche Gesellschaft und Kriminalität: zur Sozialgeschichte Preußens im Vormärz*, Göttingen, 1976.

29. See Koselleck, *Preußen zwischen Reform und Revolution*; and E. Fehrenbach, Verfassungs- und sozialpolitische Reformen und Reformprojekte under dem Einfluß des napoleonischen Frankreichs, in Berding & Ullmann (eds), *Deutschland zwischen Revolution und Restauration*.

30. Klein, *Von der Reform zur Restauration*, especially chapter 2.

31. In B. Vogel, *Allgemeine Gewerbefreiheit. Die Reformpolitik des preußischen Staatskanzlers Hardenberg*, Göttingen, 1983.

32. H-P. Ullmann, *Staatsschulden und Reformpolitik. Die Entstehung moderner öffentlicher Schulden in Bayern und Baden, 1780–1820*, Göttingen, 1986.

33. See Vogel, *Allgemeine Gewerbefreiheit* for the acceptance of Smith's ideas in Hardenberg's circle. More generally see Keith Tribe, *Governing economy: the reformation of German economic discourse 1750–1840*, Cambridge, 1988.

34. The point of the term was that before these imperial knights had stood in an "immediate" relation to the Holy Roman Empire. Now their relationship to the German Confederation, seen as in some way as a continuation of the imperial tradition, would be mediated

through state rulers. Strictly speaking sovereignty had shifted from the imperial/confederal to the territorial state level, although the theoretical implication of the idea of a "mediatized" relationship, as well as the privileges granted to Standesherren somewhat contradicted this position. On the concern with restoring the social if not the political position of these nobles see E. Kraehe, *Metternich's German Policy: Vol. 2: The Congress of Vienna*, Princeton, 1983, especially pp. 317–26. See also Heinz Gollwitzer, *Die Standesherren. Die politische und gesellschaftliche Stellung der Mediatisierten, 1815–1918: Ein Beitrag zur deutschen Sozialgeschichte*, Göttingen, 1964. The Confederal Act of 1815 was compelled to make a "modern" distinction between private rights and public power in its defence of these privileges. See Article 14 of the Deutsche Bundesakte of 8 June 1815, reprinted in E. R. Huber (ed.), *Dokumente zur Verfassungsgeschichte: Vol. 1: 1803–1850*, 3rd edn., Stuttgart, 1978, pp. 84–90 (85).

35. See Hohendahl, Literary criticism in the epoch of liberalism, and Harro Segberg, Germany, in Dann and Dinwiddy, *Nationalism in the age of the French Revolution*, pp. 137–156.

36. On the episode with Goethe see Theo Stammen, Goethe und das deutsche Nationalbewußtsein im beginnenden 19. Jahrhundert, in *Heimat und Nation. Zur Geschichte und Identität der Deutschen*, Mainz, 1984, edited by Klaus Weigelt. On national monument building see George L. Mosse, *The nationalisation of the masses*, New York, 1975. On trying to construct a sense of Bavarian political identity see Werner Blessing, *Staat und Kirche in der Gesellschaft. Institutioneller Autorität und mentaler Wandel in Bayern während des 19. Jahrhunderts*, Göttingen, 1982; and M. Harnisch, *"Für Fürst und Valerland". Bayern 1848–1871*, Munich, 1990.

37. Wolfram Siemann, *"Deutschlands Ruhe, Sicherheit und Ordnung". Die Anfänge der politischen Polizei 1806–1866*, Tübingen, 1985.

38. We possess two good overviews of German liberalism: James Sheehan, *German liberalism in the 19th century*, Chicago, 1978; and Dieter Langewiesche, *Liberalismus in Deutschland*, Frankfurt, 1988.

39. For an interesting account of how this national conception, perhaps focused on the Zollverein, could also be linked to a shift to a modern social conception in which industrial growth was seen as central see Rudolf Boch, *Grenzenlose Wachstum? Das rheinische Wirtschaftsbürgertum und seine Industrialisierungsdebatte 1814–1857*, Göttingen, 1991.

40. On the war of 1792 see T. C. Blanning, *The origins of the French revolutionary wars*, London, 1986. The seminal work which has stimulated interest in the changing meaning of boundaries and how they relate to identities is P. Sahlins, *Boundaries: the making of France and Spain in the Pyrenees*, Berkeley, 1989. Generally on the history of what were

"German" boundaries and how they changed their meaning see A. Demandt (ed.), *Deutschlands Grenzen in der Geschichte*, Munich, 1990. For a more theoretical consideration of the shift from "frontiers" to "boundaries" see A. Giddens, *The nation-state and violence*, Cambridge, 1985.

41. See the essay by Hans-Dietrich Schultz, Deutschlands 'natürliche' Grenzen, in *Deutschlands Grenzen in der Geschichte*, pp. 33–88.

42. For a general and comparative approach which sees the gendarmerie in relation to modern state-formation see the chapter by Clive Emsley, Gendarmes, peasants and state formation. On the decline of vagrancy and banditry see Carsten Küther, *Räuber und Gauner in Deutschland: das Organisierte Bandenwesen im 18. und frühen 19. Jahrhundert*, Göttingen, 1976.

43. See Article 18 of the Confederal Act of 1815 in Huber (ed.), *Dokumente zur Verfassungsgeschichte 1803–50*, p. 90.

44. In the south German states there was a period of apparent reverse movement as some towns were allowed to enforce a stricter right of settlement (*Heimatsrecht*), but this in turn was a reaction to the increased movement made possible by the larger territorial state. In Prussia the state by the early 1840s moved to enforce a uniform obligation to provide poor relief to people who had been resident for three years or more. This is dealt with in H-U. Wehler, *Deutsche Gesellschaftsgeschichte: Vol. 2: 1815–1845/49*, Munich, 1987.

45. I have studied the particular problems this created for the city-state of Hamburg, especially in relation to such matters as right to poor relief for people who were born in another German state but had either resided continuously in Hamburg for a number of years or had given birth to children while in Hamburg.

46. For the major imperial legislation of 1731 see Mack Walker, *German home towns: community, state and general estate 1648–1871*, Ithaca & London, 1971, chapter III, Guilds, and the appendix which translates the edict into English.

47. See Andreas Griessinger, *Das symbolische Kapital der Ehre*, Frankfurt, 1981.

48. See Wolfgang Schieder, *Anfänge der deutschen Arbeiterbewegung: Die Auslandsverein im Jahrzehnt nach der Julirevolution von 1830*, Stuttgart, 1963, especially pp. 93–109; and Friedrich Lenger, *Sozialgeschichte der deutschen Handwerker seit 1800*, Frankfurt, 1988.

49. There are many kinds of policing and the meaning of the word "Polizei" also shifted from meaning general control of internal affairs (including social policy) to the specialized forces responsible for the maintenance of law and order. The subject is beginning to receive the attention it merits. See Clive Emsley, *Policing and its context 1750–1850*,

London, 1983, as well as his chapter in this book, Peasants, gendarmes and state formation. On political policing see Siemann, *"Deutschlands Ruhe, Sicherheit und Ordnung"*. On the continuing use of soldiers in the absence of specialized police forces, but also more generally on state power and notions of order and the general interest see Alf Lüdtke, *Police and State in Prussia, 1815–1850*, Cambridge, 1989. Lüdtke has recently edited a useful collection of essays under the title *"Sicherheit" und "Wohlfahrt"*. *Polizei, Gesellschaft und Herrschaft im 19. und 20. Jahrhundert*, Frankfurt, 1992.

50. On the contradictory attitudes towards the Zollverein see Hans-Werner Hahn, "Mitteleuropäische oder kleindeutsche Wirtschafts-ordnung in der Epoche des Deutschen Bundes", in *Deutscher Bund und deutsche Frage 1815–1866*, Vienna, 1990, with many further references to the literature. Boch, *Grenzenloses Wachstum?* considers some of the social visions linked to the Zollverein.

51. I discuss this problem in my book *Nationalism and the state*, Manchester, 1982, especially chapter 8. The tension was summed up neatly by John Iliffe in his *A modern history of Tanganyika*, Cambridge, 1979, p. 121: "Control required powerful allies with obedient followings. Administration required efficient agents who could impose uncongenial innovations."

52. This theme is very well examined in Celia Applegate, *A nation of provincials: the German idea of Heimat*, Berkeley, 1990. From a different perspective the relationship between locality, confession, popular politics and the national question is examined for the three different "regions" of the Rhineland – those under Prussian, Bavarian, and Hessian rule – in Jonathan Sperber, *Rhineland radicals: the democratic movement and the revolution of 1848–1849*, Princeton, 1991.

53. See Kraehe, *Metternich's German policy*, for the negotiations of 1814–15.

54. There is no really good, up-to-date general study of the German revolution in English. The best recent German study is Wolfram Siemann, *Die deutsche Revolution von 1848/49*, Frankfurt, 1985.

55. For how this was perceived by the Rhenish bourgeoisie, see Boch, *Grenzenloses Wachstum?*; and by the radical and Catholic mobilizers of popular political action – Sperber, *Rhineland Radicals*.

56. Sperber, *Rhineland Radicals*, is especially good on demonstrating this.

57. For an English translation of the constitution of 1849 see G. Hucko (ed.), *The democratic tradition: four German constitutions*, Leamington Spa, 1987.

58. See Anselm Doering-Manteuffel, Der Ordnungszwang des Staaten-systems: Zu den Mitteleuropa-Konzepten in der österreichisch-preuß-ischen Rivalität 1849–1851, in *Die Herausforderung des europäischen*

Staatensystems, edited by Adolf Birke and Günther Heydemann, Göttingen, 1989, pp. 119–40.

59. On policing powers, in addition to Siemann, *"Deutschlands Ruhe, Sicherheit und Ordnung"*, see idem (ed.), *Der "Polizeiverein" deutscher Staaten. Eine Dokumentation zur Überwachung der Öffentlichkeit nach der Revolution von 1848/49*, Tübingen, 1983. On economic coordination see Helmut Rumpler, Das 'Allgemeine Deutsche Handelsgesetzbuch' als Element der Bundesreform im Vorfeld der Krise von 1866, in Rumpler (ed.), *Deutsche Bund und deutsche Frage*. On the argument that the increase in the power of the territorial state can go along with, not against, the effectiveness of various inter-state co-ordinating institutions, see Giddens, *The nation-state and violence*.

60. This argument is very indebted to Lothar Gall, *Bismarck: the white revolutionary*, 2 vols, London, 1986.

61. This key distinction, and its importance within the liberal middle-class political movement forming in Prussia is considered in Shlomo Na'aman, *Der deutsche Nationalverein. Die politische Konstituierung des deutschen Bürgertums 1859–1867*, Düsseldorf, 1987.

62. *Ibid.*, for this argument.

63. On the way annexation was handled and contributed to nation state-formation see Hans Patze (ed.), *Staatsgedanke und Landesbewußtsein in den neupreußischen Gebieten (1866)*, Marburg/Ulm, 1985, G. Zang (ed.), *Provinzialisierung einer Region. Zur Entstehung der bürgerlichen Gesellschaft in der Provinz*, Frankfurt, 1978, and Peter Baumgart (ed.), *Expansion und Integration. Zur Eingliederung neugewonnener Gebiete in den preußischen Staat*, Cologne, 1984. The "feedback" of institutional traditions from "new" Prussian provinces into "old" Prussia is a theme of Heide Barmeyer, *Hannovers Eingliederung in den preußischen Staat. Annexation und administrative Integration 1866–1868*, Hildesheim, 1983. A brief summary of her argument can be found in English in Geoff Eley, "Bismarckian Germany", in *Modern Germany reconsidered 1870–1945*, edited by Gordon Martel, London, 1992, pp. 1–32.

64. For one fine regional study in English see Dan White, *The splintered party: national liberalism in Hessen and the Reich, 1867–1918*, London, 1976.

65. I provide some details on this so far as Hamburg is concerned in a review article: Hamburg – the German city of laissez-faire, *The Historical Journal*, 1992.

66. Quoted in Eley, Bismarckian Germany, p. 10.

67. See Hucko (ed.), *The democratic tradition*, for the text of the constitution of 1871.

68. For an English-language treatment of such disputes see Frank Eyck, *The Frankfurt parliament 1848–49*, London, 1968, especially chapter 7.

69. See William Carr, *Schleswig-Holstein 1815–1848: a study in national conflict*, London, 1963.
70. See Article 188 of the constitution of 1849, in Hucko (ed.), *The democratic tradition*, p. 114.
71. There should be a study of the conception of "historical" nationalities within nineteenth-century European liberal traditions. The subject has been considered in detail so far as Marx and Engels are concerned, but in this instance they imitated rather than conflicted with contemporary liberals. See, for example, Ian Cummins, *Marx, Engels and national movements*, London, 1980.
72. See Wilhelm Mommsen, *Stein, Ranke, Bismarck. Ein Beitrag zur politischen und sozialen Bewegung des 19. Jahrhunderts*, Munich, 1954.
73. William Carr, *Origins of the wars of German unification*, London, 1991.
74. Eley, *Bismarckian Germany*, p. 16.
75. For this sense of a liberal vision see Langewiesche, *Liberalismus in Deutschland*, especially pp. 164ff.
76. For the idea that modern society is formed around cultural "zones" based on a language and national culture see Ernest Gellner, *Nations and nationalism*.
77. See Jürgen Kocka, Das Problem der Nation in der deutschen Geschichte, in idem, *Geschichte und Aufklärung*, Göttingen, 1989, pp. 82–100; G. A. Ritter, *Die deutsche Parteien, 1830–1914*, Göttingen, 1985; Stanley Suval, *Electoral Politics in Wilhelmine Germany*, Chapel Hill, 1985, for examples of integration and extending political participation.
78. Still of great interest on the lack of satisfactory national symbols is Theodor Schieder, *Der deutsche Kaiserreich von 1871 als Nationalstaat*, Cologne and Opladen, 1961. See now idem, *Nationalismus und Nationalstaat. Studien zum nationalen Problem im modernen Europa*, edited by O. Dann and H-U. Wehler, Göttingen, 1991. See also Elizabeth Fehrenbach, *Wandlungen des deutschen Kaisergedanken, 1871–1918*, Munich, 1969. A similar argument is developed in the recent book by Thomas Nipperdey, *Deutsche Geschichte 1866–1918. Bd.II. Machtstaat vor der Demokratie*, Munich, 1992.

CHAPTER SIX
National histories and national identities among the Serbs and Croats

Wendy Bracewell

A national identity is one of the many ways of answering the question "who are we and why are we here?" National identity has been perhaps the most salient of the group loyalties which have defined people's lives in modern times, but a consciousness of shared characteristics and a sense of national community was also to be found among collectivities in the pre-modern era. Such a sense of community draws on objective attributes (a common language, history, territory, religion, and so on), yet it is not natural or pre-ordained. It must be imagined into existence; must exist in the minds of the nation as well as in concrete reality. Both the character and the boundaries of such an identity can change, adjusting to new circumstances. Yet how and why do particular elements, out of an infinity of possibilities, become meaningful components of a national identity? And what determines the boundaries of such identities, making them more or less inclusive?

This chapter examines the shifting content and function of the national identities of the Serbs and Croats through the medium of national histories. These have the advantage for the student of national identity both of interpreting the nation to itself ("history tells us who we are"), and of influencing the nation's development ("history tells us who we should be"). They also have disadvantages in that they are usually produced by an educated elite, and are not always representative of popular views of identity. Yet comparing the interpretations promulgated in these texts with actual national loyalties can often reveal something about the relations between national ideologies and national identities. Rather than surveying the development of historiography as a whole among the South Slavs, here I focus on particular Serb and Croat national histories in the periods under foreign rule, during the national revivals, and within the Yugoslav state, concentrating on the changing religious, social and political factors influencing the formulation of national identities.

The Serbs and the Croats offer an instructive example for the study of national identities. These two peoples share common Slavic origins and speak closely related dialects. They are usually differentiated on the basis of religion (Serbs being Orthodox, Croats Catholic), tradition (usually characterized by the division between the Byzantine and the Latin world), and history (periods of independent state existence having been followed by Ottoman rule in the case of the Serbs, and by Hungarian and Habsburg rule in the case of the Croats). In spite of these distinctions, it is difficult to draw sharp boundaries between the territories they have settled. Centuries of migration and warfare left the frontier regions settled with an intricate jigsaw of peoples, with Serbs and Croats (and other ethnic groups) living intermixed in Slavonia, Northern Croatia, Dalmatia, Bosnia and Hercegovina. Unlike the situation in most of Western Europe, where the development of national identities was so closely linked with the concurrent development of states that the whole process is described as the formation of the nation-state, in south-eastern Europe national identity emerged separately from, and often in opposition to, the multi-national empires of the Habsburgs and Ottomans. Here national communities drew on their pasts to bolster their claims to political rights. At the same time, they looked for allies in their struggles, encouraging more inclusive visions of community: Slavism, Illyrianism, Yugoslavism, as well as a sense of a European identity. Thus the study of Serb and Croat identities allows us to examine the interplay between particularist national identities and more inclusive integrational identities.

Both Serbs and Croats have long traditions of political and cultural distinctiveness that persisted under alien rule. In both Serbia and Croatia, the establishment of medieval states laid the foundations of national communities and cultures. Incorporation into foreign empires did not lead to assimilation. On the contrary, the administrative structures of both the Ottoman and the Habsburg Empires preserved and legitimated national distinctions. In the Ottoman Empire, the religious and civil administration of the Orthodox community (*millet*) was entrusted to the Orthodox church, which united the Serbs of the Empire under the aegis of an ethnarch (the Patriarch of Peć). In the Habsburg Empire, the subject peoples were often represented by historic entities which preserved a political function when incorporated into the empire. The emphasis on legal and historical privileges would give a national coloration to the struggles of both the Croatian nobility and the Serb immigrants against their Habsburg sovereign. While ideas of Serb or Croat national distinctiveness were preserved, however, broader types of identity were also evolving among the South Slavs in the early modern period. Religious and cultural affinities bound together the Eastern Orthodox world in a sense of community, giving Serbs a sense of participation in Orthodox Slavdom. Among both Serbs and Croats linguistic similarities also contributed to a sense of Slavic unity, buttressed by myths of common descent and traditions of reciprocity. Illyrism and Yugoslavism would be later variants of this sense of Slav linguistic, cultural and spiritual solidarity. Thus there were two strands in South Slav collective identities: one narrower, more restricted in definition; the other broader, based on wider definitions of community. These two types of identity were not mutually exclusive. On the contrary, they were often closely intertwined.

Annals and chronicles formed the mainstay of Serbian and Croatian medieval historiography. These began their story with the Flood and narrowed in scope to focus on a particular kingdom and its dynasty. Such histories located a people in the universal course of human events, giving notice that the nation existed (indeed, implying that it represented the culmination of all human history), and embodying the identity of the nation in its rulers. The practice of representing the dynasty as the embodiment of the nation was more fully developed by Serbian historians under Ottoman rule in another genre of national history: the *žitije*, or lives of Serbian saints and rulers. These biographies glorified the Nemanjić dynasty of Serbian rulers (and several of the Serbian despots) as part of the process of creating a cult around the hallowed Serbian royal lineage. With the Ottoman conquest of the Serbian lands, the Orthodox church became the religious and secular representative of the Serbian people in the millet system. From 1557 to 1766 the autocephalous Patriarchate of Peć embodied the authority and traditions of the medieval Serbian state. The identification between the Serbian church and the Serbian state was symbolized by the day-to-day celebrations of the lives of Serbia's saintly rulers in the liturgy. Such lives formed an important part of the *Srbljak*, a menaion, or compilation of services and prayers dedicated to the Serbian saints, arranged according to the liturgical year.[1] Taken as a whole, this compendium of saints' lives provides an answer to the question posed explicitly by Patriarch Pajsije in his life of Tsar Uroš (1642): "Where did the Serbs come from, and to what purpose?" The answer was framed in terms of religion and state tradition, since Serbdom was embodied in these saintly rulers, uniquely chosen by God, "to the honor and glory of all the Serbian race and to the shame and reproof of other-believers".[2] Indeed, the Christ-like Serbian prince Lazar was depicted as accepting martyrdom at the Battle of Kosovo in order to redeem his people.[3] Even under alien rule, the Serbian church ensured that the Serbs could look back to a glorious independent past, and look forward to the promise of its resurrection.

By the eighteenth century, the Serbs were divided among several empires, in part living in diaspora. The Serb community in Southern Hungary, open to the influence of Western ideas, was the most active intellectual center, but it was also subject to a variety of pressures – threats to its privileges from the Court in Vienna; Uniate propaganda; the attempts by Hungarian magnates to enserf the free Serb peasantry. Serbian ecclesiastics and notables responded by calling history to their defense. The Serbian histories of the eighteenth century emphasized the past glory of the Serbian state; the continuity of the tradition inherited by the Serbian Church; and the legitimacy of the Serbs' claims to privileges within the Habsburg Monarchy. Historians of the eighteenth century also added a new element to their concerns with the Serbian state tradition and Serbian Orthodoxy: the place of the Serbs in the wider context of Slavdom, particularly Eastern Orthodox Slavdom. Approaching the history of the Serbs within this ethnic and religious framework, it was possible to view all the scattered Serbs as one body, in a way which an emphasis on the narrow Serbian state tradition could not. This theme could also provide a way of formulating new aspirations for the unification of the Serbs, their liberation and eventual independence, aspirations that would be voiced at the turn of the century, with the outbreak of an insurrection across the Danube in the Paşalik of Belgrade.

The work of Archimandrite Jovan Rajić is an example of this type of national history. Although entitled *The History of the Various Slav Peoples and Especially the Bulgarians, Croats and Serbs* (1794–95), its gravamen was made clearer on the titlepage, which printed the word "Serbs" in a font many sizes larger than the rest of the title. This work began with the history of all the Slavs, especially the South Slavs and the Russians, continued as a history of the medieval Serbian kingdoms, particularly Rascia under the Nemanjići, traced the history of the Serbian despots, and ended up in the fourth volume focusing on the Serbs under Habsburg rule in Southern Hungary. The work is full of internal contradictions, epitomized by Rajić's stated intention "to describe the Serbs with an unbiased pen, as is dignified and befitting, to glorify them and to deliver them out of the darkness of oblivion into the light of history". Rajić concentrated throughout on defending the Serbs' claims to the dignity of historical nationhood against the lies and distortions of their enemies, and in spite of their own ignorance of their glorious past. Although inconsistent in execution, Rajić's history has a clear message for the Serbs: it is division that poses the main threat to the nation: "Neither sword nor flame conquered the Serbs, but rather disunity."[4]

Rajić set his history in the context of the Slav community. One important tie that bound a great part of the Slavs together was Orthodoxy. Orthodoxy was certainly an important badge of identity for the Serbs in the Habsburg lands, in a state which recognized religious community as a basis for political and legal rights. Orthodox Slav unity could also serve the purpose of overcoming that division which Rajić saw as having brought about the fall of the Serbs from imperial glory. This was part of the attraction of Russia for Rajić, and the reason that he struggled so hard to fit the Russians into his history, though they did not quite fit his conception of a South Slav history. He could look to Russia, the great Orthodox empire, as an example and an inspiration for the Serbs. The Orthodox Church helped to spread the Serbian name to new areas: from texts such as Stojan Šobat's catechism of 1772, for example, an Orthodox Vlach in the Habsburg lands would have learned that the answer to the question "who are you?" was: "I am a man, a Serb, and an [Orthodox] Christian".[5] But Orthodoxy was not the only tie that bound together the South Slavs; for it left out the Catholic Croats whom Rajić also included in his history. Here Rajić turned to language and common descent as demonstrating South Slavic community. While Orthodoxy could unite the Serbs through religion, an ethno-linguistic Slavism could map out a different path to South Slav unity.

Rajić's ideas of Serb identity (the centrality of Orthodoxy to the definition of Serbdom; the continuity of Serbian state tradition; the relations of the Serbs to the other South Slavs) had political implications, though they were not clearly spelled out. What they might mean in practice is implied in the frontispiece to Volume II, in an engraving borrowed from the work of Hristofor Žefarović. This was a portrait of Tsar Dušan in glory, trampling the trophies of war – including defeated Turks – underfoot, and surrounded by the coats-of-arms not only of the Nemanjić crown lands, but of all the Balkan lands (led by those of Serbia, Bulgaria and Illyria), proclaiming the message of South Slav unity in a revival of Dušan's empire under Serbian leadership. A Serb identity is here enriched by combining the Serbian state tradition with the idea of South Slav unity to create a national mission of Serbian unification which would also include other Slavs. The influence of these ideas can be traced in the programmes for Serbian statehood that circulated among the Habsburg Serbs at the time of the Serbian insurrection.[6]

Views of a Serbian identity based on state tradition and confession were challenged in the nineteenth century by a new concept of identity, popularized among the Serbs by Vuk Karadžić, an East European disciple of Herder. For Karadžić, the truest expression of the nation lay in the language of the peasantry, and it was language, and not religion or political tradition, that was the primary determinant of national identity. In his view, all those who spoke štokavian (one of the three major variants of Serbian and Croatian) were Serbs. The effect was to broaden the definition of Serbdom to include the large numbers of Catholic and Muslim štokavian speakers in Bosnia and Croatia. (Karadžić's formulation virtually denied the existence of a Croat nation, for he considered only those few who spoke čakavian to be Croats, since he considered kajkavian speakers Slovenes.) Karadžić's ethno-linguistic definition of national identity laid the basis for a modern nationalism among the Serbs: secular, politicized and mass-based. This nationalism legitimated the authority of a new, secular and native elite within the new Serbian state and provided the basis for its aspirations in the nineteenth and twentieth centuries, particularly in regard to the South Slavs beyond its borders. Serbia's foreign policy was driven by the aim of eventually embracing all those lands inhabited by Serbs – broadly defined – in one state. This state would not be a revival of the medieval Serbian state uniting the Orthodox and the other Slavs of the Balkan Peninsula under Dušan's banner, as envisioned in Žefarović's engraving and Rajić's writings. Instead it would be based on the principle that each nation (historically and ethno-linguistically defined) has the right to a sovereign state covering the territory on which it lives. Although it would cover much the same territory, its citizens would be defined as Serbs, and the fact of their common identity would be the justification for the existence of the state. This could be seen as a sort of Slavism in which Serbs would play the role of Piedmont, liberating and unifying their South Slav brethren, either under the Serbian name or, in another variant, as "Yugoslavs".

The view of Serb identity which underpinned this nationalism was consolidated through the educational system of the independent state of Serbia. Popular histories, especially those written for schools, give a good overview of its content and functions. The works of Milenko M. Vukičević, a prolific writer of popular histories, including *Istorija srpskog naroda u slici i reci* (Belgrade, 1912) and *Istorija srpskog naroda za srednje škole* (Belgrade, 1902–4 , and in five further editions), provide a good example of such writings.[7] His version of Serbian history began with the Slavs, whom he claimed had all originally been called Serbs, implying that the Serbs were the oldest Slavic tribe from whom all the others had descended. Vukičević defined "the fatherland of the Serbian people" as "all those lands in which the people speak the Serbian language".[8] Vukičević never claimed openly that the Croats did not exist as a separate people (though other Serbian writers of similar textbooks were more explicit in calling them Serbs). But by including Croatia, Slavonia and Dalmatia among the provinces where the Serbian language was spoken and identifying them as part of the fatherland of the Serbian people, he left the issue ambiguous. However, in all but the last, more Yugoslav-oriented edition of his textbooks he ignored Croatia, giving the impression that its affairs were of little direct relevance to Serbian history. He paid much more attention to the Military Frontier and

Vojvodina, Bosnia and Hercegovina, and Dubrovnik. According to Vukičević, the lands north of the Sava and the Danube where many Serbs had settled after fleeing Ottoman rule in 1690 were historically Serbian (and not Hungarian or Croatian), since Serbs had lived there since the seventh century. Bosnia and Hercegovina, too, had been settled by Serbs since the seventh century. Bosnia's population was divided by faith into Muslim, Orthodox and Catholic, but they were all the same people (Serbs), since they were of the same origin and spoke the same language. Dubrovnik, by the same reasoning, was also Serbian. The definition of Serb identity based on descent and language had clear implications for these South Slav lands. If they were settled with Serbs and were part of "the fatherland of the Serbian people", other claims on them were invalid, and they were destined to be rejoined to the Serbian state. These interpretations of the past had a profound influence on Serb views of themselves. They shaped Serbian expectations of the character of the first Yugoslavia and the role that the Serbs would play in it.

The historical writings surveyed here chart a shift in the definitions of a Serb identity over a long period, from a view of Serbdom personified by a state and dynastic tradition and characterized by the Serbian Orthodox faith, to a definition of national identity based primarily on language and descent. These redefinitions shifted the boundaries between Serbs and non-Serbs, binding together people living in scattered territories under different rulers, and extending the Serbian name to new members. The emphasis on Serbian Orthodoxy had helped to assimilate Orthodox Vlachs; an ethno-linguistic identity helped unite the loyalties of the "Srbijanci" of Serbia proper and the "prečani" Serbs from across the Sava and Danube. The success of the ethno-linguistic definition of Serbian identity was not complete, however. Although many Serbs believed, after Karadžić, that all štokavian speakers were Serbs, only a few Catholic intellectuals followed the logic of this argument or accepted the leading role of the Serbian nation as in the best interests of the South Slavs, and proclaimed themselves Serbs. Other Croats passionately resisted the simple equation of language with identity. Whether or not it was accepted by all those it claimed as Serbs, this definition of identity legitimated the aspirations of the new Serbian state to unite the Serbian people in the territories beyond its borders, particularly in Vojvodina, Bosnia-Hercegovina, Kosovo and Macedonia. Neither Slavism nor Yugoslavism was inimicable to these aspirations; indeed, they could offer a different means to the same end of uniting all Serbs in one state.

The circumstances of the Croats in the sixteenth and seventeenth centuries were not propitious for the assertion of a common identity. The lands that had made up the medieval kingdom of Croatia were divided, and Croats found themselves under seven different political juristictions: autonomous Dubrovnik; Venetian Dalmatia and the islands; the Ottoman interior; and within the Habsburg Empire, the Military Frontier; Istria; parts of Hungary; and Croatia and Slavonia. These divisions had contributed to the development of regional identities, reinforced by differences of dialect. Nonetheless, an awareness of traditions of Croat community and a common identity persisted. The awareness of a common tradition is apparent in the writing of histories, which affirmed the antiquity of the Croats by tracing their origins since biblical times, claimed a share of the glory and might of the Slavs and recounted the history of the medieval Croatian state, before focusing on the author's own region. Two common strands persist over a long period in the construction of a Croat national identity. Their weakness and division attracted the Croats to the greater Slav collectivity. Slav might could enable them to stand against their Venetian, Ottoman, German or Magyar overlords and Slav diversity could mitigate their own divisions. But this tendency to seek support among their Slavic kin was accompanied by the development of a narrower and more exclusive Croat identity, which usually drew on the traditions of the Croatian state and its historic privileges.

Both of these strands can be traced in the histories of the Croats written in the seventeenth century by Juraj Rattkay and by Pavao Ritter Vitezović. Rattkay, member of a Croatianized noble family of Hungarian origins and a canon of the Zagreb Cathedral, published his *Memoria regum et banorum regnorum Dalmatiae, Croatiae et Slavoniae* in Vienna in 1652. Elaborating on earlier speculations, Rattkay traced the origins of all the Slavs to Croatia. Rattkay structured the development of Croatian history after their loss of a native dynasty around the institution of the Ban (or viceroy) appointed from the Croatian nobility, rather than around the Hungarian or Habsburg kings. At a time when the Croatian nobles were aligning ever closer with the Hungarians in their resistance to the Viennese court, this was a significant affirmation of a separate Croat political identity. Vitezović, a member of the Croatian lesser nobility, developed the ideas of Slav unity and Croatian political tradition further in his various historical writings.[9] He took the myth of the Croatian origin of the Illyrian Slavs to its logical conclusion, and extended the Croatian name to all the Slavs as a stimulus to Croat pride in its glorious past and its powerful progeny. But this nebulous claim to seniority among the Slav peoples was not a solid enough foundation for Vitezović's hopes for a "resurrected Croatia" (*Croatia rediviva*, 1700). Vitezović turned to political traditions to support Croatian pretensions to independent existence. His history of the institutions of the King, Ban and Diet, and his discussions of Croatian boundaries and privileges were all formulated to provide evidence of Croatian political continuity in its crown lands, as these were being liberated from Ottoman control and their final disposition was being debated. Such a history provided not just a myth of origins, and a defence against the fear of assimilation, but also a programme for the future.

Although they discussed the origins of the Croats in terms of common descent and language, these histories posited a national identity that was far from socially inclusive. They were constructed to serve the interests of the Croatian nobility in its resistence to the centralizing efforts of the Habsburg state. Although the Serbs were represented by an ecclesiastical elite, who employed legitimist arguments against the Habsburgs in much the same way, the religious framework of the Serb identity embraced all Orthodox believers. Among the Croats, however, it was primarily the nobility, the "political nation", who embodied the nation in the early modern period. The Croatian nobility was at variance with their Habsburg rulers in several respects in the seventeenth century, particularly with regard to the disposition of territory seen as historically part of Croatia, and over Habsburg attempts to impose absolutism. The Croatian nobles were intent on defending their territories and their political privileges. Their weapons in these struggles were those of historicism. The Croat nation's past was to be a shield for the nobility's threatened privileges in the present and a guide to its expansion in the future. The resulting emphasis on political tradition and "state right" would have a lasting influence on Croat national ideas. The equation between the nobility and the Croat nation would also be very long lasting. Even when a "modern" mass nationalism developed in Croatia in the nineteenth century, it was initially mobilized by the nobility against the threat to their privileges from the Magyars.

In the eighteenth century, however, the Croatian nobility, particularly the magnates, allied themselves closely with their Hungarian equivalents against Habsburg centralization. It was not until Magyar nationalism began to infringe on what were perceived as Croatian separate state rights – and especially the Hungarian insistence on the substitution of Magyar for Latin as the language of state at the end of the eighteenth century – that a Croat identity was seen as a source of resistance. Out of this struggle, at the beginning of the nineteenth century, developed both a modern Croat national identity and the idea of South Slav cooperation and unification (Illyrianism, Yugoslavism). In the struggle against Buda, the Croatian "awakeners" turned naturally to a weapon that had been forged earlier on behalf of the Croatian nation in the battles against Vienna: the Croatian state tradition. The legal rights of the Croatian state, reaching back to 1102 and codified over centuries were a somewhat battered shield to raise against the up-to-date field guns of liberal Magyar nationalism. In addition to these traditional noble defenses, the awakeners sought to arouse a wider national consciousness that could compete with that of the Magyars. This too relied on ideas that were ready to hand: longstanding beliefs in the common origins and national unity of all the South Slavs (Illyrians), as demonstrated by their common language. While the Croats were few and divided, the combined might of the Illyrians would be more than a match for their rivals.

The formulation of a new national identity can be traced in the approach to national history taken by the Illyrianists. Between 1839 and 1842, Ivan Švear (a parish priest in Požega) published a massive history in four volumes, *Ogledalo Iliriuma* (The Mirror of Illyrium). Like the older chronicles, it began with the flood, followed the descent of the Slavs from the ancient Illyrians, and went on to treat all the South Slav "tribes", devoting separate narratives to the histories of the Serbs and Bulgarians up to the Ottoman conquest. Most space, however, was devoted to the Croats. Švear, like the other Illyrianists, stressed the unity of the South Slavs on the basis of descent and language, proclaiming one nation from the Alps to the Black Sea. Though not everyone accepted the idea that the South Slavs were descended from the Illyrians of antiquity, "Illyrian" was a title with a long pedigree among the South Slavs (and particularly the Croats) which could encompass all the fragmented South Slav "tribes" under a neutral term. Before religious divisions and selfish interests had led to their downfall, the Illyrian tribes had successfully defended themselves against the empires of the east and west. Surely they could unite to do so once again: "This is the nineteenth century, O Serb-Illyrian brethren. (. . .) If we wish to reach our desired goal, we must go hand in hand, embracing as brothers sprung from one Slav-Illyrian mother of the Slavs, with a brave, constant and heroic stride."[10]

But these appeals met little response among the Serbs, who were creating their own identity around the newly formed Serbian state and who for the moment saw no advantage in submerging themselves in a greater Illyrian whole; nor from the Slovenes, who were developing their own ethno-linguistic national idea. Illyrianism was really primarily a Croat idea, arising out of Croat traditions and aimed at specifically Croat problems. Švear's work illustrates this nicely. In spite of the broad conception of his Illyrian history and his appeals for South Slav unity, his work had a distinctly Croat bias. It was not just that the bulk of the work was devoted to their history. Even in his discussion of Illyrian brotherhood he gave preeminence to the Croats: according to Švear, "Croat" was the original name of the Slav peoples, and the Serbs, as well as the other Slavs, were descended from them.[11] This made it possible for Švear to emphasize the unity of the people of Croatia proper, Dalmatia, and his native Slavonia , under the single name of "Croat" (a term which had by this time become commonly restricted to the narrow area around Zagreb).[12] He also devoted much space to the problem of defending Croatian rights against Magyar nationalist aspirations, using the familiar arguments of state right, as well as the natural right of nations.

As a result, the "Mirror of Illyrium" reflected a recognizably Croat face. The identity which Švear's work – and the Illyrian movement – helped to define was not Illyrian or South Slav, but rather Croat, overcoming regional particularisms, dialect differences and social divisions to unite the Croat people in a single national identity under one name (Illyrian was eventually replaced by Croatian), and one literary language. These were significant achievements, but they were solidly rooted in ideas that had already been mapped out in the seventeenth century. Their main novelty was that of other modern national identities: they included the common people firmly within the definition of the nation.

The state-building implications of Švear's vision were more

ambiguous (as were those of the Illyrian movement). On the one hand, if the South Slavs were one nation, they had the potential and the right to reunite and resurrect their lost empire. This would not be a revival of Dušan's Slavic empire as pictured by Rajić and Žefarović, nor the Great Serbia implied by Serb ethno-linguistic claims. The golden age to be reclaimed was that of the mythical Illyrian empire when all the Slavs were united in brotherly equality, each respecting the individuality of the other "tribes". Precisely what its contours might be was not immediately apparent. References to the eastern and western empires that it had repulsed in the past suggested that the reborn Illyrian empire would imply the dismantling of the Habsburg and Ottoman Empires. The emphasis on the unity of the Croats, on the other hand, opened up the possibility of a more limited Croatian solution, either independent or within a Habsburg framework. And the use of state-right arguments implied even more limited responses to specific Magyar pressures. All these possibilities were also inherent in Illyrianism as a political movement, and were relevant in different circumstances.

After Švear's initial, not particularly scholarly attempt at a national history, a series of Croatian histories were published in the nineteenth century, largely by historians of a Yugoslav orientation (Šime Ljubić, Tade Smičiklas, Vjekoslav Klaić, Ferdo Šišić).[13] However, these histories were even less "Yugoslav" in their conception than Švear's had been, and concentrated more narrowly on the history of the Croats. Tade Smičiklas's remarks in the preface to his *Poviest hrvatska* (1882) were typical: he stressed the national unity of the South Slavs, particularly at the level of the common people, but then proposed a framework for a national history that was based on "Croatia's eternal resistance to foreign domination".[14] These narratives were structured around states and rulers, with the Kingdom of Croatia receiving the greatest attention and Dalmatia and Dubrovnik being treated in parallel. As in the seventeenth century, the version of the past that best informed the identity of the Croat nation in the eyes of these historians was one that affirmed its historic rights in an independent state, held in unbroken succession since the rule of the medieval Croatian kings.

More interesting, perhaps, is the way in which these historians treated relations with the other South Slav nations. It is striking that the Illyrian movement was treated as the Croat national awakening, with little attention to its South Slav ideas. The "Yugoslav" belief that the Serbs and Croats were (or should be) one people with two names was scarcely visible in these works. The Serbs were treated as a separate nation with distinctive religious and political traditions. Where the claims of the two nations came into conflict, these historians took a distinctly Croatocentric stand. Bosnia-Hercegovina was the main arena of competing claims between Croats and Serbs, becoming a particularly sore point after it was occupied by Austria in 1878 and annexed in 1908. Both state-right arguments and ethno-linguistic evidence were advanced in these texts to demonstrate Croat claims. These were national histories, the focus on the Croats alone, and issues were discussed largely in terms of their implications for the Croats, rather than in a consistently South Slav or Yugoslav framework.

The allegedly Yugoslav orientation of Croatian historiography was a hotly debated topic during the national resurgence of 1970–71 in Croatia. Criticisms were voiced that Croat historians "had not succeeded in fulfilling their debt to time and to their people," and that Croatian history "was not carrying out its social function".[15] One of the causes for complaint was the lack of any recent synthesis of Croatian history, so that plans had been made to reissue a new edition of Šišić's *Pregled povijesti hrvatskog naroda* (first published in 1916). Although some critics lamented the lack of a history that Croats could respond to as a truly *national* (or nationalist?) version of their past, in fact Šišić's scholarly account of the history of the state was still appropriate to the identity and aspirations of the Croats, even in a new context. This suggests that the character of the Croatian national identity had not changed all that much in more than 50 years. Through their efforts towards South Slav cooperation, the Illyrianists had succeeded in integrating Croatians, Slavonians and Dalmatians in a single, socially inclusive Croat identity. Although Croats were primarily Catholic, and confession was an important marker of the difference between Croat and Serb, the universalism of the Catholic Church meant that religion did not have the same cohesive force among the Croats as Serbian Orthodoxy did among the Serbs. With their multitude of dialects, the Croats also found language a fragile bond, at least until the Illyrianists succeeded in introducing a single literary standard. The national histories surveyed above demonstrate the importance that historic tradition and state rights took on in the construction of an integral Croat identity.

What was the relationship between national histories and supra-national history? So far South Slav or Yugoslav ideas have been discussed in the context of narrower national histories and national identities. Was there a distinctive Yugoslav tradition in history writing, and how did it interact with individual national identities? It was not really until after the establishment of the Kingdom of the Serbs, Croats, and Slovenes that an attempt at a modern Yugoslav history was published: V. Čorović's *Istorija Jugoslavije* (Belgrade, 1933). This was a monument to the unitarist version of the Yugoslav idea promoted in interwar Yugoslavia, depicting Yugoslavia as the apotheosis of the Serbian state tradition. A more concerted attempt to provide a synthesis of Yugoslav history was made after the Second World War, when Tito gave Marxist historians the task of "stamping out nationalistic interpretations of the cultural achievements and legacy of the past"[16] and producing a history that would be appropriate to the new socialist "brotherhood and unity" of the Yugoslav nations. This, in theory at least, could not simply be a compilation of the separate (bourgeois) histories of each nation, but would be a new synthesis, given unity by tracing the socio-economic evolution of Southeast European society from feudalism through bourgeois capitalism to socialism. In fact, the multi-volume history of Yugoslavia that was begun after the war failed signally to achieve these goals. Published in two volumes, under the title *History of the Peoples of Yugoslavia* (*Historija naroda Jugoslavije*, 1953, 1960), it presented the histories of the lands and provinces included in Yugoslavia in piecemeal fashion, so that they could neither be read as "national" histories, nor as a larger whole. The first two volumes went up to the end of the eighteenth century, but a third projected volume was never completed, because the editorial team could not reconcile differences over the interpretation of contested issues in the national histories of the nineteenth century.

These differences were brought into the open in 1972, with the publication of *The History of Yugoslavia* (*Istorija Jugoslavije*) by Ivan Božić, Sima Ćirković, Milorad Ekmečić and Vladimir Dedijer. The work caused a storm of controversy in both the academic and the popular press.[17] Most of the complaints dealt with the problems of nationalism and national identity, focusing on the section that treated the nineteenth century. Critics objected to the title of the book, which was not only inaccurate (since it covered a long period before the creation of the state of Yugoslavia) but also implied that the history of the *peoples* of Yugoslavia was essentially that of the emergence of the joint *state* of Yugoslavia. Critics claimed that the disproportionate attention devoted to Serbia created the impression that Yugoslavia was the natural culmination of Serbian statehood – and that the interpretation of "Yugoslavism" advanced in the book was only a cloak for Serbian hegemony (a criticism that was also being made of the Yugoslav state). Croat critics were nettled by the tendency to ignore the Croatian state tradition (a topic that had reemerged as a theme of resurgent Croat nationalism), in contrast to the treatment given Serbian statehood. Others complained that the whole Yugoslav question was treated as one of Serb-Croat relations, while the other nations received only minimal coverage. Muslim critics, for example, decried the short shrift given to the Bosnian Muslims – seeing in it a denial of their separate national identity. Ekmečić complained that the book's critics assumed that "national statehood in the past is not only the main theme of history but also the only theme of our history" and that "the study of history is the national question and an instrument in the creation of a national consciousness".[18] The problem was not only that history and identity were closely intertwined, but that there was no agreement over the character that a Yugoslav consciousness or identity should take. Under these circumstances, a history that would integrate the South Slav nations into a Yugoslav framework was impossible to carry out to everybody's satisfaction. In contrast, multi-volume national histories of the peoples of Yugoslavia proliferated: a five-volume *History of the Slovenian People*, a three-volume *History of the Macedonian People*, a planned eight-volume *History of Montenegro*, a six-volume *History of the Serbian People* . . . [19]

It now seems that not only a Yugoslav history, but also a Yugoslav union is an impossibility. The debates over national histories versus a Yugoslav history were symptomatic of deeper divisions over the nature of the Yugoslav state. The bitter conflicts that have now engulfed the people of the Yugoslav lands in warfare were increasingly openly expressed from the early 1980s. Political and economic disputes were phrased in national terms; and the boundaries of national identities were drawn more and more sharply, while any common Yugoslav identity was discredited. National histories played an important role in these processes: both as a means of shaping national consciousness and as a vehicle for national arguments. But perhaps more interesting than the somewhat predictable efforts to rediscover themselves in their pasts have been the attempts made by both Serbs and Croats to use history to define and discredit the identity of their enemies. Both of these have implicated claims to a European identity.

One way in which the past has been used to blacken a national identity is the Serbian characterization of the Croat nation as "genocidal", based on the experiences of the Second World War. In Pavelic's quisling Independent State of Croatia (NDH) the fascist Ustašas carried out an appalling slaughter of Serbs, Jews, Gypsies and anti-fascist Croats. The supression of divisive aspects of the past as an aid to "brotherhood and unity" in Tito's Yugoslavia made this a taboo topic, but the lack of open discussion allowed the fears and hatreds generated during the war to ferment unexamined. Serbs felt that the Croats had never accepted responsibility for these crimes; Croats believed that Ustaša crimes had been exaggerated in order to link any manifestation of Croat national individuality with fascism. In the 1980s a dispute over the number of victims of the war, particularly in the notorious Jasenovac concentration camp, brought this into the open. The statistics were hotly debated: while Croat historians and politicians minimized the numbers of victims, the Serbian tendency was to inflate them.[20] Serbian writers reiterated that the entire Croat nation bore a responsibility for the crime of mass genocide, implying that there had been widespread Croat support for Ustaša crimes.[21] Some went so far as to claim that a genocidal tendency against the Serbs was a characteristic of Croatian national identity: "Genocide against the Serbs . . . is a specific phenomenon in our [Serb] centuries-old common life with the Croats. The protracted development of the genocidal idea in certain centers of Croat society . . . took deep root in the consciousness of many generations."[22] This view of the Croats as innately genocidal and fascistic struck a chord with many Serbs in the atmosphere of crisis from the end of the 1980s, while Croat nationalists did little to dispel Serb fears. In the first flush of electoral victory in 1990 old nationalist symbols were revived with no attempt to purge them of the taint they had acquired by association with the Ustašas and the NDH. Serbs in Croatia justified their refusal to accept an independent Croatian state in 1990–91 by their fears that they would again be threatened with genocide. It only took a small step for them to claim that all Croats were Ustašas, a sentiment frequently expressed by Serb fighters in the war in Croatia in 1991–92. Furthermore, Serbian commentators saw in German support of Slovene and Croatian independence proof of a joint dedication to a Fourth Reich. The effect was to put a new twist to Croat attempts to rediscover a specifically Central European identity in their past. These commentators recognized Croat "Europeanness" – only to reject that identity as historically compromised.

In turn, by claiming a European identity, the Croats raised doubts about whether Serbs could be considered Europeans. This too was based on interpretations of national history, this time rooted in the distant past. Those who saw the essence of a Croat identity in its European heritage stressed Croatia's Catholic and Habsburg past – as the "antemurale Christianitatis" Croatia had been on the very frontline of Europe. But if Croatia was on the frontier of Europe, everything across that border was outside. Croat claims to a European identity were often a way of denying such an identity to the Serbs. From this perspective, the Serb identity had been shaped by its Byzantine and Orthodox heritage and the legacy of five hundred years of Ottoman rule. This representation can be characterized as "orientalist" in the sense used by Edward Said, in that it characterizes the Orient as primitive, violent and despotic, contrasting it with a modern, rational, and democratic West, and uses these dichotomies as a justification for action.[23] The forces of history had allegedly made the Serbs incapable of accepting the liberal democracy and civil society that the Croat and Slovene democratic movements demanded in 1990 (summed up in the cry "Europe Now!"). Instead, Byzantine and Orthodox traditions had fostered authoritarianism and the instrumentalization of religion, while Ottoman rule had habituated the Serbs to corruption and cruelty. As Franjo Tudjman, president of Croatia, put it: "Croats belong to a different culture – to a different civilization – from the Serbs. . . . Croats are a part of Western Europe, part of the Mediterranean tradition. . . .   The Serbs belong to the East. Their church belongs to the East. . . .   They are an Eastern people like the Turks and the Albanians. They belong to the Byzantine culture. . . .   Regardless of the linguistiç similarities, we cannot be together."[24] Parenthetically, although these rhetorical strategies were bitterly contested by Serbs, similar orientalizing discourses had been used much earlier by Serbs against the Albanians in Kosovo, and more recently against the Muslims in Bosnia. Precisely where the East begins is open to debate. What is apparent is that history can be used to contruct a national identity for the "Other" as well as for oneself.

The identities examined here have changed and adapted, yet they retain a recognizable continuity. They were not conjured out of thin air in the nineteenth century, as some, misled by the novel aspects of modern nationalism, seem to think. In order to inspire loyalty, these nationalisms had to be perceived as genuine, to be grounded in experience (actual or vicarious). Such a sense of collective experience could be acquired through national histories. These might be reshaped to fit changing perceptions, but they were also constrained by the existing historical tradition: history, like identity, was not entirely contingent. Earlier themes were constantly reworked in new conditions so that, for example, state right among the Croats and Orthodoxy among the Serbs were recurring elements in their identities. The attempts at a Yugoslav history discussed here, however, did not express a shared experience that could engage the loyalties of all the peoples of Yugoslavia in an overarching identity. Nor does it appear that Europe can provide a common identity in which particularistic conflicts might be submerged, when each attempt at inclusion in Europe carries with it an exclusion of those perceived to be "Other".

Notes

1. Such compilations had been published as early as the sixteenth cenury (Božidar Vuković, *Praznični minej*, Venice, 1536–38); the first full version of the *Srbljak* was published in 1761, and then reprinted in 1765 in Venice.
2. Pajsije Janjevac, *Žitije cara Urosa*, in *Stare srpske biografije*, ed. Dimitrije Bogdanović, Beograd, 1968, pp. 252, 263–4.
3. For the theme of martyrdom and resurrection in Serbian cult writings and elsewhere, see Thomas A. Emmert, *Serbian Golgotha: Kosovo, 1389*, New York, 1990, especially pp. 61–78.
4. *Istorija raznyh slavenskih narodov naipače bolgar, horvatov i serbov*, III pp. 241–42, see also III pp. 87, 110–11; IV pp. 37, 121, 188.
5. Cited in V. Djerić, *O srpskom imenu po zapadnijem krajevima našega naroda*, Biograd, 1914, p. 64.
6. For Žefarović's work and programmes for Serbian statehood among the Habsburg Serbs, see Ivo Banac, The Role of Vojvodina in Karadjordje's Revolution, *Südostforschungen*, 40, 1981, pp. 31–61.
7. For Vukičević, and his eventual turn to Yugoslavism, see C. Jelavich, Milenko M. Vukičević: from Serbianism to Yugoslavism in Dennis Deletant and Harry Hanak, *Historians as nation-builders*, London,

1988.

8. *Istorija srpskog naroda za srednje škole*, vol. 1 (1911), p. 3; (1914), pp. 1–2, and *Istorija srpskog naroda u slici i reci*, 1912, p. 4.

9. For Vitezović, see the work by Catherine Simpson, *Pavao Ritter Vitezović: defining national identity in the Baroque age*, London, Ph.D. thesis, 1991.

10. *Ogledalo Iliriuma*, IV, p. 476. See also III, p. 349.

11. *Ibid.*, III, pp. 146, 205; IV, pp. 475, 517.

12. *Ibid.*, IV, pp. 205, 517.

13. Šime Ljubić, *Pregled hrvatske poviesti*, 1864; Tade Smičiklas, *Poviest hrvatska*, 1879, 1882; Vjekoslav Klaić, *Povjest Hrvata*, 1899–1911; Ferdo Šišić, *Pregled povijesti hrvatskog naroda*, 1916.

14. *Poviest hrvatska*, p. xxiv.

15. Quoted in J. Šidak, Hrvatska historiografija, *Historijski zbornik*, 1971/72.

16. Josip Broz Tito, The Role of the LC in the further development of Socialist social relations and current problems in the International Workers' Movement and the struggle for peace: Socialism in the world in *VIII Congress of the LCY*, Belgrade, 1965, p. 40.

17. M. Ekmečić, Odgovor na neke kritike "Istorije Jugoslavije" (XIX vijek), *Jugoslovenski istorijski časopis* 13, nos. 1–2, 1974, gives a list of critical reviews, pp. 217–18, footnote 1.

18. Ekmečić, pp. 220, 222.

19. B. Grafenauer, *Zgodovina slovenskega naroda*, Ljubljana, 1954–62; *Istorija na makedonskiot narod*, Skopje, 1969; *Istorija Crne Gore*, Titograd, 1967–, *Istorija srpskog naroda*, Belgrade, 1981– .

20. For a discussion of these statistics, see Ljubo Boban, Jasenovac and the Manipulation of History, *East European Politics and Societies*, 4, 1990, no. 3, pp. 580–92 and V. Žerjavić, *Opsesije i megalomanije oko Jasenovca i Bleiburga*, Zagreb, 1992.

21. See, for example, M. Bulajić, *Never again: genocide of the Serbs, Jews and Gypsies in the Ustashi Independent State of Croatia*, Belgrade, 1991, and S. Kljakić, *A conspiracy of silence: genocide in the Independent State of Croatia and concentration camp Jasenovac*, Belgrade, 1991 (pamphlets published and distributed by the Ministry of Information of the Republic of Serbia during the war in Croatia).

22. Vasilije Krestić, O genezi genocida nad Srbima u NDH, *Književne novine*, 15 Sept. 1986, p. 5, quoted in Ivo Banac, Yugoslavia: The Fearful Asymmetry of War, *Daedalus*, 1992, no. 2, p. 157.

23. Edward Said, *Orientalism*, New York, 1979, and see Milica Bakić-Hayden and Robert M. Hayden, Orientalist variations on the theme "Balkans": symbolic geography in recent Yugoslav cultural politics, *Slavic Review*, 51, No. 1, Spring 1992, pp. 1–15.

24. *New Yorker*, 18 March 1991, p. 74.

Part II
European perspectives

CHAPTER SEVEN
Core and periphery: Eastern Europe

Martyn Rady

The terms "core" and "periphery" originate in systems-theory and in attempts undertaken mainly in the 1960s and 1970s to explain the economic, social and political relationship between western countries and the third world. Systems theorists sought to establish a larger and more sophisticated model of capitalist exploitation than the conventional Marxist-Leninist critique of imperialism. They stressed, in particular, the global nature of capitalism and the world-wide division of labour between the "core" manufacturing regions and the "peripheral" producers of primary products. In its search for new markets, so it was argued, the core squeezed the periphery into a condition of economic dependence. This condition impeded the development of the periphery by forcing its economic activity outwards and a new form of "plantation capitalism" emerged. Thus, international capitalism not only transformed the existing relations of production in the countries it chose to exploit but also introduced a new measure of dependence and deprivation.

It was not long before the theory of dependence found its way into historical writing. One of the first to apply systems theory to historical development was Daniel Chirot, who sought to interpret the experience of nineteenth-century Romania with reference to its place in the contemporary "world economy".[1] But it was Immanuel Wallerstein who popularized the notions of core and periphery among historians by applying systems theory on a grand scale to the European and Atlantic economies.[2] Such has been Wallerstein's influence that the terms "core" and "periphery" are now commonly employed by historians without reference to, or even knowledge of, the theoretical context in which they were first placed.

A part of Wallerstein's analysis involves the relationship of western to eastern Europe. Broadly, Wallerstein argues that the creation of "strong states" in the west during the middle ages gave them an advantage in a late medieval "crisis of feudalism". The western monarchies sought a new form of "surplus appropriation" either by opening up markets in the New World or, alternatively, by developing unequal trading relations with the countries of eastern Europe. As it was, Poland-Lithuania, Hungary, Bohemia and East-Elbian Germany suffered a disadvantage relative to the west on account of the weakening of authority caused there by the Mongol-Tatar and Turkish invasions. Given the conjuncture of economic circumstances, the "slight edge" enjoyed by the west over the East European monarchies became of critical importance in determining the future course of events. Eastern Europe was accordingly forced into a condition of close dependence upon foreign trade and so it became a peripheral region of a core consisting of England, the Netherlands, and parts of France, Germany and Italy. The intensity of trading relations between core and periphery transformed the nobilities of eastern Europe into a capitalist class of feudal landowners, who thereupon imposed on the peasantry a form of "coercive cash-crop economy" or of "colonial capitalism": the "second serfdom" of Marxist legend. Thus, "the slight edge of the fifteenth century became the great disparity of the seventeenth and the monumental difference of the nineteenth."[3]

As with all macro-theories, Wallerstein's model may be easily faulted on details. There are plenty of scholars who have argued that his system does not apply to their precise area of expertise and that it is therefore too simplistic. Others have given the opinion that Russia and Ottoman Turkey, both of which Wallerstein presented as separate "world systems", were more closely integrated into the European and Atlantic economy than Wallerstein allows.[4] One Hungarian historian voiced his disbelief that the condition of his countrymen in the sixteenth and seventeenth centuries should be compared to the plight of negroes in the colonies. Others pointed out that the advantages enjoyed by the core operated as a challenge to the countries of the periphery and thus fostered rather than impeded economic, social and political advance.[5]

The harshest criticism of Wallerstein was delivered by fellow

Marxists who were swift to denounce the centrality which he gave to trade rather than to class interaction. The notion of a "world economy" was thought particularly unsettling since the proper level of analysis was considered, after Marx, to be the state. Wallerstein was additionally found guilty of the charge of "neo-Smithianism" by presuming that feudal landowners would automatically presume it to be in their best interests to "truck and barter" and to convert themselves into agricultural entrepreneurs.[6] None of Wallerstein's critics thought, however, to make use of Friedrich Engels's pertinent advice: "Anyone who attempted to bring the economy of Tierra del Fuego under the same laws as are operating in present day England would obviously produce nothing but the most banal commonplaces."[7]

Wallerstein's analysis was based on extensive reading of secondary texts, mostly published in English. On the whole, his critics have done little more than re-read the same literature, adding nuances and interpretations of their own. As far as eastern Europe is concerned, the ideas of both sides are largely based on a partial historical writing: for in the former Soviet bloc the only scholarly works which might be published through the medium of English tended to be those of a thoroughly orthodox stamp. There is, however, a less familiar literature which calls into question many of the basic premises on which both Wallerstein and his critics have relied.

General studies on the East European economy during the sixteenth century have relied extensively upon the example of Poland. Although Wallerstein himself realized the limitations of the "Polish model" for eastern Europe as a whole, other systems theorists have been far less circumspect. As a consequence, the emergence of an international market in agricultural commodities during the late fifteenth and sixteenth centuries is frequently made responsible for the establishment of servile labour relations not only in Poland but in all the countries of eastern Europe.[8]

The relationship between the international grain trade and the institution of serfdom in Poland is a historical commonplace, which has been made familiar to western audiences through the work in particular of Marian Małowist.[9] But it is of a much older vintage than even Małowist. Montesquieu himself noted that, "Some of the [Polish] lords possess entire provinces; they oppress the husbandmen in order to have greater quantities of corn which they send to strangers to procure the superfluous demands of luxury. If Poland had no foreign trade, its inhabitants would be happier."[10] Although the plight of the peasantry worsened significantly during the sixteenth and seventeenth centuries, the sufficiency of Montesquieu's and Małowist's explanation for this phenomenon is open to debate.

Certainly, the importance of the cereals trade for the Polish economy cannot be denied. At the end of the sixteenth century, grain accounted for 70 per cent, and later on 80 per cent, of total Polish exports to the west.[11] Nevertheless, as a proportion of the total harvest, the amount of grain exported to the west at this time was probably under ten per cent. Thus, it had probably not risen significantly as a percentage of volume since the fourteenth century.[12] Moreover, it is evident that only a part of Poland, the region along the Vistula, contributed grain for the export market. The institution of the folwark (the demesne manor organized for intensive cereal production and worked by corvée labour) was confined largely to the crown and magnate estates in this zone.[13] On the latifundia in Lithuania and eastern Poland, rents continued to be paid in kind rather than in labour services and demesne farming was less significant. Cash rents were paid in Royal Prussia and around Poznan and Danzig, where large peasant farms were also common.[14] Thus, not only was the Polish agricultural economy less export-oriented than is frequently presumed, but Polish peasant society retained a greater diversity than the blanket description of "serfdom" allows.

If the "Polish model" hardly suffices for Poland, it is even less adequate as an explanation for agrarian change in other parts of eastern Europe. In Bohemia, peasant mobility was restricted by law at the close of the fifteenth century. Over the next century and a half, demesne farming increased and *robota* obligations rose from a few days a year to three or four a week. Yet Bohemian agricultural produce was not serving an international market but was destined overwhelmingly for local consumption.[15] The same pattern of new restrictions and impositions on the peasantry may be observed in Transylvania and Muscovy, neither of which were notable contributors to the world economy.

An even greater difficulty emerges in the case of Hungary. The principal export item from Hungary was heavy-bodied cattle, which accounted for over 90 per cent of total export value in the mid-sixteenth century.[16] Cattle were driven on the hoof from the

Hungarian Plain to markets in Austria, southern Germany and Italy. The Hungarian beef trade was well organized and administered through such centres as Kecskemét, Cegléd and Debrecen. Yet the actual breeding and grazing of cattle was overseen by a free, wage-earning peasantry, who worked primarily for local merchants but who also traded cattle of their own.[17] The condition of this group was markedly different from that of the serfs who were tied to estates producing cereals for the home market. Instead, therefore, of exercising a corrosive effect on peasant freedoms, Hungary's participation in the international economy may in fact have had the contrary consequence.

A further objection to the notion that it was the development of a "colonial economy" in the sixteenth century which was responsible for serfdom in Eastern Europe lies in regard to chronology. For there is no clear correlation between the growth of the international market in agricultural goods and the process of enserfment. In Poland, it is usual to regard the imposition of servile labour obligations as occurring in the sixteenth century and as speeding up in the seventeenth. Already by the 1470s, however, peasants in the diocese of Cracow (which was not in any case a notable grain-exporting region) were working three days *robota* a week.[18] Limitations on peasant mobility were first imposed in 1496 and seigneurial jurisdiction over the serf population was made complete in 1521. In Prussia, Silesia and Hungary, legal restrictions on peasant movement were also recorded in the early sixteenth century; however, these enactments came after a much longer process of erosion, going back over a century.[19] In Bohemia, the earliest legislation limiting the legal rights of the peasantry can be traced back to the mid-fifteenth century, but it was not until after the Battle of the White Mountain (1620) that labour obligations began to register a sharp rise.[20] In Transylvania there is some evidence of an increase in labour obligations beginning in the 1440s and of the imposition at around the same time of restrictions on peasant movement.[21]

The imposition of labour obligations and the tying of the peasantry to the soil, which may be regarded as criteria both of serfdom and of a "coerced cash-crop economy", cannot therefore be attributed to changes in the structure of international trade. The evidence strongly suggests that the process of enserfment in Eastern Europe was a gradual one, spread over several centuries, and that it moved at a different pace according to region. In some places, it does not even seem to have occurred at all.

The principal alternative to Wallerstein's explanation for enserf-ment rests on the idea of a "late medieval depression". This is the opinion traditionally favoured by east European historians and it approximates the conventional demographic explanation. The Black Death and accompanying epidemics created a fall in cereal production and a labour shortage. In both western and eastern Europe, there was a "seigneurial reaction" as landowners sought to preserve their revenues and to retain control over the diminished labour market. The reaction failed in the west, leading to a pattern of enfranchisement and to the formation of a wage-earning peasantry. In eastern Europe, however, the reverse occurred. Despite attempts by the various monarchs to preserve peasant freedoms, the nobility triumphed. An upturn in corn prices in the late fifteenth century made it additionally profitable for landowners in the east to extract labour services from their peasants. The peasants were now made to work the demesne, the size of which was already swollen because landowners had taken over vacant peasant farms. Feudal rents in cash and kind were gradually superseded by labour obligations, and the leasing out of demesne land came to an end.[22]

The triumph of the seigneurial reaction in the east has been variously explained in terms of the numerical size and power of the nobility, the weakness of the region's towns, constant warring, Mongols, Turks and Hussites, currency debasement and the extrem-ity of the demographic crisis there. Most of these interpretations presuppose, however, that feudalism and serfdom are exclusively economic phenomena. Only very rarely have historians examined the legal and institutional character of the changes which took place in eastern Europe and which facilitated the triumph of the region's nobility over its peasantry.[23]

It is common to make the River Elbe a dividing line in the early modern period. To the west lay *Grundherrschaft* and a predominantly free peasantry; to the east was *Gutsherrschaft* and serfdom. The divi-sion was not in reality as geographically convenient. A transitional zone of *Wirtschaftsherrschaft*, where the lord used little robot labour but exploited instead his monopoly rights, affected parts of Austria and Germany and extended also into Hungary, and there were parts of eastern Europe where serfdom was unfamiliar.[24] What is important to notice, however, is less the vagaries and imprecision of the line as its antiquity. For, as far as the medieval peasantry were concerned, the line of the River Elbe marked an important point of legal change.

We can roughly say that peasant freedoms were more keenly expressed and articulated in western Germany and in Austria.[25] In this area, the peasant *Gemeinde* possessed strong powers of legal autonomy. The *Gemeinde* constituted a *universitas*, in token of which peasant communities in south-west Germany and Franconia possessed their own seals and even had their own *Rathäuser*. They commonly elected their own headmen and *Schöffen* and often had the right to appoint the parish priest. West of the Elbe, these institutions were lacking only in Bavaria, where for fiscal reasons they had to be created from scratch by Duke Ludwig the Rich in the 1460s.

These far reaching rights of self-government were manifested in the contemporary legal literature. Austria and Germany west of the Elbe are also the lands of the *Weistümer*: written customaries of law which regulated jurisdiction, services, payments, rights to pasture and woodland, and inheritance. The *Weistümer*, which may be variously known as *Dinghofrodeln* (in Alsace), *Öffnungen* (in Switzerland), *Banntaidingen* (in Austria) or *Rügen* (in Saxony and the Sudetenland), were neither the expression of primitive folk law nor impositions laid down by the local lord. They emerged (as indeed did all customary provision) by way of agreement, out of the interaction of *Herrschaft* and *Genossenschaft*.[26] Framed in writing, the *Weistümer* were intended to be *zersagt* und *zerlesen*, in the manner of a song. The ubiquity of the *Weistümer* may be demonstrated by reference either to the seven-volume collection published last century by Jacob Grimm, or to the more recent publication of 600 Alsatian texts.[27] As one might expect in view of the relative underdevelopment of its peasant institutions, Bavaria has yielded few examples of *Weistümer*.

What of the situation east of the Elbe? Although the surviving sources tend to be far from illuminating, few local institutions of peasant self-government appear in Eastern Europe before the thirteenth century. Until this time, a large proportion of the rural population lived in communities whose primary purpose was to provide specific services and products for the local castellan or lord.[28] Within individual villages there were substantial variations in terms of status and obligation, which the modern description of "semi-free" only serves to conceal. The German *Ostsiedlung* had, however, a transforming effect on legal institutions in the countryside and introduced a new measure of uniformity. In order to attract settlers, villages were granted various exemptions and newcomers were often given extensive privileges. Their rights, which were enshrined in charters, usually encompassed a measure of self-government and freedom from the performance of onerous duties. In time, the rights granted to migrant *hospites* were extended to already existing communities. Thus, in Bohemia by the fourteenth century the *ius Theutonicum* had merged with the older *ius Boemicum*, and nearly all peasants enjoyed roughly the same rights.[29]

In eastern Europe, however, the introduction of German legal norms was not accompanied by the establishment of powerful organs of self-government. Although elected *Schöffen* played a part in local jurisdiction right up until the eighteenth century, the peasant community was frequently headed by a hereditary office-holder, the *Schultheiss*, who combined judicial and administrative functions. The *Schultheiss* was usually descended from the founder or *locator* of the settlement. He counted amongst the wealthiest of the peasantry (holding a double *Bauerngut*), and mediated between the village and the landowner. At an early stage, however, the office was bought out either by townsfolk, local noblemen or landowners. As a consequence, the jurisdictional and administrative rights belonging to the *Schultheiss* became an adjunct either of seigneurial or of municipal justice.[30] An alternative, which may be demonstrated among the rural German community in Transylvania, was that office-holders acquired noble rank and thereupon ceased to play a part in communal activity.[31]

The principal instrument of local self-government and autonomy was thus lost to the East-Elbian peasantry as early as the fourteenth and early fifteenth centuries. The peasant *Gemeinde* functioned thereafter in only an attenuated form and acquired few of the rights enjoyed by rural communities farther west. Unsurprisingly, since the *Genossenschaft* itself was so weak, *Genossenschaftsrecht* was rarely articulated. Legal provisions originally ceded by charter were thus seldom reinforced by the codification of customary principles and, while plenty of examples of *Landrecht*, *Lehnrecht* and *Stadtrecht* survive, *Weistümer* are entirely lacking.[32]

An analogous situation prevailed in Hungary where, except for Transylvania, German settlement was sparse in rural areas. The native peasant communities in Hungary enjoyed only very rudimentary rights of self-government and their *villici* were usually appointed by the local lord. The rights of the peasantry were nowhere codified in Hungary, but had instead to be determined in litigation by peasant assessors chosen by the lord.[33] Significantly, the only rural community in the kingdom of Hungary to frame its customs in writing was the largely self-governing Szekler community in Transylvania.[34]

The relative absence of sophisticated instruments of peasant autonomy was compounded in eastern Europe by the extensive powers attaching to the local nobilities. On the one hand, the nobility enjoyed almost exclusive representation in the various parliaments and diets and in the local and county assemblies. These institutions took the lead in raising patrimonial rights to the status of custom of the realm and in reducing countryfolk to the legal condition of serfs. On the other, individual noblemen possessed strong powers of immunity which frequently permitted them to exercise high justice on their own estates and to adjudicate in matters wherein they themselves were litigants. In the absence of any clearly enunciated peasant custom, it was easy for local landowners to add to their presumed rights. One Bohemian jurist noted that nobles commonly omitted details of labour obligations when describing their estates on the Land Tables. For they were then free to extend the length of the *robota*.[35] Conceivably also, as has been indicated for the duchy of Wrocław, the publication of Roman Law texts and of the *Constitutio Carolina* (1532) strengthened the landowner's hand by freeing him from the obligation to declare for his subjects their own law.[36]

The imposition of serfdom was therefore facilitated by the particular legal and institutional disabilities of the medieval east European peasantry, and in the extensive powers attaching to the region's nobility. This imbalance was evident well before the onset of the late medieval agricultural depression. Once this struck, the nobility were forced to act to preserve their incomes and they took the simplest route of squeezing their tenants.[37] The strengths of communal autonomy and the relative weakness of the nobility in the region west of the Elbe prevented landowners from following the same course and so led to an increasing divergence in the history of these two parts of Europe.

Historians are fond nowadays of finding "fault lines" in Europe and the civil war in Yugoslavia has renewed interest in the supposed fissure between the Catholic and Orthodox parts of the continent.

When seeking the origins of civil society and of the *Rechtsstaat* (with both of which the Orthodox world is allegedly unfamiliar), it is more profitable to look at the legal division of Europe than at its religious and cultural clefts. The first critical line of legal change, which as we have seen appeared during the middle ages, followed very approximately the course of the River Elbe. To the west of this line were relatively powerful village communities and *Weistümer*; to the east lay the *Weistümer*-less region where "through entirely legal means the lords were able to set themselves up as despots of their villages".[38]

There is, however, a second legal division which follows the course of the Rhine rather than that of the Elbe. During the late fifteenth and sixteenth centuries, Germany and the Habsburg lands proved highly receptive to the influence of Roman Law. Roman Law on the one hand bridged the gap between conflicting customs and helped to standardize procedures. It thus provided in Germany a convenient mechanism for arbitrating breaches of the *Landfriede*. On the other, it inspired the compilation of already existing laws and customs, which accompanied the sixteenth-century trend towards territorial consolidation.[39] The principles of Roman Law were familiar enough in the late middle ages and were far from being despotic maxims. Nevertheless, the process of codification usually led to an increase in the powers of the ruler by way of an elaboration and extension of his sovereign and regalian rights. Additionally, as lawyers began to conceive of their role as *Fürstendiener*, so they increasingly interpreted the law to the prince's advantage.[40] The old republican elements in Roman Law, as epitomized by the tag *Quod omnes tangit ab omnibus approbetur*, were thus obscured by a new stress on the principles *Quod principi placuit legis habet vigorem* and *Princeps legibus solutus est*.[41]

The admission of Roman Law had a profound effect upon the constitutional history of the region east of the River Rhine. Roman Law sharply distinguished between public and private spheres. Otto von Gierke argued last century that this distinction had a tendency to dissolve society into two parts: an omnipotent state and atomized individuals. As a consequence, it amplified the authority of the ruler while permitting little room for the development of independent associations.[42] More obviously, the notions of sovereignty embedded in Roman Law cut clean through the older dualist construction according to which the law emerged out of the interaction of the ruler and the political nation and of which the prince was solely the guardian. In Roman Law, the legislative power was an adjunct of *Landeshoheit*, the repository of which was the sovereign ruler. Under its influence and that of the lawyers, the prince was transformed into the author of the law and the delicate medieval balance between *Regiment* and *Stände* tilted decisively in favour of the former.

For all their talk of *legibus solutus*, jurists seldom permitted the ruler to legislate in an arbitrary fashion. The monarch was still bound to observe "the traditional rights and liberties of his subjects". An obvious difficulty emerged, though, in matters wherein the law itself was silent and where traditional rights and liberties were uncertain. West of the River Rhine, in England, Holland and France, it was understood that where the law was silent the citizen was free. The stress laid in Roman Law upon the legislative omnicompetence of the ruler led, however, to a presumption of the very reverse in the lands east of the Rhine. In Germany and the Habsburg Monarchy, the presumption of the law tended always to be in favour of the ruler and of his servants. Where the law was silent, the ruler had the right to issue ordinances which interfered with the subject's freedom.[43] The autocratic principle found its fullest expression on the signpost in Baden made famous by Treitschke: "It is permitted to travel on this road".[44] But the same principle was equally evident in the flood of intrusive mandates, decrees and police ordinances published by the rulers of Central and Eastern Europe during the course of the sixteenth and seventeenth centuries.[45]

The institutions of serfdom and of noble privilege, which persisted in a large part of eastern Europe from the middle ages to the nineteenth century, may have added to the region's relative condition of backwardness. At least, during the eighteenth and nineteenth centuries they were generally believed to be obstacles both to progress and to the raising of state revenues. At the same time, rulers and their advisors in eastern Europe became convinced that their lands laboured generally under a disadvantage and that unless changes were introduced they would be defeated or outstripped.

Given the accumulation of authority vested in the ruler, it is not surprising that all plans for reform in eastern Europe should have been predicated on princely intervention. Cameralists like Hörnigk, Schröder, Justi and Becher converted the mercantilist prescriptions fashionable in western Europe into princely programmes which were to be administered by a loyal bureaucracy: the wheels and gears of the machine of state over which the ruler presided as the foreman. Cameralists were convinced of the importance of harnessing and disciplining the workforce in the interests of the "common good", of eradicating idleness with firm police action, of regulating relations between employers and workers, and of eliminating wasteful consumption.[46]

The ideas of the Enlightenment were additionally championed by the princely courts of eastern Europe. Stripped of their libertarian content, they became the intellectual artillery for the destruction of those institutions which interposed between ruler and subject. Under the impact of the Enlightenment, Roman Law principles were supplemented by ideas based on a rationalistic natural law.[47] The prince, while still retaining his sovereign rights, was promoted to the office of first servant of the state. And the state itself was given the objective of securing the "public good" and even the "bliss" (*Glückseligkeit*) of the population. As Christian Wolff explained in 1756, it was the duty of the ruler, "to muster all his powers and diligence to devise those means beneficial to the promotion of the common weal and security and to make all necessary preparations for their deployment"; and it was the obligation of subjects, "to consent and accede to any given instructions which are considered by the ruler to be beneficial to them".[48]

The excesses of seigneurial lordship and of noble privilege were among the first victims of the new science of the state. During the course of the eighteenth century, the Habsburg rulers imposed limitations on the use of corvée labour, restricted the jurisdictional rights of landowners and took the lead in demonstrating how the grant of free tenancies could improve yields. In the 1780s, the peasantry were granted personal mobility and the right to hereditary tenures, and they were relieved of many onerous and customary banalités. The nobility's freedom from the payment of taxation was directly challenged by plans to impose a uniform land tax. The explanation for these innovations was that existing conditions stood in the way of improvement and that the monarch was uniquely empowered by the nature of his office to act in support of the common welfare. The way out of the social and economic stagnation typical of those countries which lay east of the Elbe, was thus found in autocratic remedies characteristic of the lands eastward of the Rhine.

The belief that progress and the common good could be achieved by regulation from above found its most complete expression in the work of Joseph II and in the 700 or so edicts a year for which his government was responsible. Joseph's nineteenth-century successors continued his work at a slower and more circumspect pace. Yet many of the assumptions underlying Habsburg policy in the nineteenth century were still Josephinist in inspiration. Not only was Habsburg policy centralizing and anti-feudal, but it was predicated on the belief that an activist government and bureaucracy were the most appropriate instruments for ensuring progress. Commerce, moral education, agriculture and railways were all thus considered suitable objects for a highly interventionist government.[49] This was particularly so during the neo-absolutist period of the 1850s, when the servants of the monarch did not have to worry about constitutional niceties. The discretionary powers attaching to the administration, which originated in the autocratic principle of the law, provided additional opportunities for over-regulation, while the manifold activities of government swelled the size of the meddlesome imperial and royal bureaucracy.

It would be hard to make the case that "modernization" in the Habsburg monarchy was "state-led". Intervention was seldom matched by government investment. The preferred instruments of fiscal policy were tax-breaks and selective subsidies, both of which were often designed to attract foreign capital. For all their interest in railway construction (the *Ministerrat* seems to have discussed little else, even when the railways were in private ownership), Bruck and Baumgartner probably achieved less than Freycinet in France. The most ambitious investment programme in the whole history of the monarchy, Koerber's proposed injection of a billion crowns into transport, never obtained budgetary approval.

Nevertheless, it was in the realm of conviction rather than in the realm of reality that the presumed role of government exercised the greatest influence. This was particularly so once the notion of the state fused with the nationalist and moral perceptions of liberals and Hegelians. Thereafter, the state simultaneously embodied the *Volk* and "the march of God in the world". It became, as Gyula Szekfü wrote in 1920 of Habsburg Hungary, "our one and only pride, to which we dedicated and sacrificed every freedom and grand idea. We fattened it up into a Leviathan, which devoured and digested everything . . . ".[50] Beyond the metaphysical, government was still perceived as the institution best equipped to ensure material progress. The works of Fichte, List and particularly Rau, all of whom were advocates of the ruthless application of *Gesetz und Zwang* in the economy, found an eager readership in Central and Eastern Europe. It is possible to argue that the étatist philosophy of the nineteenth century, which spilled over into the interwar years in eastern Europe, contributed to the intellectual appeal of communism in the 1940s.[51]

In Eastern Europe today there is a profound and exaggerated awareness of how backward the region is in comparison to the west The condition of relative retardation is not a new feature of eastern Europe, but has its roots in differences in historical and legal development which may be traced back to the middle ages. It is not of course an ineluctable condition. In the framing of their new constitutions, the governments of eastern Europe have evinced their strong commitment to the principles of the *Rechtsstaat* and to political pluralism. Furthermore, as the countries of Eastern Europe become more closely integrated within Pan-European organizations, the possibility of their repudiation of democratic and liberal values becomes increasingly remote.

The greater danger is that the governments of Eastern Europe may yet in time return to cameralist economic remedies. If the present strategy of privatization and marketization fails to yield the expected economic transformation, Eastern Europe may find itself locked into the role of providing cheap labour and raw materials for its western neighbours. In this event, the retained economic power of the state and the weight of historical tradition could lead to extensive government intervention in the economy as fresh attempts are made to engineer an industrial breakthrough.[52] Although entirely in keeping with solutions adopted in the region over the last two centuries, neo-cameralism would be a desperate resort. Amongst much else, the historical experience of eastern Europe should have demonstrated that the amplification of the powers of government does not provide a fast route from the European periphery to membership of the core.

Notes

1. Daniel Chirot, *Social change in a peripheral society: the creation of a Balkan colony*, Academic Press Inc, 1976.

2. Immanuel Wallerstein, *The modern world-system: capitalist agriculture and the origins of the European world-economy in the sixteenth century*, Academic Press Inc, 1974.

3. *Ibid.*, p. 99.

4. Michael North, Untersuchungen zur adligen Gutswirtschaft im Herzogtum Preussens des 16. Jahrhunderts, *Vierteljahrschrift für Sozial- und Wirtschaftsgeschichte*, 70, 1983, pp. 1–20; Hans-Heinrich Nolte, Zur Stellung Osteuropas im internationalen System der frühen Neuzeit. Aussenhandel und Sozialgeschichte bei der Bestimmung der Regionen, *Jahrbücher für Geschichte Osteuropas*, 28, 1980, pp. 160–97; Hermann Kellenbenz, Immanuel Wallerstein, The modern world-system, *Journal of Modern History*, 48, 1976, pp. 685–92.

5. György Granasztói, Beszélgetés Pach Zsigmond Pállal, *Történelmi Szemle*, 25, 1982, p. 168; Iván Berend and György Ránki, Foreign trade and the industrialisation of the European periphery in the nineteenth century, *Journal of European Economic History*, 9, 1980, pp. 539–84; Läszló Makkai additionally suggested that the cities of southern Germany may have exerted an economic pull in the middle ages similar to that of the later Atlantic economy: Feudalizmus és az eredeti jellegzetességek Europában, *Történelmi Szemle*, 19, 1976, pp. 275–6.

6. Robert Brenner, The origins of capitalist development: a critique of Neo-Smithian Marxism, *New Left Review*, 104, 1977, pp. 25–92; Verl F. Hunt, The rise of feudalism in Eastern Europe: a critical appraisal of the Wallerstein "World System" Thesis, *Science and Society*, 42, 1978, pp. 43–61. Criticism of Wallerstein was primarily confined to obscure theoretical journals: a summary of these together with a belated defence of Wallerstein is given in Robert A. Denemark and Kenneth P. Thomas, The Brenner-Wallerstein debate, *International Studies Quarterly*, 32, 1988, pp. 47–65.

7. Friedrich Engels, *Anti-Dühring*, II/i, Peking 1976 edition, p. 187.

8. According thus to Daniel Chirot: "The clearest example of the transformation of a free peasant rural economy is the one which took place in Eastern Europe. In Poland, the sixteenth century was a period of marked increases in cereal exports (chiefly to Amsterdam). The quantity commercialized was large enough to have a profound influence on Polish social structure. Feudal dues were raised, and whereas before the peasants had been either free or only lightly burdened by feudal obligations, in the sixteenth century they were reduced to a servile state, prohibited from moving and had large dues (labor dues paid in work on noble demesne) imposed on them as the nobility moved to the world grain market . . . A similar transformation prevailed in much of the rest of Eastern

Europe, particularly in East Germany, Livonia, Silesia, Bohemia and Hungary." Daniel Chirot, The growth of the market and servile labor systems in agriculture, *Journal of Social History*, 8, 1975, pp. 68–9.

9. Marian Małowist, The problem of inequality of economic development in Europe in the later Middle Ages, *Economic History Review*, 2nd Series, 19, 1966, pp. 1–14.

10. Baron de Montesquieu, *Spirit of the Laws*, Book 20, ch. 23, trans. Thomas Nugent, New York, 1949, p. 329.

11. A. Mączak, Der polnische Getreideexport und das Problem der Handelsbilanz (1557– 1647), in Ingomar Bog (ed.), *Der Aussenhandel Ostmitteleuropas 1450–1650*, Cologne, 1971, p. 33.

12. Maria Bogucka, North European commerce and the problem of dualism in the development of modern Europe, in Vera Zimányi (ed.), *La Pologne et la Hongrie aux XVIe-XVIIIe siècles*, Budapest, 1981, pp. 13–14; Witold Kula, *An economic theory of the feudal system: towards a model of the Polish economy 1500–1800*, NLB, 1976, p. 93, citing tentative estimates of A. Wyczanski. Bogucka gives a figure of between 5.8 to 6.6 per cent for the proportion of the harvest sent abroad. Her figure is based on exports through Danzig. Although Danzig was the leading entrepot for Polish grain, some smaller quantities evidently passed through Riga, Elbing, Königsberg and Stettin.

13. Roughly three-quarters of the arable in Great and Little Poland was owned by the middle and lesser gentry. On their estates the demesne principally served to meet household needs.

14. Andrzej Kaminski, Neo-serfdom in Poland-Lithuania, *Slavic Review*, 34, 1975, pp. 252–68.

15. Leonid Żytkowicz, Trends of agrarian economy in Poland, Bohemia and Hungary from the middle of the fifteenth to the middle of the seventeenth centuries, in Antoni Mączak, Henryk Samsonowicz, Peter Burke (eds), *East-Central Europe in transition: from the fourteenth to the seventeenth century*, Cambridge, 1985, pp. 68–69.

16. Gyözö Ember, *Magyarország nyugati külkereskedelme a XVI. század középén*, Budapest, 1988, p. 731. The cattle trade was not a new phenomenon and probably accounted for 50–60 per cent of Hungarian exports in the 15th century.

17. *Magyarország története 1526–1686*, I, ed. Zs. P. Pach, Budapest, 1987, pp. 347–50.

18. Żytkowicz, p. 64; peasants on the estates of the diocese of Gniezno also owed labour services of 2–3 days a week by the mid-fifteenth century.

19. In Hungary, the earliest royal attempts to preserve the right of free peasant movement against noble encroachments were recorded in 1397 and 1405: *Decreta Regni Hungariae*, ed. F. Döry, G. Bónis and V. Bácskai,

Budapest, 1976 pp. 155, 195–6; in Silesia, grants of German law to peasant communities cease around 1400: Richard C. Hoffmann, *Land, liberties and lordship in a late medieval countryside: agrarian structures and change in the Duchy of Wrocław*, University of Pennsylvania Press, 1989, p. 312, and additional labour services were imposed: ed. P. Ludwig, J. J. Menzel, W. Irgang, *Geschichte Schlesiens*, I, Sigmaringen, 1988, 5th edition, p. 343; for Prussia, see the ordinances of 1412, given in *Akten der Ständetage Preussens unter der Herrschaft des deutschen Ordens*, ed. M. Toeppen, I, Leipzig, 1874, p. 199.

20. William E. Wright, *Serf, Seigneur and Sovereign: agrarian reform in eighteenth-century Bohemia*, Minnesota, 1966, pp. 8–9.

21. Lajos Demény, *Parasztfelkelés Erdélyben 1437–1438*, Budapest, 1987, pp. 54, 75–77; Ştefan Pascu similarly notes a gradual deterioration preceding the sixteenth century: *Voievodatul Transilvaniei*, III, Cluj-Napoca, 1986, pp. 74–5.

22. Zs. P. Pach, The development of feudal rent in Hungary in the fifteenth century, *Economic History Review*, 2nd Series, 19, 1966, pp. 1–14. Pach notes the similarities in this regard between Hungary, Poland and Bohemia.

23. Two leading economic historians in the west, writing from quite different standpoints, have indicated the insufficiency of commercial factors as an explanation for the enforcement of servile labour relations in eastern Europe and both have suggested the importance of institutional and political relationships: M. M. Postan, Economic relations between Eastern and Western Europe, ed. F. Graus, K. Bosl et al., *Eastern and Western Europe in the middle ages*, Thames and Hudson, 1970, pp. 170–174; Robert Brenner, Agrarian class structure and economic development in pre-industrial Europe, *Past and Present*, 70, 1976, p. 57.

24. Alfred Hoffmann, *Wirtschaftsgeschichte des Landes Oberösterreich*, Salzburg, 1952; Anton Špiesz, Czechoslovakia's place in the agrarian development of Middle and East Europe of modern times, *Studia Historica Slovaca*, 6, 1969, p. 61.

25. For much of what follows: Günther Franz, *Geschichte des deutschen Bauernstandes vom frühen Mittelalter bis zum 19. Jahrhundert*, second edition, Stuttgart, 1976, pp. 52–67.

26. Karl Kollnig, Probleme der Weistumforschung, in Günther Franz (ed.), *Deutsches Bauerntum im Mittelalter*, Darmstadt, 1976, p. 412.

27. Jacob Grimm, *Deutsche Weistümer*, I–VII, Göttingen, 1840–78; Karl Kollnig, *Elsässische Weistümer. Untersuchungen über bäuerliche Volksüberlieferung am Oberrhein*, Frankfurt, 1941.

28. Christian Lübke, *Arbeit und Wirtschaft im östlichen Mitteleuropa*, Stuttgart, 1991, p. 9, notes that *Dienstorganisation* is common in the Árpád,

Přemyslid and Piast kingdoms, but can scarcely be found among the neighbouring Slavonic groups.

29. František Graus, *Deutsche und slavische Verfassungsgeschichte*, *Historische Zeitschrift*, 197, 1963, p. 301; a similar development is evident in Silesia: Hoffmann, p. 20.

30. Hence the adage, "Was dem Schultheissen geschah ist dem Herrn geschehen": given in Karl Heinz Quirin, *Herrschaft und Gemeinde nach mitteldeutschen Quellen des 12. bis 18. Jahrhundert*, Göttingen, 1952, p. 65. Quirin regards the court of the Schultheiss as being from its inception a "herrschaftliche Niedergericht", *Herrschaft und Gemeinde nach mitteldeutschen Quellen des 12. bis 18. Jahrhundert*, p. 29.

31. Ed. Béla Köpeczi, *Erdély története*, I, Budapest, 1986, pp. 333–34.

32. Richard Schröder and Eberhard von Künssberg, *Lehrbuch der deutschen Rechtsgeschichte*, sixth edition, I, Leipzig, 1919, p. 761. Jacob Grimm notes the absence of *Weistümer* in the following lands: Upper Saxony, Meissen, Brandenburg, Mecklenberg, Pomerania, Silesia, Lusatia, Moravia, Styria and Carinthia; and their rarity in the Tyrol (!), Salzburg, Upper Austria and Bavaria – *Deutsche Rechtsalterthümer*, I, Berlin, 1956, p. xi. Both Schröder and, more recently, Heide Wunder, Peasant organization and class conflict in Eastern and Western Germany, *Past and Present*, 78, 1978, p. 49 interpret the lack of *Weistümer* east of the Elbe by reference to the legal sufficiency of the original charters of settlement. With respect to Wunder, there is a substantial difference between *Weistümer* and *Handfesten*, both in their appearance and the quantity of rights which they enumerate. The latter are almost always terse, vague and concerned overwhelmingly with the rights belonging to the *Schultheiss*.

33. Imre Hajnik, *A magyar birósági szervezet és perjog az Árpád-és a vegyes-házi királyok alatt*, Budapest, 1899, pp. 97–9.

34. In 1555, published in *A Nemes székely Nemzetnek Constitutiói, privilégiumai és . . . törvényes itéletei*, Pest, 1818, pp. 40–51.

35. Kenneth J. Dillon, *King and estates in the Bohemian Lands 1526–1564*, Brussels, 1976, p. 13

36. Hoffmann, p. 359. Although local law "broke" both land law and imperial law, the obligation of proving the applicability of *Partikularrecht* always rested on the plaintiff.

37. This point is cogently made by Robert Brenner in: Economic backwardness in Eastern Europe in light of development in the West, in ed. Daniel Chirot, *The origins of backwardness in Eastern Europe: economics and politics from the middle ages until the early twentieth century*, California, 1989, pp. 31–7.

38. Jerome Blum, The rise of serfdom in Eastern Europe, *American Historical Review*, 62, 1957, p. 824.

39. Legal codification was not confined just to the larger principalities of the Empire. In Moravia, the territorial consolidation of the estates of the bishopric of Olomouc, which was undertaken by Stanislaus Thurzó during the first decades of the sixteenth century, was augmented by the publication of a *Prawa Manska*, Olomouc, 1538.

40. James Q. Whitman, *The legacy of Roman Law in the German Romantic Era*, Princeton, 1990, pp. 54–7.

41. On the republican elements in Roman Law which were later obscured by absolutist constructions: Quentin Skinner, *The foundations of modern political thought*, II, Cambridge, 1978, pp. 124–34; ed. J. H. Burns, *The Cambridge history of medieval political thought*, Cambridge, 1988, p. 47.

42. Discussed by Michael John, *Politics and the law in late nineteenth century Germany: the origins of the civil code*, Oxford, 1989, pp. 114–15; on the problems encountered by classical Roman Law in accommodating corporate bodies within its framework: W. W. Buckland, *A text-book of Roman Law from Augustus to Justinian*, Cambridge, 1966 (third edition), p. 174.

43. László Péter, "Volt-e magyar társadalom a XIX. században? A jogrend és a civil társadalom képződése", *Változás és állandóság. Tanulmányok a magyar polgári társadalomról* (Hollándiai Mikes Kelemen Kör), 1989, pp. 74–5; by the same author, Montesquieu's paradox on freedom and Hungary's constitutions 1790–1990, *The New Hungarian Quarterly*, 123, Autumn 1991, pp. 3–14.

44. Heinrich von Treitschke, *History of Germany in the nineteenth century*, 7 volumes, London, 1915–19, 2, pp. 668–89, cited by James J. Sheehan, *German liberalism in the nineteenth century*, Methuen, 1982, p. 37. Treitschke, however, interpreted the signpost as an example of bureaucratic nonsense comparable to the numbering of trees.

45. Discussed at length in Marc Raeff, *The well-ordered police state: social and institutional change through law in the Germanies and Russia, 1600–1800*, New Haven, 1983; more recently, Roland Axtmann, "Police" and the Formation of the Modern State. Legal and Ideological Assumptions on State Capacity in the Austrian Lands of the Habsburg Empire, 1500–1800, *German History*, 10, 1992, pp. 39–61.

46. Axtmann, pp. 49–55.

47. Although the purpose behind the new civil law codes drawn up in the late eighteenth and nineteenth century was to supplant Roman Law with natural law, this intention was not fulfilled: see thus Kaunitz's comments on the Codex Theresianus as given in Henry E. Strakosch, *State absolutism and the rule of law: the struggle for the codification of civil law in Austria 1753–1811*, Sydney, 1967, p. 90.

48. Axtmann, "Police", p. 44.

49. On the nineteenth-century legacy of Josephinism, Josef Redlich,

Das österreichische Staats- und Reichsproblem, I, part 1, Leipzig, 1920, pp. 40–41, 45; Herbert Matis, Leitlinien der österreichischen Wirtschaftspolitik, Adam Wandruszka and Peter Urbanitsch, *Die Habsburgermonarchie 1848–1918*, I, Vienna, 1973, pp. 29–31.

50. Gyula Szekfü, *Három nemzedék és ami utána következik*, Budapest, 1989, p. 270.

51. Jerzy Jedlicki, Die unerträgliche Last der Geschichte, *Transit. Europaische Revue*, 2, 1991, pp. 21–2.

52. The strategy of "slow" privatization, adopted in most of the region in order to avoid macroeconomic destabilization, means that governments continue to occupy the commanding heights of the national economies and will probably continue to do so until at least the end of the century. In Hungary, more than two years after the collapse of communism, 80 per cent of industry was still state-owned. Moreover, it is often the case that the share capital in privatized businesses turns out on closer inspection to be owned by state-run banks.

CHAPTER EIGHT
Towards a European history of the petite bourgeoisie

Jonathan Morris

This chapter is an exploration of how the history of a social stratum might be written in a European context, in this case the history of the *petite bourgeoisie* in the nineteenth century. One approach to this problem is to develop a model of social and political behaviour amongst a stratum that one could expect to see repeated across different nations if broadly similar economic conditions existed. Such a model did exist to explain petty bourgeois behaviour during capitalist modernization, but has now been rejected by scholars. By reviewing this debate, I hope to indicate some paths towards a new European history of the *petite bourgeoisie*.

Petty and petite bourgeoisie

The current vogue amongst historians for employing the *petite bourgeoisie* as both a descriptive term and a category of social analysis stems from a reaction to the perceived inadequacies of the analysis of those scholars and political activists who followed (and vulgarized) Marx in writing of a petty bourgeoisie whose status and position was progressively weakened with the development of capitalism culminating in its disappearance into the mass of the proletariat.

Marxists viewed the existence of the petty bourgeoisie as indicative of a certain stage within the advance of capitalism. The petty bourgeoisie inhabit a world in which the final vestiges of guild production have been abolished, but full capitalist maturity has not been reached. The *Communist Manifesto* advances this view succinctly. With the development of capitalism "the lower strata of the middle class – the small tradespeople, shopkeepers, and retired tradesmen generally, the handicraftsmen and peasants – all these sink gradually into the proletariat, partly because their diminutive capital does not suffice for the scale on which modern industry is carried on, and is swamped in the competition with the large capitalists, partly because their specialized skill is rendered worthless by new methods of production".[1] Indeed

> as modern industry develops they even see the moment approaching when they will completely disappear as an independent section of modern society to be replaced, in manufactures, agriculture and commerce, by overlookers, bailiffs and shopmen.[2]

Accordingly, they

> fight against the bourgeoisie to save from extinction their existence as fractions of the middle class. They are therefore not revolutionary but conservative. Nay more they are reactionary, for they are trying to roll back the wheel of history.[3]

Marx and Engels conceded that there was a chance that the petty bourgeoisie would act in a revolutionary manner during this fight, but only in order to restore the older forms of production. This was the ideology of petty bourgeois socialism which dissects "with great acuteness the contradictions in the conditions of modern production", proves "incontrovertibly the disastrous effects of machinery and division of labour, the concentration of capital and land in a few hands, overproduction and crises", but whose positive aims aspire

> either to restoring the old means of production and of exchange, and with them the old property relations and the old society, or to cramping the modern means of production and of exchange within the framework of the old property relations that have been, and were bound to be, exploded by those means. In either case it is both reactionary and utopian.

Its last words are: corporate guilds for manufacture, patriarchal relations in agriculture'.[4]

This analysis appeared to solve both the historical and political problems associated with the petty bourgeoisie. To the practitioners of praxis it provided an explanation for the failure of their ideas to achieve popularity amongst the petty bourgeoisie, the backward-looking nature of the stratum, and also the comforting thought that with the disappearance of the petty bourgeoisie this barrier would be overcome. Political activists preached the message of impending proletarianization in the hope that opening the eyes of the petty bourgeoisie to the reality of their situation would persuade them to push the wheel of history forwards, instead of vainly struggling to turn it anti-clockwise.[5]

Historians, meanwhile, found in petty-bourgeois socialism an explanation of the stratum's radicalism in the early nineteenth century and its failure to develop into a revolutionary consciousness, whilst the increasingly reactionary nature of the grouping as the century progressed was attributed to contemplation of its imminent extinction. This interpretation has found favour amongst serious scholars (including many non-Marxists) as well as vulgarizers, and is now perhaps most associated with those explanations of the rise of fascism in the twentieth century in which "status anxiety" amongst the lower middle classes is a significant feature.[6]

The historians who now opt to write of the *petite bourgeoisie* dissent with the foregoing analysis at almost every juncture. Given the ideological baggage that the term "petty bourgeoisie" now carries, it is no surprise that scholars such as Geoffrey Crossick and Heinz-Gerhard Haupt, organizers of the round table seminars on the European *petite-bourgeoise* held between 1979 and 1990, should have explicitly stated that they

> decided to write of a *"petite bourgeoisie"* and *"petits bourgeois"* because of a wish to shift attention from the pejorative and, more importantly, narrowing implications of the older term "petty bourgeoisie".[7]

The adoption of the *petite bourgeoisie* as the preferred unit of analysis was also sparked by concern over the wide range of occupational groupings encompassed within the petty bourgeoisie. The historians of the *petite bourgeoisie* did not concern themselves with peasant proprietors, regarding them as essentially primary producers rather than manufacturers and retailers, whilst the white-collar lower middle classes were excluded on the grounds that they were employees rather than self-employed economic agents. Instead they adopted the working definition of the *petite bourgeoisie* as those whose livelihood was derived from both their own capital and their own labour, that is by working in their own enterprises with or without the employment of additional labour.[8] In the nineteenth century this usually meant shopkeepers and master artisans. Inevitably, though not exclusively, this work has focused on urban small proprietors.[9]

The desire to avoid confusion between very different forms of *petite bourgeoisie* also means abandoning comparative analysis of European areas in which the development of capitalism occurred along fundamentally different lines, and where such strata as the urban intellectuals of Romania have been identified as members of the petty bourgeoisie.[10] Indeed, because the modernizing core of Europe incorporated regions of different states, rather than nations themselves, it might be argued that regional, rather than national, analysis is more appropriate to an understanding of the *petite bourgeoisie*.

This work has challenged many of the assumptions inherent in previous thinking about the petty bourgeoisie, notably those concerning the effects of modernization upon the *petite bourgeoisie*, and the politicization of the stratum. I shall review these topics in the next two sections of this essay. In particular, it has raised important considerations about the comparative analysis of the *petit bourgeois* experience in Europe that will be the subject of the final part of this paper.

Modernization and the petite bourgeoisie

The interpretation of the economic fortunes of small traders and master artisans during what is now described as modernization, which I use here to indicate a transition to concentrations of capital in both manufacturing and distribution, along with the development of a mass market for consumer consumption, was central to the new thinking amongst historians of the *petite bourgeoisie*. Above all they refuted the deterministic view that the advance of mass manufacture and machine production inevitably implied the disappearance of the small scale sector.

Even within industries in which factory production became the norm, opportunities existed for small producers. Small workshops might supply components to the factories, they might be contracted to undertake repair and maintenance work for large producers, or utilized to cope with periods of excessive demand. Conversely, small workshops remained the centres of production for those goods for which demand was sufficiently irregular or insubstantial to mean that large scale manufacture was not commercially viable.

The development of machine technology was often beneficial to small and medium sized producers. In 1902, for instance, Milanese bakers enthused over an electric kneading machine that was small enough to be installed in most bakeries and reduced the number of workers needed in an enterprise. Various attempts to institute large-scale factory type production of bread in Milan in the last years of the nineteenth century all failed, however, not least due to what appears to be consumer resistance to the finished product. The proportion of overall bread production taking place in the smallest bakeries actually increased between 1879 and 1913.[11]

The appearance of department stores and chain multiples has often been used as a way of extending the thesis of petty bourgeois decline in the face of the concentration of capital into the retail sector. This can be challenged on several counts – these enterprises could help attract clients to small shops located in their vicinity, whilst often their reliance on artisan suppliers gave a significant boost to the *petite bourgeoisie* as a whole. The most important point, though, is simply that the retail market expanded so rapidly that these enterprises did little to check growth in the sector as a whole. Urbanization brought increasing numbers of customers into the retail market, whilst the appearance of stores trading in in gramophones, bicycles, and domestic appliances, along with new services, such as those provided by photographers, provided new opportunities for small traders. In Germany the ratio of customers to retailers halved between the 1860s and 1890s, whilst between 1895 and 1907 the numbers of shops increased by 42 per cent as compared to an 8 per cent growth in the nation's population, a pattern repeated throughout Europe.[12]

This is not to deny the overall effect of the advance of large-scale production in certain sectors – the number of industrial firms registered for the French business tax, the *patente*, fell significantly in the later nineteenth century, whilst the size of these, as measured by their contributions, grew – but one must remain aware that the story was less one-sided than earlier analysts presupposed. In 1901 three-quarters of all French manufacturing enterprises were those of domestic producers, independent masters or family enterprises. Amongst the quarter of businesses which employed any non-family labour, 80 per cent employed fewer than six wage labourers.[13]

The recent re-evaluations of French industrialization suggest the small manufacturing sector can play a dynamic role in the transition to modernity. Large-scale entrepreneurs would sub-contract production to a network of small-scale enterprises thus avoiding committing themselves to the concentration of production before a mass market had been definitively established. Small manufacturers gained access to the distribution chains of such entrepreneurs, and relied on them for the provision of capital and credit. Taken to the extreme this pattern replicated the putting-out system, with firms now working the materials supplied by the entrepreneur to produce goods he then sold through his distribution chain. This system did not necessarily preserve craft production – the small enterprises within the network usually employed simple machine technology – but it did offer a niche for small business.[14]

This pattern was far from unique to France, although it was particularly suited to the French market.[15] In England there was a period between the introduction of the sewing machine in the 1860s and the establishment of factory production after the 1880s when the shoe-making industry functioned in this fashion.[16] Similar networks made their appearance in most European economies: in Austria, for example, the expansion of small-scale production for the consumer market in Vienna took place within the framework of the so-called *Verlagssystem* that linked artisan production to the capitalist market economy . This was notable for being developed in conjunction with the control of the still extant guild organizations.[17]

In general, the *petit bourgeois* enterprises which most frequently gained from modernization did so by virtue of their integration into networks which served the interests of larger capital. Retailers became part of distribution networks controlled by large-scale wholesalers or manufacturers, small manufacturers supplied factories with components or undertook work which was unsuitable for large-scale production. These beneficiaries did not challenge or compete against the concentration of capital, but compromised with it. They were nominally independent, but relied on larger scale players for operating capital or for access to the market.

It is difficult to quantify such degrees of dependence. Blackbourn has estimated that of those whom conservatives defined as the *Mittelstand* in Germany during the 1890s – that is the peasantry, the master artisans and the shopkeepers, a definition rather closer to that of the petty than the *petite bourgeoisie* – only around a third of the 8 million or so members of this group were actually independent.[18] In Paris it has been suggested that only 5.1 per cent of craftsmen were independent by 1847 and a mere 1.9 per cent could be so described by 1901.[19]

The development of capitalism also altered the essential skills necessary for effective survival in business. It is true, of course, that some craft skills were eroded by the development of machine technology. What seems to unite the *petite bourgeoisie*, however, is more the nature of the new skills need to survive under the conditions of maturing capitalism. Above all these were business techniques, rather than trade specific ones. Grocers, for instance, abandoned old skills such as chocolate making, realizing that the key to success lay in meeting the rising demand for advertised brand name products through efficient stocking systems and the development of effective links to suppliers. Bookkeeping, stock control and cash flow management all became more important than the specific skills associated with the trade in which they were exercised.[20]

In effect what occurred was the transformation of the *petite bourgeoisie* from craftsmen (including retailing craftsmen) into small businessmen. During the nineteenth century the *petite bourgeoisie* of those who worked their own capital (that is capital they had obtained for themselves) became increasingly fragmented into dependants and independents, masters and small businessmen, although these classifications (and *mentalités*) were far from exclusive and coexisted in many individuals.

A deterministic view of the casting down of the *petite bourgeoisie* into the proletariat as a by-product of capitalist modernization appears to fall, therefore, as a range of opportunities opened up for the *petite bourgeoisie* during this transition from guild production to full-blown capitalism. The economic space occupied by the *petite bourgeoisie*, however, was effectively defined with relation to large capital, in that the small proprietors occupied those spaces left or made available to them by modernization. In this sense Marx's description of the petty bourgeoisie as "ever renewing itself as a supplementary part of bourgeois society" could still be applied to the *petite bourgeoisie*, providing one recognizes that the fluctuating nature of the stratum was caused by new entrants profiting from the possibilities provided by modernization as much as by the demise of former members in the face of the advance of capitalism.

Politics and politicization amongst the petite bourgeoisie

Does this mean, then, that the *petite bourgeoisie* sought only to turn back the wheel of history to previous forms of the organization of production and distribution, as Marx suggested? Or that their failure to achieve this goal led them to turn from "revolutionary" means to "reactionary" ones, in the manner suggested by social theorists? Was it the case that a particularly pronounced form of this progression could account for the German tragedy of the twentieth century?

It is not difficult to build the case that this is indeed what happened. In the 1848 upheavals in France, *petit bourgeois* participants called for the imposition of uniform tariffs and uniform working conditions within trades, and joined forces with workers in attempts to set up conventions that would regulate industries.[21] In the June 1848 pre-parliament in Hamburg, masters argued that a social parliament should be established in parallel with the political parliament meeting in the Frankfurt Paulskirche. This social parliament would control all matters of industrial, commercial and social legislation. The intent was clearly the establishment of control over the capitalist process that was held to have undermined their position (a position which vindicates the stress that recent historians have laid on the development of capitalism, rather than industrialization, as the critical *petit bourgeois* experience of the nineteenth century).[22]

As the century advanced, these demands became more pronounced, particularly in the wake of the Great Depression. In Germany, historians of both master artisans and shopkeepers traced the evolution of various *petit bourgeois* associations into national organizations that called for controls on large-scale capitalism and a return to a strong guild system.[23] The same pattern can be discerned

in Austria. In both states, these movements were likewise support-
ive of the extreme right. Stöcker, leader of the Social Conservatives
in Germany, and Karl Lueger, the head of the Christian Socials
in Vienna, both developed their constituencies within the master
artisan organizations of their respective countries. It was Lueger's
conquest of the Viennese craft guilds, the representative institutions
of what was still the largest class grouping in the restricted Viennese
electorate, that enabled him to become Mayor of the city in 1897.[24]

Anti-Semitism was a key part of these extremists' appeal to the
master artisan's institutions. It would seem that this performed two
main functions. First, Jews served as a convenient symbol for those
forces which were undermining the master's position, notably the
growing numbers of self-employed workers in various trades who
worked outside the realm of guild production. Secondly, it enabled
the drawing of an equation in which the master artisans were seen
as belonging to a national community, whilst their competitors did
not. This of course did not apply only to self-employed journeymen.
Department store owners and peddlers could both be denounced as
Jews, whilst the cooperative movement was inspired by unpatriotic
socialists.

Of course, the facts do not bear such an analysis out.[25] The point
to emphasize here is that the key to the protest that was being
registered was against the nature of capitalist development itself.
At a German conference of master-artisans in Germany in 1892, a
militant master-tailors' leader stated that

> as far as we are concerned the Jewish question is solved at the
> moment in which only men who have learned a craft – practi-
> cally and theoretically – are able to operate craft workshops.[26]

Volkov argued that the anti-modernism amongst German master
artisans in the depression years before the end of the century was
reproduced in the depression of the late 1920s with disastrous
consequences.[27]

The call for a return to controls over methods of production and
the numbers of producers in Austria and much of Germany was
associated with a guild system which had survived formally in
these states until the 1860s, in contrast to the abolition of the
guilds elsewhere in Europe during the French revolutionary era.
These demands appeared to be met by the authorities. Guilds were

revived in Austria and Germany in the 1880s, and membership of these was made obligatory under certain circumstances in Germany in 1897. In the 1890s new taxation laws that penalized large department stores were introduced in various German states and the imperial legislation regarding apprenticeship regulations was tightened in 1908.

In these concessions some historians discerned elements of what was called *Mittelstandspolitik*, a strategy for the incorporation of the *petite bourgeoisie* into a conservative bloc to act as a social defence against the seduction of the working class by socialist or other subversive ideas. It seemed that the guilds and craft chambers had actually been revived by government itself in order to give the masters and retailers the conviction that they had a voice within the system. As Winkler wrote:

> The *Mittelstandspolitik* of the Empire was the result of massive pressure on the part of interest groups, . . . however . . . in the case of handicrafts, the organisation of group interests was not so much autonomous as officially implemented.[28]

He went on to make the case that the development of social protection under the Empire, and its denial in the Weimar Republic, accounted for lower middle class support for Nazism.

More recent historians of the *petite bourgeoisie* have raised many objections to the ways in which anti-modernism has been used to explain the actions of the stratum both in the late nineteenth and early twentieth centuries, as well as part of an explanation of the long term origins of fascism. One obvious objection is that these anti-modernist sentiments only surfaced on a cyclical basis; in times of economic prosperity progressive attitudes could be found amongst the *petite bourgeoisie* (although this does not discredit the argument that *petit-bourgeois* attitudes during the depression of the 1890s were repeated during that of the 1930s).

A comparative analysis of the European *petite bourgeoisie* suggests a sufficiently shared experience of the nineteenth century to throw doubt on the deterministic explanations of Nazism as the end-product of anti-modernism and social protectionism. Although the demands for the reintroduction of guilds were peculiar to Austria and Germany (where these institutions were only formally abolished in the 1860s, as opposed to the French revolutionary era), *petit-bourgeois* associations in France, Belgium and Denmark all called for restrictions on large-scale capital towards the end of the century, with department stores attracting particular attention. Politically these movements often identified with extremist and excluded movements.

Again these demands drew responses from the state. In the 1890s new taxation laws that penalized large department stores were introduced in France, whilst there was a a tightening of the legislation concerning co-operatives in Italy. In the 1900s Denmark moved against the multiples, whilst Italy simplified the bookkeeping requirements for small businesses and decriminalized simple bankruptcy in 1903. In Belgium Catholic governments keen to develop a social barrier against their Socialist rivals rivals set up an Office for the Middle Classes in 1899 within the Ministry of Industry and Labour, which became a Department of·the Middle Classes in 1906. These attempted to improve apprenticeship and encourage vocational training, and were particularly active in promoting the formation of *syndicats bourgeois* – trade associations which sometimes took on functions such as bulk purchasing at discount prices.[29]

Whilst traces of *Mittelstandspolitik* can be found in several states, it is arguable as to how far the associations set up to defend craftsmen and retailer interests were actually incorporated into a wider conservative bloc. There are many examples of their changing their political allies in order to achieve the best overall result for the movement – for example the growth of *petit bourgeois* support for the Liberal Hansabund in Germany in the wake of the Conservative administration's financial reforms of 1909.[30] These demonstrations of political autonomy amongst the *petite bourgeoisie* call into question the motives behind government policies – it could be argued that governments simply responded to political pressures rather than creating them, and that the success of the *petite bourgeoisie* in winning concessions was a tribute to their increasing importance and involvement in the political sphere following the democratization of politics.

Most importantly, however, it can be argued that the apparently anti-modernist reaction I have outlined above was only manifested within some parts of the *petite bourgeoisie* – those elements who felt threatened by modernization. It does not take into consideration the large proportion of the stratum who may have accommodated themselves to the new patterns of production and exchange that resulted from modernization. Bakers in Milan, for example, who appear to have been resistant to the threat of large-scale manufacture, were not to be found bemoaning modernization, but remained loyal to a political tradition that might best be described as one of democratic liberalism.[31]

It is crucial to consider also the responses of those members of the *petite bourgeoisie* who were effectively, or even formally, dependent on large scale capital. Many of those in such a position had graduated into it, i.e. experienced this position as a form of social mobility, rather than as the culmination of diminishing independence. These new members of the *petite bourgeoisie* were unlikely to be tempted into anti-modernism with its call for a return to a past in which they had not shared. There is plenty of evidence, however, that many of these new *petits bourgeois* were prepared to recognize their own lack of independence from large-scale capital, to the point of becoming leading figures in socialist parties that maintained at least a formal opposition to the concept of private property. Innkeepers played a significant role in the development of the German SPD, both in terms of their own membership and through their provision of rooms for meetings, whilst several studies in France have emphasized the importance of the *petite bourgeoisie* within the SFIO.[32]

This serves to highlight the difficulties encountered in studying the *petite bourgeoisie* by focusing on national associations of masters and retailers. The fact that many of these displayed anti-modernist characteristics is well worthy of study, but cannot be held to be representative of the complete experience of the *petite bourgeoisie*. In 1895, for example, of the three million or so small workshop proprietors in Germany, less than half were self-employed masters in traditional crafts which qualified for guild membership, and half of these were resident in rural areas.[33] Those excluded from the guilds experienced modernization in a very different manner, many as beneficiaries of the processes that those within these associations opposed.

The diversity of *petit bourgeois* experience during modernization raises some important questions about the validity of making comparisons between the various national *petite bourgeoisies*. In one sense the more recent studies of the *petite bourgeoisie* confirm a commonality of experience that suggests caution in attempting to discern the causes of particular twentieth-century phenomena in the experiences of the nineteenth century *petite bourgeoisie*. Analysis of the effects of modernization, however, indicates the considerable variety of ways in which this was experienced by the *petite bourgeoisie* within every state. Given this, a comparative analysis of the stratum at national level must be regarded as having only limited value.

Units of comparative analysis

Crossick and Haupt, in their commentary on the historiography of the *petite bourgeoisie* suggest that

> at the level of national comparisons, similarities might be more striking than differences, especially in daily existence and experiences. The interesting contrasts might be less those amongst countries, and more the distinctions between types of town.[34]

This is surely true. While the economic functions of the *petite bourgeoisie* are broadly similar in whatever city or country they are operating in (that, after all, is how we managed to define them as members of the *petite bourgeoisie*), the local commercial environments in which they operate are not. It was at local, rather than national, level that *petit bourgeois* associations were strongest, and most permanent, whichever country we examine. Given the criticism of the connection made between the anti-modernism of national associations of the *petite bourgeoisie* and the economic fortunes of the stratum, it is vital to note that local associations often encompassed the various parts of the *petite bourgeoise* in terms of independence, size, or whatever, yet might well contain alternative divisions between trades, or within them, that could only be explained by reference to specific features of the commercial environment. Consequently local studies might produce very different readings of political activity amongst the *petite bourgeoisie*, situated within the context of the diverse effects of modernization upon the stratum.

Comparisons between cities serve not only to highlight these locally specific features, but also to identify common features of the *petit-bourgeois* experience that do not emerge from national studies focused on the anti-modernist paradigm. I will attempt to demonstrate this through a comparison of the shopkeeper movements in

Paris and Milan between 1880 and 1905, making use of Philip Nord's work on the French capital and my own on the Italian commercial centre.[35]

It was the failure of the state authorities to alter the shop licensing legislation to discriminate against department stores in Paris that sparked the formation of the shopkeeper association, the *Ligue syndicale du travail, de l'industrie et du commerce*, in the French capital in 1888. By the mid 1890s it had over 140,000 members (though many were non-Parisians). In Milan, the *Federazione generale degli esercenti* was also founded in 1888, two years after the shopkeeper newspaper *L'Esercente* was set up in the aftermath of an attempt by the city council to alter the terms of a local sales duty on retail goods in a way that would have endangered the advantages derived from the duty by suburban shopkeepers. By 1899 there were 5,000 members of the Federation, and the newspaper boasted a similar-sized circulation.[36]

Both these movements were of groups who believed themselves to be disadvantaged within the commercial environment, but that disadvantage was not necessarily a simple product of modernization. In the Parisian case, although the department stores clearly did represent a modernization of the retailing sector, the divisions between shopkeepers were primarily ones of location arising from the creation of favoured and unfavoured locations by Haussmann's rebuilding of the capital. The *Ligue* attracted those proprietors who had found themselves in back street locations, unable to compete with their peers on the main boulevards where shoppers attracted by the department stores concentrated their attentions.

In Milan, the spatial division was even more obvious. The sales duty was applied to each individual good in the city centre, whilst in the suburbs the duty was calculated on overall turnover, using a lower set of tariffs. The resultant lower prices in the suburbs were attractive to shoppers from the city centre as a duty free allowance enabled them to bring a certain quantity of goods back through the city walls without charge. It was attempts to lower this duty free allowance that sparked the shopkeeper movement in 1886 with the result that most of its members were suburban traders. Although it later sought to extend its influence into the city centre, municipal proposals to abolish the tax distinction led to a series of splits within the movement along zonal lines.

The manner in which these movements arose also accounted for the composition of their membership and leadership. In Paris, for instance, there was a predominance of luxury goods traders such as jewellers, goldsmiths and watchmakers, along with clothiers and tailors. These, of course, were those trades most directly affected by competition from the department stores. In Milan, however, butchers, bakers and grocers were to the fore in a movement of food and drink provisioners. These were the trades most commonly practised in the suburbs and which had most to lose from a change in the city tax regulations. Conversely luxury craft traders tended to be congregated in the city centre, were relatively secure against threats from department stores (of which there were only two), and remained within their own trade associations. As important as the fact that different trades dominated these movements, however, is the fact that shopkeepers from the same trade were divided over membership of both movements by their different situations – bakers in the Milanese city centre and jewellers located on large Parisian boulevards were most likely not to be participants in these movements or to share their goals. Membership cannot be explained by anti-modernism alone.

Certainly elements of anti-modernism existed in both movements. The *Ligue syndicale* had identified cheap mass manufacture and department store retailers as the enemy, and it did not hesitate to point to the German origins of many manufactured products and the Jewish antecedents of several department store owners in an attempt to win support for its case through the manipulation of xenophobia. As Nord points out, however, such strategies were common amongst politicians of all persuasions, and should not be allowed to detract from what he sees as a fundamentally radical-republican philosophy amongst the *liguers*.[37] In Milan, however, *L'Esercente* suggested that the scapegoat role once occupied by the Jews had been taken over by the shopkeepers themselves. "what centuries ago happened to the Hebrews now repeats itself for the shopkeepers: After him, into him, he's a Jew. Were they rogues, murderers, thieves, those sons of Israel? Eh! but they were Jews. And one didn't reason beyond that."[38]

This statement was made during the depression years of the 1890s when the paper repeatedly condemned what it portrayed as the "unfair competition" of the consumer co-operatives. When the business cycle turned, however, a rapprochement with even those co-operatives who utilized the same principles as department stores was effected, again suggestive of the need to treat "anti-modernism" as an intermittent feature. Furthermore, the Milanese shopkeepers were equally swift to condemn what they saw as outmoded forms of commerce – such as street markets and peddling – and disparaged tailors and haberdashers for continuing to sell by bargaining with customers instead of using a fixed price (one of the reasons these retailers did not feature in the movement).

A comparison of the Parisian and Milanese movements demonstrates that shopkeeper politics were much more flexible than the model of a progression from anti-modernism to right wing extremism suggests. These movements not unnaturally supported those political factions which advocated policies closest to their own and were prepared to change their allies if they found it expedient to do so. In Paris the shopkeeper movement was associated in turn with Republicans, Boulangists, anti-Semites and the anti-Dreyfuss coalition (all of whom developed specific programmes tailored to *Ligue* concerns), but was then increasingly integrated into an anti-Socialist business coalition whose membership included precisely those elements against whom the original movement had fought. In Milan the movement was initially associated with the alliance of Radicals and Republicans known as the Democrats who drew their support from the city suburbs, and suburban shopkeepers tended to return to this alliance whenever they felt their positions under threat. At other times, with the Democrats wooing the pro-cooperative Socialists, the movement drifted towards the conservative Moderate alliance. After the Moderates united the two tax zones of the city, *Federazione* representatives participated in a Democrat administration between 1899 and 1904, but found themselves unable to work with the Socialists and turned back to the Moderates in order to defeat it.

In both Paris and Milan, then, chosen partners might come from various parts of the political spectrum. Furthermore, a variety of political positions contended within the movements themselves. Although both movements arrived at anti-Socialist positions, these were not accompanied by extremism: in the Parisian case there was a passage from the radical to the conventional right, whilst in Milan parts of the shopkeeper movement moved back towards the Democrats once they abandoned the Socialists after 1905. This is suggestive of political autonomy within the *petite bourgeoisie*, not its incorporation into the right.

It would be better to interpret the increasing participation of the shopkeeper movements in wider business coalitions as indicative of their greater integration into the mainstream political economy. By the 1900s the depression had lifted, perhaps making an accommodation between department store owners and small shopkeepers easier to reach in Paris as was suggested by small shopkeeper participation in the campaigns of the *Federation des commercants-detaillants* against Sunday closing led by the department store owner Georges Maus.[39] In Milan the unification of the suburban and city centre tax zones created the conditions for the development of a wider shopkeeper identity throughout the city, aided by the arrival of an economic upturn. Increasing labour militancy led to the development of links with larger scale proprietors such as hoteliers, who recruited from the same workforce, whilst experience of the consumer-orientated policies of the Socialists led to a more general identification of shopkeeper interests with those of the business community.[40] Again there is a sense here of the transition of the *petite bourgeoisie* into small businessmen.

Comparison of shopkeeper movements in Paris and Milan demonstrates that studies of the *petite bourgeoisie* at a local level are revealing of both a complexity and a concreteness that necessarily disappears if one moves to the plane of national comparisons. Participants in *petit bourgeois* movements at the local level are often missing at the national one where traditional petty bourgeois movements with anti-modernist tendencies grab the attention. At the local level issues that relate more specifically to the commercial environment than simply the "modernization" of production and exchange were often responsible for mobilizing a wider *petite bourgeoisie*. As the Milan and Paris examples demonstrate, however, the *petite bourgeoisie*, and even the constituent trades within it, are as likely to be divided as united over even local issues.

Towards a European history of the petite bourgeoisie

This essay has shown how those historians and social scientists who write about a *petite bourgeoisie* have rethought the work of earlier generations of scholars who chose to follow Marx in writing of a petty bourgeoisie. The picture of a petty bourgeoisie in economic decline seeking political salvation through anti-modernism has been revised in the light of the diverse experiences of the *petite bourgeoisie* during modernization and the variety of political strategies this engendered. National comparisons suggest more similarities than differences in this pattern but, though providing a caution against explaining particular twentieth-century phenomena in the light of general nineteenth-century ones, they often ignore much of the reality of nineteenth-century *petit bourgeois* experience. National movements tend to be unrepresentative of the diversity within the stratum, whilst trying to link together the very different situations of the *petite bourgeoisie* in large industrial cities and small provincial towns to produce a national aggregate experience is more useful in illustrating this diversity than it is in providing elements for a comparative analysis.

Local studies provide better materials for a comparative history of the *petite bourgeoisie* as they are more successful at encompassing the range of *petit bourgeois* experience, and moving the debate on from the anti-modernism thesis. Multiplying and comparing examples may also help demystify some national peculiarities. In England, for instance, where there were few lasting national movements amongst the *petite bourgeoisie*, provoking considerable debate about English exceptionalism in resisting anti-modernism, there was none the less considerable *petit bourgeois* involvement in local politics, usually through the medium of participation in Economy or Ratepayers' parties which sought to keep down local taxation.[41]

Contrasts between different types of town provide one way forward, as Crossick and Haupt suggested. Of particular importance, however, are comparisons between similar types of towns or cities, especially those in different countries. In such studies the role of the state would certainly appear as a factor in determining *petits bourgeois* experience, but it would no longer be allied to the nation as the unit for comparative analysis. Such an approach should prove a more effective way of working towards a European history of the *petite bourgeoisie*.

Notes

1. Karl Marx, Friedrich Engels, *The communist manifesto*, Penguin edition, London, 1967, p. 88.
2. *Ibid.*, p. 108.
3. *Ibid.*, p. 91.

4. *Ibid.*, p. 109.

5. The Socialist, Ugo Fantoni, berated Italian shopkeepers, for instance, because of their failure to recognize that their class was destined to disappear. "By persisting in your indifference, by not making common cause with the workers of the world", he scolded them, "you demonstrate that you don't have the dignity of men, you neglect that sentiment of foresight and *amour propre* that every man, especially in poor circumstances, should jealously preserve". Ugo Fantoni, *Agli Esercenti*, Milan, 1896, p. 5.

6. A full review of this literature is not possible here. A guide is provided in Philip Nord, *Paris shopkeepers and the politics of resentment*, Princeton, 1984, pp. 8–17. One well-known scholar to be influenced by such explanations is Lipset whose analysis of petty bourgeois behaviour encompasses both early support for democratic movements and later reactionary activity in terms of economic developments. Seymour Martin Lipset, *Political man*, New York, 1963, pp. 129–33.

7. Geoffrey Crossick, Heinz-Gerhard Haupt, Shopkeepers, master artisans and the historian, in Crossick G., Haupt H.-G. (eds), *Shopkeepers and master artisans in nineteenth-century Europe*, London, 1984, p. 26n.

8. The sociologists Bechhofer and Elliot have played the greatest role in advancing these definitions. See Frank Bechhofer, Brian Elliot, Persistence and change: the *petite bourgeoisie* in industrial society, *Archives Européennes de sociologie*, XVII, 1, 1976, pp. 76–9.

9. One exception is Jean-Claude Farcy, Rural artisans in the Beauce during the nineteenth century, in Crossick, Haupt, *Shopkeepers and master artisans*, pp. 219–38.

10. Irina Livezeanu, Between state and nation: Romanian lower middle class intellectuals in the interwar period, in Rudy Koshar (ed.), *Splintered classes*, New York, 1990, pp. 165–9.

11. Machine impastatrici, *L'Esercente*, 26 January, Milan, 1902; Il pane, *Città di Milano*, Milan, July 1914, p. 4. On the failure of factory-sized bakeries in Milan see Jonathan Morris, *The political economy of shopkeeping in Milan 1886–1922*, Cambridge, 1993, p. 255.

12. David Blackbourn, Between resignation and volatility: the German *petite bourgeoisie* in the nineteenth century, in Crossick, Haupt, *Shopkeepers and master artisans*, p. 41.

13. Heinz-Gerhard Haupt, The petite bourgeoisie in France, 1850–1914, in Crossick, Haupt, *Shopkeepers and master artisans*, pp. 97–8.

14. On these aspects of French industrialisation see Roger Price, *An economic history of modern France 1730–1914*, London, 1981, pp. 96–9; Patrick O'Brien, Caglar Keyder,, *Economic growth in Britain and France 1870–1914*, London, 1978, pp. 164–71; Heinz-Gerhard Haupt, *Storia sociale della Francia dal 1789 a oggi*, Bari, 1991, pp. 74–83.

15. For a review of the ways in which these patterns developed see Friedrich Lenger, Beyond exceptionalism: notes on the artisanal phase of the labour movement in France, England, Germany and the United States, *International Review of Social History*, XXXVI, 1, 1992, pp. 6–8.

16. Geoffrey Crossick, The *petite bourgeoisie* in nineteenth-century Britain, in Crossick, Haupt, *Shopkeepers and master artisans*, pp. 68–9.

17. Josef Ehmer, The artisan family in nineteenth-century Austria: the *embourgeoisment* of the *petite bourgeoisie* in, Crossick, Haupt, *Shopkeepers and master artisans*, pp. 199–206.

18. David Blackbourn, The *Mittelstand* in German society and politics, 1871–1914, *Social History*, II, 2, 1977, p. 419.

19. Heinz-Gerhard Haupt, The petite bourgeoisie in France, 1850–1914, in Crossick, Haupt, *Shopkeepers and master artisans*, p. 101.

20. On grocers see Morris, *The political economy of shopkeeping in Milan*, p. 56; Geoffrey Crossick, Shopkeeping and the state in Britain, in Crossick, Haupt, *Shopkeepers and master artisans*, p. 243; Alain Faure, The grocery trade in nineteenth-century Paris: a fragmented corporation, *ibid.*, pp. 155–174.

21. William H. Sewell, *Work and revolution in France*, Cambridge, 1980, p. 259.

22. Shulamit Volkov, *The rise of popular antimodernism in Germany*, Princeton, 1978, pp. 103–4.

23. *Ibid.*; Robert Gellately, *The politics of economic despair: shopkeepers and German politics*, London, 1974.

24. See John Boyer, *Political radicalism in late Imperial Vienna*, Chicago, 1981.

25. Certainly Jewish emigration from eastern Europe had produced an inflow of traders and craftsmen who had not passed through the apprenticeship system and there were undoubtedly concentrations of such people into certain trades. In 1895, however, only 5 per cent of peddlers in Germany were of Jewish origin, whilst 20 per cent of the Jewish labour force in the country was engaged in the industrial and handicraft sector, compared to 35 per cent of the German labour force. Volkov, *The rise of popular anti-modernism*, pp. 217–8.

26. Quoted in *ibid.*, pp. 314–15.

27. *Ibid.*, pp. 343–53.

28. Heinrich Winkler, From social protectionism to national socialism: the German small-business movement in comparative perspective, *Journal of Modern History*, 48, 1, 1976, p. 3.

29. In 1906 there were around 100 such *syndicats* in existence; by 1913 there were 689. Ginette Kurgan-van-Hentenryk, A forgotten class: the petite bourgeoisie in Belgium 1850–1914, in Crossick, Haupt, *Shopkeepers and master artisans*, p. 130.

30. Blackbourn, Between resignation and volatility, p. 52.
31. This did not prevent them from frequently switching their allegiance from one political party to another, but was the starting point from which the programmes of the main political groupings were judged.
32. Robert Michels, *Political parties*, New York, 1968, p. 269; Haupt, The petite bourgeoisie in France, p. 111.
33. Volkov, *The rise of popular antimodernism*, p. 20.
34. Crossick, Haupt, Shopkeepers, master artisans and the historian, p. 22.
35. Nord, *Paris shopkeepers*; Morris, *Political economy of shopkeeping in Milan*. See also Jonathan Morris, I bottegai e il mondo dei Bagatti Valsecchi in Cesare Mozzarelli, Rosanna Pavoni (eds), *Milano fin de siècle e il caso Bagatti Valsecchi*, Milan, 1991, pp. 377–85.
36. Figures taken from Nord, *Paris shopkeepers*, p. 7; Morris, *Political economy of shopkeeping in Milan*, p. 126.
37. Nord, *Paris shopkeepers*, pp. 295–301.
38. Respingiamo i rimproveri del signor Antoniotti, in *L'Esercente*, Milan, 8 April 1888.
39. Although Nord argues that this was a cynical manoeuvre on the part of Maus. Philip Nord, The small shopkeepers' movement and politics in France, 1888–1914, in Crossick, Haupt, *Shopkeepers and master artisans*, pp. 186–7.
40. This suggests that shopworkers increasingly regarded themselves as ordinary workers operating within the usual framework of industrial relations, rather than apprentices acquiring a trade skill, implicitly recognising the transformation of the *petite bourgeoisie* into small businessmen.
41. On English exceptionalism see, for example, Geoffrey Crossick, The emergence of the lower middle class in Britain, in Geoffrey Crossick (ed.), *The lower middle class in Britain 1870–1914*, London, 1977, pp. 39–48. On Economy parties and the *petite bourgeoisie* see E. P. Hennock, *Fit and proper persons*, London, 1973, pp. 312–16.

CHAPTER NINE
Working-class identities in Europe, 1850–1914

Dick Geary

The opinion that the development of industrial production and the modernization of technology would lead to the creation of a labour force increasingly monolithic in its interests and identity was stated classically by Karl Marx in the *Poverty of Philosophy* and more famously in the *Communist Manifesto*.[1] In this prognosis factory labour and the employment of modern machinery would iron out differences in skill and levels of remuneration. Workers would come to see their community of interests against employers, who would also become aware of shared interests and organize themselves. Thus capital and labour would confront one another in the most decisive conflict of modern society. For Marx the consequence was to be a revolutionary working-class politics.

At a general level it is undeniable that the growth of the European labour movement in the late nineteenth and early twentieth century was in some way related to the processes of urbanization and industrialization, which brought more and more workers together in factories and new residential districts and which saw an ever larger percentage of the labour force become dependent on wage labour.[2] Yet the relationship between these general developments and the emergence of "class" identity is more than a little problematical. In the first place and somewhat ironically the politics and language of class pre-dated the onset of wide-spread factory production. Radical Chartists in Britain, the members of revolutionary secret societies that sprang up in France in the 1830s and 1840s, those who died or were arrested on the barricades in Paris, Berlin, Dresden, Leipzig and Vienna in 1848–49 were not members of the new factory proletariat (in any case still so small in numbers in continental Europe) but members of the so-called "degraded" artisan trades of joinery, shoemaking and tailoring. Their problem was not the factory owner, the new industrialist, but the merchant capitalist, who did not labour with his hands but possessed economic power simply through the possession of capital. He was no Samuel Smiles but the "parasite". "Artisan socialism", which specifically addressed itself to wage labourers, was a consequence of increased dependence on merchants in industries dominated by the putting-out (domestic) system and competition from sweated industries. It was not a function of the new factory/industrial order in most cases.[3]

For a none-too-short period of time after the mid-century organizations of labour, in some cases of a socialist hue, remained dependent upon artisans, as the work of Sewell, Moss and Hanagan has demonstrated for France, and that of Kocka, Renzsch, Offermann, Eisenberg and Breuilly has shown for Germany. The idea that the factory operatives of Milan constituted the early vanguard of Italian labour politics has also been displaced by a recognition of the role of artisans in the woollen industry of the Biella region and skilled printers and textile workers around Milan.[4] In fact it is clear that the most modern industrial sectors based upon mechanized factory production were, at least initially, oases of calm in otherwise turbulent societies. In Britain it was in towns with strong craft traditions – towns such as Huddersfield – that Chartism was to prove most attractive, whilst the factory operatives of Halifax distanced themselves from radical politics. As the most authoritative study of industrial Lancashire has argued, the relationship between labour protest and factory production was an inverse one in the middle of the nineteenth century:

> the consequences of modern factory production were to be expressed in the first evidences of that reformism which has since characterized English working-class movements . . . The consolidation of mechanized, factory industry in the second half of the nineteenth century was the occasion of class harmony more than class conflict.[5]

Later – between 1910 and 1920 – the militancy of some British engineering workers was not located in the most modern factories of the automobile industry, such as Coventry, but in the older centres of production. In the French case research has shown that strikes and radical working-class politics between 1870 and 1914 were dominated by artisans or skilled workers, whereas the unskilled and often female labour of the mechanized textile industry were much less likely to engage in activities testifying to some form of class awareness.[6] Michelle Perrot has even spoken of the "calm of the large factories".[7] Significantly the labour force of the most modern and highly mechanized factories, where mass production by semi- or unskilled workers was the rule, was the least likely to engage in conflict with employers, join trade unions or give overt support to left-wing politics. The unskilled of the large textile factories in Germany, workers in the largest metal plants in the Ruhr, employees of Bayer, BASF and Hoechst rarely went on strike and in the main refused to participate in union or socialist activities. Strikes in Germany were much more common in small and medium-sized concerns, whilst the Free Trade Unions and the German Social Democratic Party recruited primarily from the skilled.[8] In fact the labour movement of all European countries on the eve of the First World War was overwhelmingly recruited from skilled males.[9] Thus to be an industrial worker in no way necessarily implied commitment to class-based forms of action.

It is certainly impossible to relate forms of working-class politics simply to "objective economic interests". The degree of organizational solidarity and political radicalism varied enormously from one country to another. Thus British "labour aristocrats" (printers, skilled engineering workers) might have constituted the vanguard of sectional and collaborationist politics in Great Britain, but in Germany they gave their support to the class-based and ostensibly Marxist policies of the SPD and were disproportionately present in the revolutionary upheavals in Tsarist Russia. Even within one country the political identities of workers cannot be reduced to occupational factors: whereas French miners in the Nord and Pas-de-Calais generally gave their support to reformism, those of the Southern Massif were better described as syndicalists. Attempts to explain anarcho-syndicalism in both France and Spain as a function of small-scale artisan production may have some mileage in the craft trades of Paris and the Catalan textile industry; yet the French syndicalist movement also embraced unskilled porcelain workers, whilst Spanish syndicalism did not prove attractive to operatives of the small-scale textile industry of the Basque province of Guipuzcoa.[10] In short the political expression of working-class identity cannot be reduced to occupational or industrial structures. Rather the picture is one of massive national and regional diversity. This further suggests that the prime determinants of at least the political identity of workers is to be found *outside* the workplace in factors such as residence, popular culture, the attitudes and behaviour of other social groups, and above all the role of the state. To these factors we will return below.

The existence of national and regional differences in working-class formation does not imply, of course, that no meaningful national and cross-national generalizations can be made about the identity and behaviour of workers. We have already seen that degraded artisans reacted to their predicament in Britain, France and Germany in not dissimilar ways around the middle of the century. The predominance of skilled males in labour organizations was still a more or less universal phenomenon in 1914. Everywhere women and the unskilled proved difficult to organize for groups speaking the language of class and class conflict. Specific occupational groups also revealed marked similarity in at least their industrial behaviour across national boundaries. Dockers were volatile, difficult to organize and demonstrated syndicalist tendencies in the ports of many countries. Printers were almost invariably the first to organize and used their industrial muscle to achieve collective bargaining in several states. In the decade before the outbreak of the First World War engineering workers became increasingly prominent in various forms of labour protest in Austria, Britain, France, Germany, Italy and Hungary, as they were again in the upheavals at the end of the war. Miners, working in dangerous conditions underground and often living together in relatively isolated communities, developed almost everywhere a powerful occupational solidarity. The relationship between such solidarity and *class* solidarity, however, could prove extremely complex. In Britain most miners eschewed Chartism and after the turn of the century were the last important group of organized workers to affiliate to the TUC. The concerns of German miners seem to have concentrated to a very large extent on conditions in the mines rather than the social order more generally, as became clear in the revolutionary upheavals in the Ruhr between 1918 and 1920.[11] In any case cross-national similarities in *industrial* behaviour, explicable in terms of workplace experience, did not translate into similarities in *political* identity, where, as we have seen, the picture is rather one of fragmentation and dissimilarity. One reason for such fragmentation is to be found in the nature of industrial growth itself.

The most fundamental fact about economic growth and techno-logical modernization is its *uneven* nature. Most obviously the rate and timing of industrialization varied enormously from one Euro-pean country to another. There is no doubt that early but relatively gradual industrialization in Britain facilitated strong craft unions, the development of collective bargaining and a less confrontational system of both industrial relations and politics than the later but much more rapid and capital-intensive economic changes experi-enced in Imperial Germany. Equally the different pace and timing of the process of industrialization in different countries produced national labour forces of very different structure. No less important, however, was uneven development *within* national boundaries. Here the British experience of *relatively* uniform urban and indus-trial growth was very definitely the exception rather than the rule. In many countries the industrialization of some regions was accompanied by the marked de-industrialization of other areas: Ger-many's southern and eastern provinces remained largely untouched by the changes which characterized Saxony, Berlin and the Ruhr. In France much of the *midi* remained unaffected by industrialization and if anything Languedoc de-industrialized. The gap between the Italian *mezzogiorno* and the industrial triangle comprising Milan, Turin and Genoa grew notoriously large; whilst Catalonia and the Northern Basque provinces were significantly more economically developed than the rest of Spain The result, of course, was that different regions within a single country possessed workforces very different in their interests and experiences; and this in turn may explain the persistence of regional variations in working-class behaviour.[12]

Unevenness characterized not only regional and national eco-nomic growth but also rates of modernization between different industrial sectors. On the one hand France on the eve of the First World War still possessed an extremely large artisanal sector, yet at the same time was in the forefront of the development of artificial fibres (rayon) and use of hydroelectric power, had pioneered a whole series of initiatives in the retail trade (the large store) and could boast one of the most advanced automobile industries in Europe. Germany in 1914 is quite rightly thought of as an industrial giant; yet side by side with the modern plants of Siemens and AEG in engineering, of Bayer, BASF and Hoechst in chemicals and the massive iron and steel works of the Ruhr there existed a large agricultural sector employing over a quarter of the labour force, domestic industry characterized the production of toys and musical instruments, large parts of the Saxon textile industry, especially in the Vogtland, and even shoemaking in the Palatine town of Pirmasens. In the occupational census of 1907 around half of those characterized as "workers" lived in small towns and villages of under 10,000 inhabitants and approximately a third of those categorized as employed in "industry and crafts" worked in firms employing fewer than five people.[13]

Technological advance within even a single industry was no more likely to produce a homogeneous workforce; and the idea that it led to an erosion of skill – deskilling or dequalification – is at best only partly true before 1914. In the first place the huge expansion of engineering before the outbreak of war created more and not fewer jobs for skilled engineers, as, for example, in the German city of Bielefeld, a centre of bicycle production. Even where new machines facilitated the employment of semi-skilled labour, those machines still needed to be set up, maintained and repaired by highly skilled men. The self-employment of skilled mechanics was also encouraged by the invention and application of gas and electric motors and the need for bicycle or motorcar repair and maintenance. The additional fact that different sectors of engineering modernized at differing rates also militated against uniformity amongst the labour force, as did the fact that even in the German engineering industry the application of the "American" system – the use of a single central power source, the systematic replacement of skilled male by less skilled female labour – was very much the exception rather than the rule. Indeed the only real attempt to introduce such a system in German engineering before 1914 was at the Bosch works in Stuttgart, where it met with significant resistance from the labour force. In the French textile industry mechanization did not lead to the employment of formerly craft workers in unskilled production, for the new jobs were often taken by those newly recruited to industry from rural backgrounds.[14]

The uneven development of industrial production thus militated against homogeneity and was more likely to further fragmentation and sectionalism rather than solidarity when left to itself. Worker could also be set against worker by the various systems of payment adopted by employers. The differential treatment of white- and blue-collar workers in the German engineering-electrical industry was at least in part the consequence of a deliberate attempt on the part of the firms to prevent the development of a community of interests between the two groups. Rudolf Vetterli's study of the Swiss Fischer engineering company at Schaffhausen brilliantly demonstrates how the existence of multiple grievances within the plant failed to result in collective action on the part of the workforce precisely because of a multiplicity of payment hierarchies. Conflicts between skilled men and their less skilled helpers could also be engendered where the skilled were offered bonus payments or piece-rates for increased productivity and yet the unskilled remained tied to hourly wages and thus had no interest whatsoever in an intensification of labour.[15] Once again the workplace scarcely functioned as the midwife of communality.

It can be argued that workers came together across skill and industrial boundaries, therefore, not as a consequence of shared economic interest but rather as a result of pressures exogenous to the shopfloor. I have argued at length elsewhere that a sense of class solidarity was most likely to develop where the role of the state was repressive or discriminatory, where the national bourgeoisie was weak or abandoned its commitment to liberal constitutional reform and where employers adopted authoritarian attitudes and refused to engage in collective bargaining.[16] I will not repeat those arguments here, but would like to stress that a sense of solidarity also had to be *created* and that this was precisely the task that the emerging socialist parties such as the SFIO, PSI and above all SPD allocated to themselves. The ability of the SPD in Germany, in contrast to any socialist sect in Britain, to recruit so many individual party members, win so many votes and spawn a host of ancilliary and leisure associations, however, was not just a consequence of the "external" factors mentioned above, but also related to various aspects of residence and popular culture: in Germany unlike Britain before the First World War the choral societies, cycling and sports organizations of Social Democracy did not have to compete on any significant level with either mass commercialized leisure or the possibility of a "modest domesticity" (Ross McKibbin), the latter made possible by the existence of working-class, single-family terraced housing.[17]

Even in Germany, however, that part of the labour movement which consciously spoke the language of class solidarity could never speak for the whole of the working class. In most countries women and the unskilled remained unorganized; and when women later became enfranchised, their voting behaviour suggested that class position was not the major determinant of their choices. The same applied to many males. In Britain and France a significant section of the workforce preferred the collaborationist politics of liberalism and voted for the British Liberal Party or the French Radical Party. It was also not unusual, though it scarcely fits any class-based model of political behaviour, for some workers to give their support to conservative or nationalist candidates. This was clearly the case in the "working-class Tory" districts of industrial Lancashire, where anti-Irish sentiment or even hostility to the local mill-owners, who were often Liberals, played a role. This last possibility raises the spectre of the compatibility of class identity *and* political conservatism, a phenomenon which was also to be found amongst the wool-shearers of Mazamet in France, who proved themselves capable of sustained strike-action against their employers yet gave their votes to the right. In the German case there also existed workers, though in no great numbers, who voted for the National Liberals before 1914, for the German National People's (Nationalist) Party in the early years of the Weimar Republic and subsequently turned to the Nazis in the economic crisis of the early 1930s. These tended to be workers who lived in company housing, such as the core labour force of Krupp in Essen, who belonged to company insurance schemes and who were members of company ("yellow") unions.[18]

A sense of class could also be countered by religious identity. Areas of high religious observance in France, Spain and Italy were often immune to socialist activity, which flourished in places of low observance and wide-spread anti-clericalism. In Belgium, Holland and Germany working-class organizations actually fractured along lines of religious confession. In the German case, for example, most Catholics who were industrial workers continued to vote for the specifically Catholic Centre Party and the SPD did badly in towns that were solidly Catholic though industrial, such as Aachen and

Cologne. German Catholics formed their own trade unions; and there were occasions, such as the industrial action at Dortmunder Union in 1911 and in the great Ruhr miners' strike of 1912, where those unions refused to collaborate with the socialist-oriented Free Trade Unions, thus jeopardizing the chances of success. In areas of mixed confession, such as the Ruhr, confessional identities often overrode class sentiment in the case of Protestant workers too. Where the SPD won votes in the first stage of elections in some constituencies, for example, but then its candidate had to withdraw from the re-run on account of insufficient votes, then the same workers who had supported the SPD in the first round voted for a conservative candidate in the second round where the other candidate was a Catholic, albeit a worker![19]

Equally divisive and more potentially explosive were ethnic divisions within the European working class. In Austria-Hungary Germans and Czechs formed separate working-class organizations. In Imperial Germany Poles formed their own union and supported Polish nationalism, except in the case of Protestant Masurians, who supported the political structure of the Empire and were loyal to the Emperor! In Northern France local workers resented the employment of relatively placid Belgian Catholics whilst the hostility between Marseilles dockers and North African workers was even greater. In Britain Irish workers were often regarded as a threat to jobs and wages by the English; whilst Irish Catholic labourers espoused the politics of Irish nationalism and their Protestant counterparts were certainly not in the forefront of English labour politics.[20]

At this point some words of qualification and caution are necessary. That workers were divided along lines of skill, occupation, age, gender, religion and ethnicity, as well as political choice, which was never simply reducible to the former elements though strongly related to them, did not invariably prevent collective action across these divides. German Catholics might belong to specifically Christian trade unions; but those unions increasingly had to behave like their socialist rivals, i.e. engage in industrial conflict and distribute strike pay, in order to survive. Those unions also joined with the Free Trade Unions in common strike action in the miners' strike of 1905. The same was true of Polish workers, whose commitment to the nationalist cause did not obscure an awareness of their identity as wage labourers. Indeed, in Imperial Germany being a Pole and a worker went hand-in-hand; and the Polish union participated in the 1905 and 1912 strikes in Germany's mining regions. Hostility to other ethnic groups was sometimes more instrumental than anything else; that is to say that workers were worried about competition from cheap labour rather than ethnicity and dropped their hostility if such a threat did not materialize. Interestingly the failure of the German trade unions to integrate the Polish workers in Imperial Germany was not repeated in France after 1918, when Polish miners who emigrated into the coalfields of North Eastern France, often from the Ruhr, became members of the native unions, albeit with considerable autonomy.[21]

The above further suggests that the crass historiography which claims that the events of 1914, when workers supported their national war efforts, also denoted the demise or absence of class consciousness, in no way necessarily follows. Not only was working-class patriotism very different in nature to the jingoism of the nationalist right, but also the same Welsh miners who volunteered to fight in August 1914 were on strike in 1915. In any case, local studies in Germany have also suggested that the working class there did *not* demonstrate the same nationalist fervour in the early days of August 1914 as other groups in the population.[22] Patriotism and a sense of class could often go hand-in-hand, as we have already seen. The German Social Democrat William Bromme reports evenings spent in working-class choral societies singing socialist songs, followed by walks home with colleagues at which patriotic tunes seemed to be favoured. The same source refers to pictures in the home of his working-class parents: pictures of Lassalle, Marx and Liebknecht, but also of the Kaiser, General von Moltke, Bismarck, and even the representations of several saints![23] There can also be found in the Bethnall Green Museum a wonderful testimony to the complexity of working-class identity. It is a banner produced by Australian dockers in the wake of the great 1889 dock strike. Its prime message is working-class solidarity across the oceans; but as well as the representation of an heroic dockworker, the banner also contains the Union Jack and Britannia. Here we have international working-class solidarity under the monarchy and within the Empire!

None of this should surprise. Workers were socialized not only in the factory and segregated residential communities, but also in schools, in armies (in continental Europe) and in national cultures.

To imagine there was one identity within the head of even a single worker would be at best foolish.

Notes

1. Karl Marx and Friedrich Engels, *Marx-Engels Gesamtausgabe*, Moscow, 1927, I/3, p. 207; Karl Marx and Friedrich Engels, in *ibid.*; 1/6, pp. 533f.
2. The significance of dependent wage labour in class formation is stressed in particular by Jürgen Kocka, *Lohnarbeit und Klassenbildung*, Berlin/Bonn, 1983.
3. Dick Geary, *European labour protest*, London, 1981, pp. 33ff.
4. W. Sewell, *Work and revolution*, Cambridge, 1980; Bernard Moss, *The origins of the French labour movement*, Berkeley, 1976; Michael Hanagan, *The logic of solidarity*, Urbana, 1980; Kocka, *Lohnarbeit und Klassenbildung*; Wolfgang Renzsch, *Handwerker und Lohnarbeiter in der frühen Arbeiterbewegung*, Göttingen, 1980; T. Offermann, *Arbeiter und liberales Bürgertum in Deutschland*, Bonn, 1979; John Breuilly, Liberalism or social democracy, in *European History Quarterly*, 1985, 1, pp. 3–42; John Breuilly, *Joachim Friedrich Martens*, Göttingen, 1984; Christiane Eisenberg, *Deutsche und englische Gewerkschaften*, Göttingen, 1986; John A. Davis, Socialism and the working classes in Italy before 1914, in Dick Geary (ed.), *Labour and socialist movements in Europe before 1914*, Oxford, 1989, pp. 198–207; H. D. Bell, *Sesto San Giovanni*, New Brunswick, 1986.
5. Patrick Joyce, *Work, society and politics*, Brighton, 1980, pp. 50 and 63.
6. James Hinton, *The first shop stewards movement*, London, 1973; Hanagan, *The logic of solidarity*.
7. Michelle Perrot, On the formation of the French working class, in Katznagelson and A. Zollberg, *Working-class formation*, Princeton, 1986, pp. 89ff.
8. Geary, *Labour protest*, pp. 70–80.
9. *Ibid.*, pp. 70–80.
10. See the articles on Britain, France and Spain by Gordon Phillips, Roger Magraw and Paul Heywood in Geary, *Labour and socialist movements*.
11. For a survey of the relationship between miners and Chartism see Roy Church, Chartism and the miners, in *Labour History Review* 56, 1991, 3, pp. 23–36. On Ruhr miners, Jürgen Tampke, *The Ruhr and revolution*, London, 1979.
12. A classic study of uneven development is Frank B. Tipton, *Regional variations in the economic development of Germany*, Middleton, 1976. The importance of regional variations in the nature of working-class

formation is stressed in the essays on France, Italy and Spain by Magraw, Davis and Heywood in Geary, *Labour and socialist movements* and by Alain Cottereau, The distinctiveness of working-class cultures in France, in Katznagelson and Zollberg, pp. 111–23.

13. Tipton, *Regional variations in the economic development of Germany*.

14. Heidrun Homburg, Anfänge des Taylorsystems in Deutschland, in *Geschichte und Gesellschaft*, 4, 1978, 2, pp. 170ff; Karl Ditt, Technologischer Wandel und Strukturveränderung der Fabrikarbeiterschaft in Bielefeld, in Werner Conze and Ullrich Engelhart (eds), *Arbeiter im Industrialisierungsprozess*, Stuttgart, 1979; Hanagan, *The logic of solidarity*.

15. Rudolf Vetterli, *Industriearbeit, Arbeiterbewusstsein und gewerkschaftliche Organisation*, Göttingen, 1978.

16. Geary, *Labour protest*, pp. 48–70; Dick Geary, *European labour politics from 1900 to the depression*, London, 1991, pp. 15–21.

17. Ross McKibbin, Why was there no Marxism in Great Britain? in *EHR* 99, 1984, pp. 303–309; Dick Geary, Arbeiterkultur in Deutschland und Grossbritannien im Vergleich, in Dietmar Petzina (ed.), *Fahnen, Fäuste, Körper*, Essen, 1986, pp. 91–101.

18. Klaus Mattheier, *Die Gelben*, Düsseldorf, 1973.

19. Dieter Groh, *Negative integration und revolutionärer attentismus*, Frankfurt am Main, 1973, p. 282f; Gerhard A. Ritter, *Die Arbeiterbewegung im Wilhelminischen Deutschland*, Berlin, 1959, pp. 73–8; P. M. Jones, Political commitment and rural society in the Southern Massif Central in *European Studies Review* 10, 1980, 3, pp. 337–56; A. Siegfried, *Tableau politique de la France de l'Ouest*, Paris, 1964; Adrian Lyttleton, Revolution and counter-revolution in Italy, in Charles L. Betrand, *Revolutionary situations in Europe*, Montreal, 1977, pp. 64ff; Gerald Brenan, *The Spanish labyrinth*, Cambridge, 1962, pp. 89ff and 152; Gabriel Jackson, *The Spanish Republic and the Civil War*, Princeton, 1965, pp. 289ff.

20. On Poles see Christoph Klessmann, *Polnische Bergarbeiter im Ruhrgebiet*. . For working-class nationalism and ethnic conflict in France see Magraw in Geary, *Labour and socialist movements*, pp. 62ff.

21. John H. Kulczycki, Nationalism over class solidarity, in *Canadian Review of Studies in Nationalism*, xiv, 1987, pp. 261–76.

22. Volker Ullrich, Everyday life and the German working class, in Roger Fletcher (ed.), *From Bernstein to Brandt*, London, 1987, p. 56; Friedhelm Boll, *Massenbewegungen in Niedersachsen*, Bonn, 1981, pp. 151ff.

23. William Bromme, *Lebensgeschichte eines modernen Fabrikarbeiters*, Jena, 1930, pp. 71ff.

CHAPTER TEN

The peculiarities of national cultures: the German case

Martin Swales

This chapter addresses some of the theoretical and historical implications of a literary-critical project concerning the particularity (to be
more precise, the *unrealism*) of German prose writing when viewed
within the generality (that is, the *realism*) of European novel fictions
from the late eighteenth century to the twentieth. It seeks to situate
these literary concerns within certain cultural, social, and historical
issues – not least because I am interested in the confluence of the
two realms, of the literary on the one hand and the historico-social
on the other.

Anybody who (like myself) works with imaginative literature is
liable to feel uncertain of his or her ground when venturing into the
territory traditionally inhabited and charted by historians. Literary
critics sometimes have the sense that they belong to a profession
which sails under the flag whose motto is "Let us ignore the facts
and get straight down to the truth." Not that I want to endorse
any simple divide between history-as-factual-accuracy on the one
hand and literature-as-mere-fantasy on the other. After all, even
Rankean notions of "wie es eigentlich gewesen ist" ("how it actually
was") imply both fidelity to precise facts and circumstances, to
archival and documentary sources, and also the need for creative,
imaginative empathy. The famous adverb "eigentlich" – "actually"
– implies both "factually" and "essentially", the former a category
of empirical testability, the latter one of intuitive truthfulness and
interpretative power. And yet, however much literary critics such
as myself may claim to have areas of overlap with historians, there

are differences. Nobody can prove that Natasha and Prince Andrew and Levin lived; but it can be proved that Napoleon did.. While novels tell stories, as do histories, and in this sense have a narrative hermeneutic in common, there are, quite simply, different categories of testability at work.

Let me begin with a general reflection on community, on what it is in the human species that generates a sense of belonging. In all kinds of ways the notion of a workable, livable community depends on the presence of corporate, shared modes of cultural mediation and signification. Language, custom, convention, ritual, symbol may provide a more primary bond in the definition of community than pragmatic (e.g. economic, geopolitical, legal) factors. For this reason, the human species may be less *homo sapiens* than *homo significans*. What has happened in Yugoslavia of late offers overwhelmingly eloquent testimony to the fact that human beings will move heaven and earth, will destroy life, property, economic livelihood, in order to reinstate cultural meanings that have been muffled for several decades. From the human need to indwell in what Lionel Trilling once called the "hum and buzz of implication", in the omnipresent textual density of attuned mentalities, of shared values and assumptions, the fierce particularity of a local culture can emerge. And in the process, notions of a larger meta-local community (such as are enshrined in those addresses that schoolchildren write in their textbooks – Birmingham, Warwickshire, England, Great Britain, Europe, the World), of concentric circles of communal allegiance, are dismissed as empty, functionalist, bureaucratic – rather than genuinely inhabited.

Yet the intimations of culture need not always be to underwrite narrow, tribal consciousness. On the contrary: one crucial function of culture is, as we might say, to put a community on the map, and we should never forget that that map is both for internal and external use. Indeed, the internal and the external use overlap. The map explains the community to itself by explaining it to the outside world. Any user of a map stands outside the being of the thing mapped; the terrain mapped has edges. As we read the map, we read our own experience from some Archimedean point outside the functioning mechanisms of that experience. That Archimedean realm may represent another kind of community, larger and more generous than the local one. It has even had names bestowed on it – *Mitteleuropa*, the European Idea – to say nothing of notions of Federation, Commonwealth, or whatever. Much of the Maastricht debate has to do with the interplay of particularist and meta-particularist issues – and with the quest for cultural significations and validations that operate on both sides of the equation.

The domain of cultural signification can, therefore, sustain a dialectic of local and meta-local, of particularist and (for want of a better word) universalist, a complex, shifting, living dialectic that, to borrow a phrase from T. S. Eliot, takes the dialect of the tribe and purifies it without emasculating it into (for example) some bland Eurospeak.

Let me turn now to the literary (but not only literary) issues that are at the forefront of my attention. When we look at European novel writing from the eighteenth century on, there is, according to most commentators, an instantly recognizable generality and universalism to the fictions that emerge from (say) France, England, Russia – in spite of their concern to be historically and socially particular; whereas the German tradition is the (particularist) exception to the European generalist rule.[1] The great dominance of the realistic novel is, we are told, the European high road, and German fictions are at best a side road, a pretty footpath; at worst, a dirt track. And, as we shall see, the dirt track is often equated with the aberrant course of German history, with the German *Sonderweg*. Let me explore in more detail the frequently asserted parallel between the history of German narratives and the narratives of German history.

There is a widespread view of German culture generally which says that it is, in all kinds of ways, intelligent, thoughtful, and sophisticated, but that it is curiously bereft of any sustained relationship to the familiar, empirically knowable facts of daily living. Instead of concerning themselves at all vigorously with outward things, the Germans, so the argument runs, attend to such pursuits as music (that supremely non-referential art), speculative philosophy, and theology (particularly when it assumes the guise of radical inwardness). Of course, even their worst detractors would concede that the Germans have produced a literature of note, but even here spiritual profundity is still very much the chief characteristic and besetting sin. German literature, it is said, is hopelessly in love with *"Geist"*, with the life of the mind, with the inward realm that (and here one glimpses the spectre of Luther) alone confers distinction, value, and, ultimately, justification. This problematic condition of inwardness reveals itself nowhere more clearly than in the works of narrative prose that issued from the German-speaking lands in the great age of European realism (that is: from the mid-eighteenth century onwards); whatever distinction that body of prose writing may have, it cannot be claimed to be the distinction of common-or-garden realism.

However overstated such a view of German culture may be, there are elements of truth to it. Certainly its prose literature from Goethe on does pose an acute evaluative problem, and it is all too tempting to register the gulf that separates it from European realism. Time and time again commentators stress the artistic mastery of German fiction, its linguistic richness, its formal sophistication and symbolic density – only then to say that, alas, the actual texts feel very learned and rarefied when compared to the achievement of Fielding, Dickens, Stendhal, Balzac, George Eliot, Flaubert, or Tolstoy. The poetry of German narrative fiction derives, so the argument runs, from a mismatch between high literary intelligence on the one hand and the cruel limitations of the social experience which provides the thematic matter on the other. "Poetic Realism", so often claimed as the characteristic mode of German fiction, is, then, little better than the artistic transfiguration of backwaterdom. Hence the constant debate in German discussions of the theory of narrative forms – poetry is, throughout the nineteenth century, pitted against prose. In the process, poetry is upheld by critics and theoreticians as, in the terms of *1066 and All That*, a Good Thing, and prose as a Bad, or at any rate irremediably Prosaic, Thing.[2]

One widespread explanation of this particular tenor of German culture refers us to the political and social history of the German-speaking lands. The argument can be summarized as follows: German literature prior to 1871 was of necessity provincial because, before that date, what we now know as Germany did not exist as a national entity in the way that the majority of European countries did: that is, as a unified nation state. The Holy Roman Empire of the German Nation meant provinces, small territories – in a word, particularism – rather than a cohesive demographic unit that could have its centre of gravity in a major capital city. Until the last three decades of the nineteenth century, Germany existed only in its language and culture; it was, to invoke hallowed terms, a *"Kulturnation"* (cultural nation) and not a *"politische Nation"* (political nation). The nation existed, as it were, only in the mind.

Hence, it was meta-national – in the spirit of the cosmopolitanism of the late eighteenth-century *Humanitätsideal*, of Goethe's *Iphigenie auf Tauris* or of Beethoven's *Fidelio* and Choral Symphony. Or one could think of Goethe's distich (which appears as number 96 of the *Xenien*):

> Zur *Nation* euch zu bilden, ihr hofft es, Deutsche, vergebens;
> Bildet, ihr könnt es, dafür freier zu Menschen euch aus.
> (To form yourselves into a *nation*, that, Germans, you hope for
> in vain; But form yourselves rather – that you can do – the
> more freely into human beings.)

But even Goethe can also lament the lack of palpable nationhood. He sees clearly its consequences for the development of the novel form, and makes the point that German socio-political experience simply cannot produce a Walter Scott. Hence, to demand the kind of fiction that handles a broad social panorama is to demand what the culture cannot give.[3]

To this we might simply respond that different countries produce different literatures – and leave it at that. But matters are not so straightforward because in so much thinking about the course of German history and culture there is an often unspoken norm that is invoked. The norm applies both to the history and to the narrative literature (the two phenomena are interlinked not just by the fact that the historical course of a nation moulds its culture but also, more specifically, by the fact that both history and narrative literature have their hermeneutic in common – both are a recital of events linked by a causal chronology.)[4] As far as history is concerned, the norm rests on the following doctrines. The proper course of historical development traced by the modern nation state entails a gradual process of bourgeois self-assertion fuelled by increasing economic power and social mobility. Gradually, the middle classes win forms of political influence for themselves by challenging feudal structures in the name of a more broadly participatory, democratic structure of government. The German lands fail to conform to this model: 1830 and 1848 mark dismal failures. Hence, when Germany does, as it were, come into line in 1871, she does so in a condition of curious disequilibrium. By the end of the nineteenth century she is, economically, a formidable power; but in terms of her social and political structures and attitudes she is out of synchrony with her times. This is the curse of the "belated nation", this is the time bomb at the heart of, to use another canonical term, the "special course of German history". The upshot is the monstrosity of the Third Reich.

The dangers inherent in such normative historical thinking are manifold. There is, for example, the tendency to absolutise one particular model of historical and political change, to invest historical events, whether of a benign or malignant kind, with the motor force of unexamined and unexplained inevitability. Above all else, there is the danger of ethical stridency: the course of German history becomes the curse.

A cognate, if less hectoring, category of normative thinking is also applied to the evolution of narrative forms. The central tenets can be summarized as follows.[5] The birth of the modern novel is inseparable from the increasing self-confidence of the middle classes. It expresses a sense of rapid economic change and development. The prevailing ethos derives from the revolutionary energies of capitalism, and the emphasis falls unashamedly on the individual. Timeless norms, inherited doctrines, and traditional paradigms no longer apply. The individual makes his or her way through the social world as best he or she can. The points of interaction between the individual self and the palpable, resistant particularities of bourgeois society are manifold: the family, the home, the school, the workhouse, the law courts, the prison. These points of interaction are points of friction and conflict, and they provide the key stages within the novel's plot sequence. The novel of bourgeois manners is a form that may be termed realistic primarily because it is concerned with the constant interplay of the characters' inner psychological life and the palpable facts (*res*) of society.[6] Those outward facts and circumstances are not merely a background to the characters' experience; they are constitutive of that experience. In this sense, the novel of European realism is philosophically naive; it is not concerned to ask questions of the kind: What is the self? How can one know that the empirically perceivable world is real? Rather, it takes for granted that both inner and outer realms are experienced truths and are experienced in interaction. It documents the particular forms of interaction that occur at a given time in a given place. The realistic novelist has no doubts that the individual's humanity – or lack of it – can be assessed only with reference to that interplay of inner and outer worlds.

Judged by such norms of realistic fiction, very little German prose writing shares the assumptions on which the European narrative tradition rests. Many German novels and stories are concerned, so the traditional view suggests, with the inward realm to the virtual exclusion of outward practicalities. Hence, German prose writing constantly raises philosophical issues. Thereby – and here the value-judgements come in – it is part and parcel of a culture whose intellectual sophistication is all too rarely engaged by and in a precise critical concern with the outer world. In consequence, that culture was powerless to deal with the institutional brutality of the Third Reich, producing that hideous paradox, explored with great eloquence by George Steiner, that camp guards at Auschwitz cherished Mozart and Hölderlin – and continued with the daily task of exterminating fellow human beings.[7] Not, of course, that the German novel, on even the most hostile of readings, can be held responsible for Auschwitz. But it has been seen as implicated in the cast of mind that could do precious little to prevent Auschwitz.

These are complex issues. Parts of the orthodox view of the historical and literary "Sonderweg" of Germany ring true. But there are aspects of it which I wish to challenge.

At the outset let me urge that we should be on our guard against the delights of normative thinking. Certainly, the German-speaking lands do have a culture of inwardness that does not have an obvious parallel in France or England. In Prussia, Pietism almost becomes a state religion in the eighteenth century. Its influence on education is profound, and hence, some of the best minds to emerge from the German schools and universities seem to cherish inner freedom rather than outward liberty; and the career that beckons so often is that of the state official, bureaucrat, and administrator. Hence (so the argument runs) the cutting edge of critical thought is never turned on the institutional status quo. But one wonders if the consequences can only be interpreted as heinous. The very intimacy of so many of the communities that make up German social experience produces a rich network of institutions (schools, universities, libraries, chapels, churches, opera houses, concert halls) that cannot simply be dismissed as the emblems of cankered inwardness. David Blackbourn and Geoff Eley among others have challenged the schematic view of what-was-wrong-with-Germany.[8] They insist that the historiographic stereotype obscures a number of features of German economic and social life which bespeak bourgeois emancipation and enterprise, genuinely civic energy. There is also the study by Mack Walker that addresses the crucial issue of urban and rural life.[9] I can best convey Walker's argument by means of the contrast with England – not least because England constitutes that historical and cultural norm of which I have been speaking. Raymond Williams draws attention to the early development of agrarian capitalism in England which ensures the demise of open strip farming.[10] In consequence, market towns spring up which provide the economic nexus for the marketing of agrarian production. The functional contrast between country and town is then exacerbated by the Industrial Revolution which moves the urban community ever further away from the rhythms of "natural life". All of this intensifies the nostalgia for a pre-capitalist, pre-industrial, and, above all, pre-urban world from which large numbers of the population have been banished. Precisely this sharp disjunction between rural and urban ways of life does not apply to the German lands, as W. H. Riehl showed in his crucial study *Land und Leute* (for which George Eliot displayed such enthusiasm).[11] It is vital to notice – and Mack Walker's study helps us in this regard – that the German social consciousness was shaped by the notion of pre-industrial but essentially *urban* culture. In the lands between Prussia to the north and Austria to the south – that is, in the "individualized land" of Riehl's cultural geography – the movement of European trade in the seventeenth and eighteenth centuries towards the north and the maritime west meant that the "hometowns" such as Ulm, Regensburg, Nürnberg, became increasingly inward-looking, tied to the relatively stable framework of the guild economy. The skilled master craftsman was the elite figure in an intimate urban world, one sustained not by the economic principles of growth-conscious competition but by custom, convention, and familiarity. The great song in praise of the German "hometown" ethos, sung at the point where their demise was irreversible, is Wagner's *Die Meistersinger von Nürnberg* of 1868.[12] In 1871 Germany joined the European norm and became, under Prussian hegemony, a unified nation state, and she did so as the bearer of a particular cultural legacy: one in which nostalgia for an earlier, more pacific world could envisage an urban community exempt from the abstraction and anonymity of the modern industrial city.

What are the consequences of this legacy for the tradition of German prose literature that concerns me? The European norm implies, as many commentators have stressed, a radical disjunction between public and private experience; the public realm is dominated by the competitive energies of the self-regulating market, whereas the private realm (of family and home) accommodates the affective needs of the self: compassion, gentleness, love. By contrast, the reality and the myth of the "hometown" in the German lands did not generate such a sharp disjunction between the public and the private persona. The public realm was not an offence to the emotional needs of the individual personality, and the private world, in its turn, bore the imprint of the corporate world outside the home. In saying this, I do not wish to impute to the German lands some kind of spiritual, paradisal condition from which conflicts are banished once and for all. German prose literature is full of the frictions between public and private imperatives such as we find in the literature of European realism. But – and this is the crucial point – the interplay of public and private realms is conceptualized differently in German prose.

I want to suggest that this different interplay engenders a different kind of realism – in both thematic and stylistic terms. The German prose tradition is, then, different from the European, it is, indeed, particular; but, in its particularity, it debates issues that are germane to the broader European experience, while never forfeiting its own particular perspective and approach. German prose, as I have already indicated, may not be realistic in the traditional sense of concerning itself abundantly with things, objects, houses, institutions; but it does nevertheless offer a profound comprehension of the ways in which individual life is caught up in the corporate pressures of a given society. Society is comprehended less in terms of physical evidence than at the level of shared values, ideas, assumptions, of all-pervasive mentality. German prose both reflects and reflects upon the consciousness of a given age in order to make us aware of how ideas, principles, and assumptions shape the characters' lives and show them to be living in a particular time and at a particular place. In the process we are alerted to the manifold ways in which social life is constituted, not only by the armchairs which the characters can or cannot afford but also by shared values and concepts, by certain agreements and conventions. If the classics of the European novel provide superb examples of a realism of fact, setting, and outward event, we should not close our eyes to the possibility of a realism of concept and idea, of discourse, of mental life. This latter possibility is, I would suggest, exemplified most richly by the tradition of German narrative prose from the late eighteenth century onwards. In my view, a great disservice has been done to that tradition by the plethora of commentators who have seen it as yet another example of the besetting German sin of inwardness. All too often it has been assumed that because German fiction concerns itself with the mental life of its characters it thereby enters some timeless realm of abstract, free-floating ideas, a Pantheon exempt from the pressures and concerns of social life. This is to do less than justice to a major narrative tradition by dismissing its products as mere pretexts for discursive philosophising, whereas time and time again German fiction shows us that the inwardness which it explores so richly is part of the narratively comprehended (that is, historicized) signature of a particular world. We are made to see (as I suggested in my remarks on Mack Walker's study of the "hometowns") that subjectivity, the mental life of the individual can bear the imprint of corporate social concerns, and conversely the public realm functions thanks to a consensus of values and assumptions anchored in the individual mind.

If it can be admitted that the mediations between literary, fictional statement on the one hand and society and history on the other work at the level of mentality, of shared inner life, then the theoretical basis of the realistic enterprise is strengthened and differentiated by the presence of a shared medium. That medium, of course, is language, language understood as socially and culturally specific discourse. Let me pursue this argument briefly. To go to a novel for confirmation of extra-literary facts (for example, to the effect that people did have the kinds of houses which Balzac or Dickens describes) is curiously wide of the mark because a novel is, by definition, a fiction and not an objective description of social data. Equally, so much of the anti-mimetic rhetoric of Deconstruction ("il n'y a pas de hors-texte") also misses the point – which is that there are intermeshing textualities that conjoin fiction and history, without making them identical with one another.[13] For example, the use of metaphor may, in certain cases, be a feature both of the aesthetic organization of the novel and also of the organization of society which it recreates and interrogates. Hence my observation at the outset of this paper to the effect that the human sense of community, of belonging, may derive as much from spiritual – that is, symbolic – data as from concrete particularities.

Let me try to conclude my argument by making three points

about the "particularly German" character of the German novel tradition. All three points suggest that the spark does jump the gap from particular to general, that the preoccupations of the German tradition do "travel", do illuminate the themes, modes, and concerns of European realism:

1. From Gutzkow and Immermann to Fontane and Raabe, to Musil, Broch, Günter Grass and Martin Walser, the German novel shows us the ways in which and the extent to which individuals are formed and deformed by the corporate mentality of their age. Many of the novels within this tradition suggest, somewhat in the spirit of Flaubert's *Dictionnaire des idées reçues*, that the characters' inwardness is socially determined, that they are, in this sense, more thought than thinking, more spoken than speaking.

2. The German novel registers the shift in values, the disturbance of psychological and cognitive signifiers which express socio-cultural change. I think under this heading of Immermann's notion of "Epigonentum", of Raabe's eavesdropping on the linguistic and affective precipitate within the individual psyche caused by industrialization and urbanization, of Kafka's comprehension of the inner processes of recognition and acknowledgment by which institutions are made to work, of Döblin's spectacular narrative collage which conveys the brutalizing shocks of the modern metropolis.

3. Many of the major German novels are not content simply to register (and, by implication, to acquiesce in) notions of the inner realm being determined by the outer. Hence, they attempt to derive registers of symbolic, even poetic intimation from the stereotyped living of the characters caught in the treadmill of conformism. I have already observed that the symbolic and poetic aspiration within German realism has often been held to be merely specious prettifying of limited social experience. But I would argue that, understood aright, that wish to make the inner processes of socialized characters into indicators of the possible dignity and cognitive value of mental life is no mere narrowly German preoccupation. Rather, it is the particular version of that battle between science and religion, between law-governed behaviour and validations of human autonomy that runs centrally through

the intellectual life of the European nineteenth century. In a novel such as Thomas Mann's *Buddenbrooks*, for example, the symbols that recur throughout the text speak both of regimented behaviour patterns and also, on occasion, of the human vulnerability and dignity (the two may be well-nigh identical) trapped within the regimentation. In an entirely precise distillation of socio- psychological mechanisms, which owe much to Fontane's art, the symbols in Mann's masterly novel both reveal and conceal, both acknowledge and repress, both articulate and regiment the flux of human feeling and consciousness.[14]

These, then, are some of the German versions of European issues. The German novel tradition expresses its finest insights in respect of the complex, unending interplay of inner and outer worlds, of private and public imperatives and promptings.

To return to the issue with which I began. It is perhaps especially in the cultural sphere that we can find statements of particularity, of of-one-time-and-of-one-placedom that are not regressive or tribal. And this is because, as we all know from our own experience of imaginative literature, the sheer quality with which socio-cultural specificity is both reflected and reflected upon makes it transcend mere localism and speak beyond its frontiers. To borrow a pun from Michel Zéraffa, cultural products can betray the mentality which they explore and from which they derive, "betray" in the sense of "bear the imprint of" – and in the sense of "repudiate the confines and intimacies of".[15]

I hope I have been able to suggest that, in terms of its prose fiction in the age of European realism, the German Cinderella may be allowed to go to the European ball. Indeed, of late there have been a number of signs of Cinderella's emergence. So much of the debate in the UK about Europe is couched in terms of surrender of sovereignty, threatened integrity of the nation, and so on. Whereas the German experience – the "belated nation", the "cultural nation" rather than "political nation", the "special course of German history" – has arguably generated a political culture that is able to explore issues of European integration with more complex and differentiated notions of selfhood, autonomy, identity, of provincialism and nationality, of periphery and centre than British history makes available to us. Perhaps Germany can now be seen not as the aberration that proves the European rule, but rather – to borrow a phrase which Robert Musil applied to Austria-Hungary just before 1914 – as a "particularly clear case of the modern world".[16]

Notes

Parts of this chapter derive from my: "Neglecting the weight of the elephant . . . " German prose fiction and European realism, *Modern Language Review*, 83, 1988, pp. 882–94. I am grateful to the editors for allowing me to draw on this material.

1. See for example Wolfang Preisendanz, *Wege des Realismus*, Munich, 1977, and Klaus-Detlef Müller (ed.), *Bürgerlicher Realismus*, Königstein/Ts, 1981.
2. See Hartmut Steinecke (ed.), *Romanpoetik in Deutschland*, Tübingen, 1984, and Gerhard Plumpe (ed.), *Theorie des bürgerlichen Realismus: eine Textsammlung*, Stuttgart, 1985.
3. Literarischer Sansculottismus in the *Hamburger Ausgabe*, vol. 12 (tenth edition), Munich, 1982, pp. 239–44.
4. See Arthur C. Danto, *Analytical philosophy of history*, Cambridge, 1985; Hayden White, *Metahistory*, Baltimore and London, 1973; and Paul Ricoeur, *Time and narrative*, trans. Kathleen McLaughlin and David Pellauer, 2 vols, Chicago and London, 1984.
5. See Ian Watt, *The rise of the novel*, London, 1957, and Raymond Williams, *The English novel from Dickens to Lawrence*, London, 1970.
6. See Roland Barthes, L'effet de réel, *Communications*, 11, l968, pp. 84–9, and J. P. Stern, *On realism*, London, 1973, p. 5.
7. George Steiner, To civilize our gentlemen, in Steiner, *Language and silence*, New York, 1970, pp. 55–67.
8. David Blackbourn and Geoff Eley, *The peculiarities of German history*, Oxford, 1984. See also: Helga Grebing, *Der "deutsche Sonderweg" in Europa 1806–1945: eine Kritik*, Stuttgart, Berlin, Cologne, Mainz, 1986; Jürgen Kocka, Deutsche Geschichte vor Hitler: zur Diskussion über den "deutschen Sonderweg" in Kocka, *Geschichte und Aufklärung*, Göttingen, 1989, pp. 101–l13; and Wolfgang J. Mommsen, *Britain and Germany 1800 to 1914: two developmental paths towards industrial society*, London, 1986.
9. Mack Walker, *German home towns*, Ithaca, New York and London, 1971.
10. Raymond Williams, *The country and the city*, London, 1973.

11. See: The natural history of German life, *Westminster Review*, 66, July 1856, pp. 51–76.
12. See Timothy McFarland, Wagner's Nuremberg, in *Richard Wagner, the mastersingers of Nuremberg*, ed. Nicholas John, English National Opera Guides, 19, London, 1983, pp. 27–34.
13. See Christopher Prendergast, *The order of mimesis*, Cambridge, 1986.
14. See Martin Swales, Symbolic patterns or realistic plenty? Thomas Mann's *Buddenbrooks* and the European novel. *Publications of the English Goethe Society*, 60, 1989–1990, pp. 80–95.
15. Michel Zéraffa, *Fictions: the novel and social reality*, transl. Catherine Burns and Tom Burns, Harmondsworth, 1976, p. 43.
16. Robert Musil, *Tagebücher*, ed. Adolf Frisé, Reinbek, 1983, p. 354.

CHAPTER ELEVEN

Britain and Europe in the later twentieth century: identity, sovereignty, peculiarity

Jill Stephenson

Recent debates about Britain's relationship with Europe have focused on its difficulties in negotiating with its western partners in the European Community (EC). For British Eurosceptics like Enoch Powell, Britain is "in Europe, but not of Europe".[1] Even British Euroenthusiasts have reservations about some aspects of both the EC as it currently operates and further economic and political integration. It would be naive to imagine that the other eleven EC countries were unanimous and unqualified in their support for the Community and all its works: the Danish referendum result in June 1992 was merely the most spectacular refutation of this. Yet there seems to be a clear acceptance that, for the eleven, there is no viable alternative to the Community, even if there have been growing reservations about the terms of the Maastricht Treaty.

Why is the British response different, and why is it so apparently grudging? Why has Britain always sought special treatment, whether in the original negotiations for membership of the EC, or in Harold Wilson's "renegotiation of the terms" in the mid-1970s, or in Margaret Thatcher's campaign for a British budget rebate in the 1980s, or in John Major's "opt-out" provision in the 1990s? Britain's political leaders have consistently represented their country as being a special case. This is not merely the posture of a particular government, or of a particular political party: only the Liberal Democrats are apparently unanimous and unconditional in their enthusiasm for European integration, while in both the Conservative and Labour parties – and in governments they have formed – there have been both cautious enthusiasts and avowed opponents.

Within Britain, the argument against proceeding at the continental Europeans' pace has been based on considerations of both domestic and foreign policy, which can be characterized as identity, sovereignty and peculiarity. In the first place, there remains a continuing preoccupation with maintaining both Britain's identity as an "independent" voice in world affairs and its "special relationship" with the United States of America, two priorities which have grown increasingly mutually contradictory as it has become clear that the "special relationship" is, and always has been, based on Britain's acknowledgment of its *dependence* on the USA, especially, but not only, in military terms.[2] In 1962 it was the Labour Party leader, Hugh Gaitskell, who "forecast that Britain's entry into the EEC might be 'the end of Britain as an independent nation' and . . . 'would mark the end of a thousand years of history'".[3] Implicit in that preoccupation is also the emotive issue of "sovereignty", a nebulous principle uniting politicians as various as Enoch Powell and Tony Benn, thus encouraging cynics to regard it as the last ditch into which opponents of European integration have been driven as their other objections have been either met or shown to be unfounded. Nevertheless, the idea of ceding sovereignty has from the start been a stumbling-block to British acceptance of Community institutions, with opposition to the future "European Executive" with supranational powers, which was proposed by the eventual founders of the Community, as early as 1950.[4] By the late 1980s, it had come to mean more than surrendering some of parliament's powers and the monarch's symbolic state functions, and was being associated, especially by Conservative Eurosceptics including Margaret Thatcher, with the betrayal of the British heritage of "never being slaves". In the somewhat bizarre view expressed by Sir John Stokes, MP, foreigners are less patriotic than Englishmen, and pressure to enter a closer relationship with the EC should be resisted, "to keep England England".[5]

Yet Britain has been closely involved with its European neighbours in the twentieth century and much earlier: "splendid isolation" was only a brief phase around the turn of the twentieth century. Participation in European alliances and wars and, therefore, at peace conferences is a part of centuries-long British tradition. Engaging in trade with European countries, too, has been customary: most recently, before Britain joined the EC, it became in 1960 a founder member of the looser alternative grouping, the European Free Trade Association (EFTA). Membership of the North Atlantic Treaty Organisation (NATO), too, has since 1949 involved Britain in co-operation on security and defence matters, not only with North America but also with several of the EC countries, in a relationship which has undoubtedly compromised the purity of British sovereignty. And Britain actually played a leading role in the establishment of the defensive Western European Union in March 1948.[6] These and other involvements have, however, been for specific limited purposes. Equally, when Britain first applied for membership of the Community, circa 1960, it seemed in practice to be primarily about trade and economic co-operation on an inter-governmental basis, with a vague and open-ended aim of political union. Since Britain's entry into the EC in 1973, however, the Community has developed functions and institutions far beyond those prescribed in the Treaty of Rome in 1957, a process increasingly resisted by British governments which – often alone among the twelve – have been reluctant to subscribe to policies and processes over whose final determination their government and parliament may have only partial control. That is perhaps not wholly unreasonable for a country whose government and parliament have had unfettered control over its own internal affairs since the power of its monarchy was reduced, by stages, over the last few centuries.[7] After all, not many other European countries can claim such a record: British autonomy has been unscathed by the cycle of war, invasion, occupation and imperialism which has violated the independence of the vast majority of European countries at some time in recent centuries.

Its singular political development is a fundamental cause of Britain's divergence from the patterns followed by other European countries of similar size and stature, and it affects Britons' view of both themselves and continental Europe. So effective were the British, especially British historians, after the Second World War in disseminating a view of Britain as the successful political model for all to emulate, that German historians were persuaded that Germany's development in the nineteenth and twentieth centuries was peculiar and untypical – in fact a *Sonderweg* (special path) – because it did not conform to Britain's development. This was a mistaken perspective, disguising the fact that the country with the most distinctive *Sonderweg* was Britain. What we may – with apologies to Blackbourn and Eley[8] – call "the peculiarities of British history" have conditioned the British to regard continental Europeans, with their border disputes, wars, revolutions and changes of political regime, as unreliable, unenlightened and backward. It may be a caricature, but the "Arthur Daley" view of a Europe characterized by "plods with pistols, iffy food, and sawn-off toilets"[9] still finds some resonance in Britain. The implication is that there is a gaping gulf between the British way of life and European traditions and practices – without much doubt left about which is superior.

Britain was singular in more than its evolution towards parliamentary democracy. In addition, its early, slow and idiosyncratic industrialization process distinguished its development from others'.[10] Industrialization evolved on a trial and error basis, deriving from indigenous ideas and inventions, whereas in other countries it was, initially at least, partly a matter of imposing foreign (i.e. British) practices and then adapting them to local conditions. The paradox in this, if Martin J. Wiener is to be believed, lies in Britons' revulsion at and retreat from the culture of their own creation, industrial society, a revulsion which is as old as the industrial processes themselves, and which helped to "entrench[] premodern elements within the new society . . . [giving] legitimacy to antimodern sentiments" which have remained predominant throughout the twentieth century.[11] While Wiener perhaps overstates his case, it can be said in his defence that the British reverence for "tradition" and the manifest complacency which has characterized the British governing class, are epitomized by a blind pride in British institutions without any serious attempt to compare them with those elsewhere. For example, in a blaze of self-congratulation savouring strongly of unselfconscious hubris, British Airways claims to be "the world's favourite airline".

Further, Britain's peculiar geographical location has seemed to justify Britons' consciousness of being outsiders, and it remains the physical expression of a profound and inherent psychological aloofness. Writing in the aftermath of the Paris Peace Conference of 1919, J. M. Keynes, while himself claiming to be "a European in his cares and outlook", characterized the prevailing view on this side of the Channel thus:

England still stands outside Europe. Europe's voiceless trem-
ors do not reach her. Europe is apart and England is not of
her flesh and body. But Europe is solid with herself. France,
Germany, Italy, Austria, and Holland, Russia and Roumania
and Poland, throb together, and their structure and civilization
are essentially one.[12]

More recently, P. M. H. Bell, writing of the inter-war years, has
put it less extravagantly: "In political, strategic *and above all
psychological terms* [my emphasis], Britain was not a Continental
power . . . isolationism was strong".[13] To argue that the British felt,
and often still feel, apart from Europe rather than a part of it is not
to assert that the continental countries, east and west, have more in
common with each other than any of them has with Britain, or that
even the continental EC countries are in some way homogeneous,
essentially similar in character and interests. Each country has its
own individual identity; each country's path of development is, as
was pointed out in the German *Sonderweg* debate in the 1970s and
1980s, special – even if some, like Britain's, are more special than
others'. The reserve with which many Britons regard continental
Europe is undoubtedly related to Britain's geographical position,
not merely as literally insular but also because Britain is constantly
on the periphery of Europe, almost regardless of where its centre
may be. The present administrative and political centre of the EC
is the Brussels-Luxembourg-Strasbourg triangle, with the balance
tilted heavily in favour of Brussels. But the unification of Germany
in 1990, together with the interest of eastern European countries,
especially Poland, Hungary and Czechoslovakia, in applying for
EC membership, suggests that the political centre of gravity may
well move eastwards, perhaps ultimately to Berlin, leaving Britain
even more distinctly on the periphery, along with Ireland, Denmark, Greece and Portugal, countries whose size and stature have
consigned them in recent centuries to a more minor role in world
affairs than that which Britain either expects or has been accustomed
to enjoy. This, then, is clearly what the Eurosceptics are determined
to resist: the erosion of Britain's historic role both in determining its
own destiny and in playing a central part in determining others'
destinies. Yet their alternative is completely illusory. The belief that
Britain, with its Commonwealth, should act as a separate pillar of
the capitalist world, and, in a sense, as a broker between North

America and Europe, kept Britain aloof from the early post-war moves towards European unity.[14] Britain's belated, and at first unsuccessful, attempts to catch the European train once it was moving acknowledged that this was unrealistic. If that was true by the 1960s, when President de Gaulle, too, continued to fantasize about a similarly dominant role for France,[15] it is incontestable in the 1990s.

*　　　*　　　*

Part of the problem in understanding Britain's relationship with Europe lies in the nature of "Britain". The question of whether there is "British nationalism", or even a "British nation", with a common identity, history and traditions, is not one to which there is an easy answer. In some respects, "Britain" is, to borrow from Metternich, little more than a "geographical expression". According to Alfred Cobban,

> the British Isles have remained the home of four nations – Irish, Scottish, Welsh, and English, as well as a number of smaller sub-nations, the Channel Islanders, Manxmen, and Ulster Orangemen.[16]

On the other hand, John Breuilly is clear that Britain is "a developed nation-state",[17] while Hugh Kearney has recently argued that the emphasis on the separate identities of the four nations of the British Isles has been overplayed at the expense of the essential common "Britannic" elements which have shaped the islands' history and character.[18] Keith Robbins more cautiously suggests that "the consolidation of British unity achieved during the nineteenth century was accomplished at too high a price", and cannot be regarded as irreversible.[19] Again, writing of Scotland and England only, Rosalind Mitchison has pointed out that

> common economic development, the free movement of people, a great body of common social provision and law, a shared language and a large part of shared religious and historical experience, have tied the two countries together in a multitude of ways.[20]

Yet there is no "British church", no "British legal system", no written "British constitution", nor even a "British education system". To quote but a few examples: conviction on the basis of uncorroborated confessions, as in the cases of the "Birmingham Six" and "Guildford Four" in the mid-1970s, among others, could not have happened in Scotland; nor is there in Scotland the bizarre saga of the Sunday trading laws which has been played out in England. Again, the ordination of women as full members of the clergy, so contentious an issue in the Church of England, is well-established in the Church of Scotland. Indeed, all four nations within the British Isles have traditions and customs which often distinguish them clearly from each other[21] – perhaps as clearly as Austrians can be distinguished from Germans, or Portuguese from Spaniards, or Croats from Serbs.

The distinguished early twentieth-century commentator on international affairs, Norman Angell, is reputed to have explained the intricacies of Austria-Hungary's nationalities' problems thus: "It is an area where every England has its Ireland, and every Ireland has its Ulster".[22] That perhaps tells us even more about Britain than it does about central Europe: like the old Austria-Hungary, but in less complex and conflict-ridden fashion, Britain is a multinational state. This is perhaps disguised, even implicitly denied, by the way in which many people (like Keynes) – apparently unconsciously – use the terms "Britain" and "England" interchangeably. In Christopher Smout's view,

> Scots can distinguish a loyalty to a smaller Scotland from that to a greater Britain, and enjoy both, whereas it would be unthinkable for the English to distinguish loyalty to a smaller England from [that to] a greater Britain.[23]

For example, Norman (now Lord) Tebbit's recent "cricket test" ("Which side do you cheer for – England or its opponents?"), which he proposed as a means of judging loyalty to Britain, failed to take into account the fact that a great many Scots (and doubtless Welsh and Irish, too) will cheer for virtually any foreign team competing against England. More prosaically, England, unlike the other three component parts of the UK, does not have its own Secretary of State for peculiarly English affairs.[24] There is no need: what is English is considered to be British, and vice-versa. The Scottish,

Welsh and Northern Ireland Offices mediate (some would rather say, enforce by decree) policies formulated by an overwhelmingly English government and enacted by an overwhelmingly English Parliament; therefore a separate Secretary of State for England would be superfluous – while there is a Conservative government, at least.

There is, then, something of a British identity crisis, which is highly relevant to the British attitude to Europe at the present time. For the Eurosceptics, two developments, that towards "ever closer union" in western Europe together with the new nationalism in eastern Europe, pose questions about the nature and future of Britain as an identifiable political entity. The former is deemed to threaten the international identity of this erstwhile world power, while the latter seems to threaten its integrity. On the one hand, all that is distinctively "British" is to be submerged in a superstate which will be either a characterless Esperanto construct or, more probably, an increasingly German-dominated federation. That is, the Germans may yet win by peaceful means what they have twice tried and failed to win by force of arms: European hegemony – now more of a total possibility than at any time since 1945, with the release of weak eastern European countries from Soviet thrall. On the other hand, the emergence of independent Baltic states, of a commonwealth of states replacing the former Russian/Soviet empire, and of successor states to the defunct Yugoslavia, has given added impetus to a revival of "home rule" sentiment in Britain, especially in Scotland. Writing in 1989, Eric Hobsbawm argued that the new "Balkanization" in the east would mean that

> most such hypothetical new European states would . . . apply for admission to the European Economic Community, which would once again limit their sovereign rights, though in a different manner from their previous situation.[25]

While this is undoubtedly true, it is nevertheless an attractive prospect for the new states precisely because they will not be left to fend entirely for themselves, while it is unlikely that any EC central political agency will be as oppressive as was the dominant Soviet power. Former Yugoslavs, in Slovenia and Croatia, for example, will willingly trade a slice of national sovereignty in return for the protection afforded by the European umbrella in the face of a revanchist Serbia.

The equivalent of this for many Scots is the attraction of not being ruled from London: that negative aim, rather than positive independence, is what a significant body of opinion from virtually all sections of society wishes.[26] A Scotland that is free of England, but not condemned to isolation and the cold winds of unprotected competition, is a compromise which has considerable appeal, and which helps to encourage pro-European sentiment in Scotland, where previously unreconstructed Labourism had promoted anti-Europeanism. Further, parts of Scotland and Wales, as well as English regions, have already had a taste of the benefits of European involvement, through grants from the EC's Regional Fund. No doubt the example of how an independent Ireland has benefited from EC membership seems an indicator of potential opportunities for a devolved or separate Scotland. But the commitment of only a relatively small minority of Scots to independence, as opposed to devolution, has led the Scottish National Party (SNP) to abandon its earlier hostility to the EC and, in 1988, to adopt the slogan of "Independence in Europe", proposed by Jim Sillars, victor of the Govan parliamentary by-election in the same year.[27] Like the SNP's 1970s' slogan, "It's Scotland's Oil", this smacked of sheer opportunism, as another manifestation of what Breuilly has appropriately characterized as the SNP's "image of 'Scotland first', seen in pragmatic terms".[28] But, with the recent proliferation of small national states, this slogan has gained credibility at precisely the same time as alienation from "English rule" over Scotland has intensified. The SNP has not, however, explained the terms in which a Scottish application for membership of the EC would be couched, while its publicity disingenuously assumes that Scotland would have considerable influence in the EC – on the scale currently enjoyed by Britain.[29]

On the wider British stage in the 1970s and 1980s, devolutionists who are pro-European, like Edward Heath and the late Alick Buchanan-Smith, saw their two enthusiasms as complementary, while ardent anti-Europeanists like Enoch Powell and Teddy Taylor were prominent active opponents of the Callaghan government's devolution proposals.[30] The argument in both areas, devolution and European integration, was about the sovereignty of the Westminster Parliament, and this linkage figured in the devolution debate. The Callaghan government's devolution legislation proposals reserved the right of Westminster to channel and supervise the implementation of EC decisions throughout the UK, ensuring that this was in keeping with overall government policy and thus denying the proposed Scottish and Welsh Assemblies a direct relationship with the EC. Even more explicitly, Leon Brittan posited an amendment that "Parliament shall retain the right to make any law for the United Kingdom or any part of it, including laws relating to matters within the legislative competence of the Assembly". It was even suggested that this could mean that increased British involvement in the EC might lead to progressively *less* authority for an Assembly.[31] This issue of internal British sovereignty has yet to be addressed in the 1990s by those who favour devolution with the United Kingdom.

Not surprisingly, the greatest fear of a diminution of (Westminster) parliamentary sovereignty is to be found at or near the political core of the United Kingdom: those who feel that they have some input into the power structure fear losing all or part of it. As this was true in the devolution debate in 1977–78, so it is also true in the debate on "ever closer union" within the EC. Conservative MPs with a large majority, who are chiefly to be found in southern England (although there are also Euroenthusiasts in this group) may feel this as long as there is a Conservative government. But in the 1980s differing patterns of political development at the centre and on the periphery helped to foster contrasting attitudes towards the question of sovereignty. Many of those on the periphery feel that they have little or no influence over the central direction of policy, and therefore have little to lose by a shift in the exercise of power from London to Brussels. This may well have been the motivation which has brought converts to the European cause from among Labour MPs. None of this, however, means that there is unanimous support for the EC on the British periphery. Fishermen in Hull or Aberdeen are positively hostile, while the Common Agricultural Policy has caused considerable disaffection, including in Wales.[32]

In Britain, then, it seems that sovereignty, when defined as the overriding authority of the Westminster Parliament, is less valued in a peripheral region like Scotland because that authority has come to seem increasingly remote and alien. Certainly, Smout is of the view that "For the first time in two centuries the political ethos of England and Scotland has profoundly diverged"[33] – as a result, or perhaps even as the cause, of the collapse of the Conservative Party in Scotland, which still calls itself the Conservative and Unionist

Association. The Conservative Party is perceived by a majority of Scots now as being an English party (a south of England party, at that), and the Thatcher governments certainly showed little comprehension of Scottish needs and susceptibilities. No doubt many in Wales and northern England would say the same. Yet the Scottish case is different. Scotland can claim to be a nation, or, at the very least, to have been a nation state within the last 300 years. After all, English enthusiasm for the Union in 1707 was based largely on fear that Scotland, as a separate polity with its own distinctive traditions in foreign policy, might revive the "Auld Alliance" with France, which had become England's most formidable foe and the sponsor of the Stewart Pretender.[34]

But within Scotland there are comparable problems: the dominance of Strathclyde Region, based on Glasgow, in terms of population size, led to growing fears in other regions, during the devolution debate in the late 1970s, that a Scottish Assembly would be dominated by Strathclyde's economic interests. This is why support for a "no" vote gathered strength in the period immediately preceding the referendum in 1978, especially in Orkney and Shetland, the territory most adjacent to the North Sea oilfields, where almost three-quarters of the votes cast were against the establishment of a Scottish Assembly.[35] For those on the periphery of the periphery, it may well seem preferable to be ruled from a distance, while bringing the centre of power closer may be perceived as potentially more oppressive. Clearly, the central authority that is most resented is that at only one remove from the periphery. As Orkney and Shetland have feared a transfer of significant power to Edinburgh from London, so, for many mainland Scots, a transfer of power to Brussels from London may be perceived as potentially preferable.

It is, in a sense, the embourgeoisement of the Conservative Party in the last couple of decades that has pointed up the national differences within the UK. Since the Union in 1707, the Scottish aristocracy has become thoroughly anglicized, with its London town houses and its offspring educated at English public schools and, often, Oxbridge. The recent diminution of the political power and influence of this British landed ruling class in politics, which means, overwhelmingly, within the Conservative Party,[36] has meant that governments of the 1980s and early 1990s have, in a way, seemed less British and more identifiably *English*, drawing their leaders from, and increasingly finding the bulk of their support in, southern England. Equally, the Labour Party in Parliament, not least in the Shadow Cabinet, and also the parliamentary Liberal Democrats, have a strong Scottish contingent, out of all proportion to the relative size of Scotland's population, while Wales remains a Labour stronghold. Even leaving aside the peculiar (and minority) appeal of the Nationalist parties in Scotland and Wales, the acute identification of the Conservative Party with England, and the reciprocal, and increasing, identification of the non-English British with the parliamentary opposition, has been one of the distinguishing features of British politics since 1979. In broad areas of Scottish society, including the professional middle classes, there has developed what can only be termed an "opposition mentality".

The Union which Scotland entered with England in 1603 was at first purely dynastic. A century later, under extreme economic pressure from the rising power of England, Scotland accepted an incorporating Union of the Parliaments, in 1707; there was, of course, no national referendum – in either Scotland or England. Simply, those who had a voice in the limited political systems of the day on both sides accepted and ratified the union – with cash incentives winning the compliance of many of the Scots.[37] This was in marked contrast to the force of arms used by the English to subdue both the Welsh and the Irish. It is the voluntary nature of Scotland's participation in the union that has become a live issue in the post-1945 period, and especially since 1979, to the extent that even the English have recently begun to notice that their side of the relationship is also voluntary, and therefore dissoluble. It remains to be seen if closer European union would head off some Scottish separatist sentiment precisely because it would promise to curb the sovereignty of the Westminster parliament. The option of a devolved Scottish political identity within Europe (as distinct from independence within Europe) would probably be more attractive to Scots, and the EC's professed commitment to "subsidiarity" would be wholly compatible with that. In fact, the centrifugal aspirations of regions and nationalities within Britain mirror similar tendencies in some of its western European neighbours, like Belgium or Spain. For that reason, there may be opposition from other member-states to any separate Scottish application for membership of the EC, lest it be seen as a precedent.

Yet in time of war, the unity of Britain has held firm, with the notable exception of a minority of Irishmen in 1914–18. Perhaps Robbins is correct to imply that this was connected with Britain's victory, while in 1918 "other multi-ethnic multi-lingual empires collapsed, to be replaced by states supposedly based on the principle of 'national self-determination'".[38] Failure in that war doomed Austria-Hungary particularly, with the subject nationalities, anxious not to be associated with that failure and its consequences, insisting on independence rather than membership of a Habsburg-led federation.[39] It may be that, in the British case, the end of Empire and the evidence, from the 1960s, of Britain's chronic industrial, economic and financial problems, has promoted a sense of failure in Britain that ignited long-smouldering nationalist feeling. Certainly, there has been much more clamour in Scotland and Wales for an arm's-length relationship with England since Britain ceased to be a world power, whereas the Scots, in particular, were more than ready to share in the spoils of Empire and overseas trade while Britain "ruled the waves".[40] By the 1980s, with the EC appearing to be a more vital and prosperous concern, looking ahead rather than living in the past, and – importantly for Labour supporters – as a capitalist club with an increasingly obvious social conscience, close association with it while by-passing the London dinosaur has come to have its attractions. But there remains considerable Unionist sentiment in both Scotland and England, while any future Labour government will face the dilemma of living up to its recent devolutionist promises which would probably consign it to perpetual minority political status in a British parliament without the current over-generous representation of Scotland which is overwhelmingly to its benefit.

*   *   *

Britain's late twentieth-century problems, which have undoubtedly enhanced the periphery's disaffection with control from London, derive in large measure from its peculiar development as a modern, democratic state. Britain's role as a naval power, with only very limited forces geared towards fighting a land war; its much earlier (and idiosyncratic) experience of the processes and consequences of industrialization; its overwhelming preoccupation with its empire; and its early and relatively smooth development from an absolute monarchy into a parliamentary democracy (albeit an imperfect one) – all have contributed to the peculiarities of British history and, above all, to the ambivalent attitude of the British towards their continental neighbours. Europeans have come to Britain as visitors or as refugees, but have not, in recent centuries – indeed since 1066 – come as conquerors, although some have tried. The British · have therefore not been compelled to accept political and/or social change imposed by force of arms, even temporarily, whereas in the last two hundred years most continental countries have experienced the dissolution of their traditional institutions and the diffusion of at least some of the power and wealth of their traditional landed elites and of their established church, whether through revolution or military defeat. For the new countries emerging from Turkish or Austrian control in the nineteenth and early twentieth centuries, imperfect indigenous systems which they developed were swept away in the Second World War and then replaced by a Soviet-style format, whose alien character has been attested to by the alacrity with which it has been rejected throughout central and eastern Europe in the late 1980s. The British experience has remained immune to all of this. Nor have the British chosen to change their much-vaunted traditions because, for some two hundred years, they have been victorious in most of the conflicts they have entered, and in all of those which directly threatened the British Isles (give or take the running sore of Ireland). Thus their system seems to have served them well – better than the systems which have, apparently, failed most of their continental neighbours at one time or another in that period. Most recently, as Vernon Bogdanor has said, the Second World War tested European countries' institutions and found them all, except Britain's, wanting.[41]

Yet this perhaps overlooks the fact that, if these Europeans had failed the test, Britain had not been put to the test – or, at least, to the same test. Even when its traditional defence, the sea, no longer afforded immunity from enemy attack, Britain had, in the Second World War, suffered only one element in the German *Blitzkrieg* strategy, the brutal aerial bombing. The armoured and motorized forces which met severely weakened resistance in other countries, after they had been softened up by bombing, were denied access to fortress Britain. This relative impregnability certainly contributed to the singularity of the British experience. While the Romans, the Angles, Saxons and Jutes, the Danes and the Vikings, all succeeded in some measure in invading Britain, and the Normans were able to consolidate their conquest of England [sic] at leisure after 1066, there has been no successful armed foreign invasion of Britain since that time. Philip II's Armada, French sponsorship of the deposed Stewarts, Napoleon's and Hitler's plans to extinguish the British challenge to their respective continental empires through conquest, all failed, and failed miserably because of the difficulty of launching a large-scale attack on mainland Britain from the sea. This ensured that Britain's defence would continue in the twentieth century to be entrusted to the navy and, from the 1930s, the air force, rather than to a land army of any size; this was not lost on Britain's ally, France, in both World Wars,[42] and seemed renewed justification for Le Bossuet's old jibe about "la perfide Angleterre".

Britain's island status could, however, work to its disadvantage. As the D-Day landings in June 1944 showed, it was extremely difficult for the Allies to launch an assault from Britain on the heavily-fortified European coast. The success of this operation was not a foregone conclusion, as both the heavy casualties involved and the establishment, in the first twenty-four hours of the invasion, of much less secure and extensive bridgeheads than had been planned, illustrate.[43] It is true that, to a minimal extent in the First World War and to a great extent in the Second, the development of military air-power posed a new threat to the island fortress by bringing warfare to Britain with the use of small and often elusive forces. But it is only since 1945, in the age of nuclear arms, that Britain has become potentially as vulnerable as the rest of Europe. Recognition of this made membership of NATO essential to Britain's future defence capability, even allowing for the fig-leaf of its "independent nuclear deterrent". This was a case of relinquishing a part of Britain's sovereignty so as to protect the remainder.[44] But the American domination of NATO has helped to disguise the fact that there has been since 1945 considerable interdependence among western Europeans on security matters, if only within Europe and not in "out-of-area" ventures like the Gulf War of 1991.

Although Britain was terribly weakened by the two world wars, its offshore location lent credibility to the purveyors of the "special relationship" theory, with Britain still, it was implied, a power (if not a "great" one) with some claim to a place alongside the United States, maintaining the fiction that it influenced the

US's ordering of international affairs and enjoying a status higher than that accorded to any individual continental European power. This was part-compensation for, part-hangover from, the days of Empire, role-seeking more than role-playing. Above all, it seemed to afford Britain an alibi for her failure to become involved in European integration after 1945, and, at the same time, it gave offence to the country that was politically the strongest in the new European Economic Community, France, seeming to justify de Gaulle's paranoia about an Anglo-Saxon conspiracy to prevent France from regaining great power status.[45] But Britain did not have the same positive motivation for European union as did her continental neighbours, because her experience of twentieth-century war was different from theirs. The original European Economic Community comprised West Germany and five of the countries which had, in whole or in part, been conquered, occupied and exploited by German forces during the Second World War: that rapprochement was in itself remarkable, in a little over a decade after the end of that war. But it was, of course, precisely those countries which hoped never to have to repeat the experience which were anxious to tie the accessible part of Germany into a peaceful union with themselves. Britain welcomed this as an arrangement which would in future prevent hostilities between rival western European powers and a consequent distortion of the balance of power, and thus preserve it from having ever again to intervene in a European war. This, Britain hoped, would leave it free to revert to what was believed to have been the *status quo ante bellum*, where Britain, the maritime power, concentrated on trade and empire.[46]

But this was a misreading of the past. Britain's concentration on trade and empire had not insulated her from Europe: indeed, in the late nineteenth century, it had brought her into conflict with other *European* powers, notably France and Russia – over colonies - and then Germany, over naval power. Although involvement in land fighting in Europe in 1914–18 was subsequently deemed by many to have been an error, in the 1930s Britain increasingly became the stronger member in the reluctant partnership with France geared to preventing German expansion once more.[47] The British were right to be cautious: the First World War had shown that, for the first time in centuries, Britain could not secure military victory on the European continent even when acting with European allies. The New World had to be brought in – to adapt Canning's dictum – to redress the balance of the Old. Thus British reluctance to open a "second front" in western Europe in 1942–43, much criticized both at the time and since, was entirely justified, from several points of view. For a start, far from opening a second front in the east in 1940, when Britain desperately needed assistance, Stalin had remained Hitler's ally, supplying him with essential war materials.[48] More substantially, the painful fiasco of the Dieppe Raid in August 1942, followed by the narrow initial success of the D-Day operations, highlighted the difficulties. In the latter, it was enough of a problem even once the New World had again directly entered the European fray, and would have been a suicide mission without it.

*   *   *

And yet, as Paul Kennedy has argued, Britain could not be indifferent to power-political developments in Europe.[49] Seen over the long term, it is the relationship with France which has been the key to Britain's attitudes to and involvement in Europe. To that extent, Britain's experience is similar to that of continental countries, whose most important – and generally their worst – relations are with their nearest neighbours. Britain's relative advantage was summed up by the nineteenth-century writer, Douglas Jerrold, thus: "The best thing I know between France and England is – the sea."[50] For England, the legacy of the Norman conquest was a protracted and ultimately doomed struggle by its kings to defend existing territorial possessions in France and to acquire more. Anglo-French antagonism and England's parallel attempt to snuff out Scottish independence gave rise in 1295 to a Franco-Scottish alliance which persisted in at least latent form for as long as the Scottish state. For their part, the French sought to capitalize on England's troubles, in the late seventeenth and eighteenth century wars between them, by using back doors in both Ireland and Scotland to divert British military resources from the continent.[51] British participation in European wars from 1689 to 1815, to maintain or redress the balance of power, was a disagreeable necessity, at first occasioned by a lingering genuine threat to the Protestant succession and French designs on the Netherlands. It was made palatable by the colonial prizes at stake, because France, the constant enemy in this period, not merely repeatedly upset the European balance of power, but also was coincidentally in possession of colonies which Britain coveted. William Pitt the Elder's reputed and apparently gnomic utterance that "we shall win Canada on the banks of the Elbe"[52] was perfectly rational – and in the end justified. It was perhaps a coincidence that France ceased to threaten the European balance of power fairly soon after losing important colonies to Britain; certainly, together these factors made possible, by halting steps, a Franco-British rapprochement when a new threat appeared in the form of the united Germany – a threat both to the balance of power in Europe and to British sea-power, and therefore, as many saw it, a threat to both British trade and the British Empire.[53]

Nevertheless, it could hardly be said that there was thereafter amity and warmth between France and Britain, as Britain's belated attempts to join the Common Market revealed. The development of the Six in the 1960s into a successful and self-confident grouping certainly made it less likely that they would woo Britain. Yet French dominance, especially while de Gaulle was President, disposed the others to favour the kind of counterweight that West Germany could not become, for historico-political reasons, at that time. The French veto of Britain's application to join in 1963 derived precisely from French reluctance to admit a potential rival. But there was more to it than that. France and Britain, while allies in the era of the two world wars, had never been truly friends. The British gave the clear impression for much of the inter-war period that the First World War, in which they had fought against the Germans and with the French, had been an aberration.[54] According to Sidney Aster, Neville Chamberlain "held France and its statesmen in near contempt".[55] The French, for their part, had considerable justification in the 1930s for believing that "the British would always fight to the last Frenchman"[56] before committing more than token British forces to battle on the continent. Further, after the Second World War, some Frenchmen could hardly be blamed for feeling resentment at the way in which Allied air forces had bombed *French* northern towns in pursuit of the German army. More than that, Charles de Gaulle, who suffered the ignominy of being given houseroom by the British during the war, and no doubt other Frenchmen, too, could not forgive the British and Americans for liberating France – something the French were signally unable to do themselves, whatever mythology has been cherished ever since. With the tables turned in the early 1960s, de Gaulle had the power to say "non" and took conspicuous pleasure in so doing [57]

Yet perhaps de Gaulle was right: British institutions and interests are possibly not compatible with those of continental western European countries. British economic development, like British political and strategic traditions, has been markedly different from that in continental countries. The major structural difference between them lies in the nature and importance of agriculture. This was a source of difficulty during the negotiations to admit Britain to the EC throughout the 1960s, and it remains a major bone of contention. In Britain's absence from the EC in its first decade or so, the founder members created a Common Agricultural Policy (CAP) which actively supports small, uneconomic farms, for overwhelmingly political reasons.[58] Typically, France has normally been seen in Britain as the villain of the piece, but even in a highly industrialized and advanced country like Germany, agriculture remains a sacred cow. As early as 1914, Britain derived a mere 7 per cent of her income from agriculture, compared with Germany's 23 per cent,[59] at a time when Germany was clearly overtaking Britain in many areas of industrial production. For example, by 1910, Germany was producing significantly more pig-iron and more than twice as much steel as Britain.[60] Even so, Britain became at an early stage, well before the First World War, an emphatically urban society, with urban needs and values increasingly dominating British politics and British culture.[61]

British farms, particularly in southern England, have tended to be relatively few in number and large, mostly over 100 hectares and some substantially larger, although small-scale farming has persisted in parts of Wales and northern England, and in Scotland with the crofters. By contrast, France has remained a country of only a few big cities, many small towns, and a large infrastructure of villages, particularly in the wine-growing areas, although there are also some large farms (of over 100 hectares).[62] In Germany, the small farmers of the south and west (again, often wine-growers), who often proved resistant to Nazi norms and demands,[63] are equally determined to maintain their farms, with EC funds. While some are prosperous, others subsist in varying degrees of economic non-viability. The less industrialized countries of the EC, like Ireland, for example, with its "'residual classes . . . especially farmers on marginal holdings or labourers without skills' . . . more characteristic of the southern Mediterranean than western Europe",[64] have also benefited from the CAP. But its entire ethos runs counter to the traditional British policy of keeping food prices low and importing various items of food to meet that aim, with a system of "deficiency payments" to support British farmers. While the British have fought a rearguard action on CAP subsidies,[65] they have also tried, and largely failed, to protect British fishermen's interests by resisting a fully free fisheries market, the prospect of which deterred Norway from joining the EC in 1973 after its application had been accepted.[66]

Issues like the CAP and fisheries' policy are eagerly seized on by British Eurosceptics as indications of the unsuitability of EC structures and decision-making processes for Britain, and of the need to keep Britain's options open in case decisions are taken which are so incompatible with Britain's interests that, in the last resort, withdrawal from the EC is necessary. Their vision is much more that of de Gaulle, of "L'Europe des patries", with inter-governmental committees through which Britain's relations with its EC partners should be channelled, instead of chains of communication and collaboration between individual regions, communities and even individuals – through the European Court, for example. This is redolent of the view taken by both government and opposition in the devolution debate of the later 1970s, that the sovereignty of Westminster must at all costs be retained in all areas of domestic policy. As long ago as autumn 1950, when the British Conservative Party represented this view at the Strasbourg Assembly, a French Catholic leader protested that that would be "tantamount to having the whole Community stricken with paralysis". To try to counteract this image, Harold Macmillan argued that, in time of crisis:

> we British will certainly be prepared to accept merger of sovereignty in practice if not in principle. . . . Britain might be united in a fit of absence of mind or by a series of improvisations, which would be particularly gratifying to my countrymen.[67]

It is true that the current constitution of the United Kingdom has been achieved by this kind of classic British pragmatism, but once issues like sovereignty (and, for that matter, devolution) have been put on the national agenda, it is difficult to wish them away. These are emotional, rather than rational, issues – whatever arguments of substance may be invoked in their defence. While Euroenthusiasts may deplore the CAP, they do not regard its vagaries as a resigning matter. On the other hand, Eurosceptics seem unable to overcome the feeling that, "If God had wanted to tie [Britain] to the rest of Europe, He would evidently not have dug the Channel."[68]

Notes

1. Speaking on "The World this Weekend", BBC Radio 4, 1 December 1991.
2. Olaf Mager, Anthony Eden and the framework of security: Britain's alternatives to the European defence community, 1951–54, Beatrice Heuser and Robert O'Neill (eds), *Securing peace in Europe, 1945–62*, London, 1992, p. 135; John Kent and John W. Young, The "Third Force" and NATO, *ibid.*, pp. 57–58.
3. Nora Beloff, *The General says no*, London, 1963, p. 140.
4. *Ibid.*, p. 59.
5. Speaking on "The Moral Maze", BBC Radio 4, 31 December 1991.
6. Richard Vaughan, *Twentieth century Europe: paths to unity*, London, 1979, pp. 72–4.
7. See the perceptive discussion of the striking of a balance of political power in England in John Breuilly, *Nationalism and the state*, Manchester, 1982, pp. 53–7.
8. David Blackbourn and Geoff Eley, *The peculiarities of German history*, Oxford, 1984. See especially the Introduction, p. 12, and the essay by Geoff Eley, The British model and the German road, pp. 100–4, 135–9, on the dangers of accepting Britain as a "model".
9. Television film, Minder on the Orient Express, Euston Films, 1985.
10. David Reynolds, *Britannia overruled: British policy and world power in the twentieth century*, Essex, 1991, pp. 11–18.
11. Martin J. Wiener, *English culture and the decline of the industrial spirit 1850–1980*, London, 1981, p. 7.
12. J. M. Keynes, *The economic consequences of the peace*, new edition published by Macmillan for the Royal Economic Society, London, 1984, p. 2.
13. P. M. H. Bell, *The origins of the Second World War in Europe*, London, 1986, p. 101.
14. Kent and Young, The "Third Force", p. 57.
15. James F. McMillan, *Dreyfus to de Gaulle: politics and society in France 1898–1969*, London, 1985, pp. 161–2; Beloff, *General*, pp. 22–5, 29, 32, 37, 39–41; Luigi Barzini, *The Europeans*, London, 1983, pp. 145–52.
16. Alfred Cobban, *The nation state and national self-determination*, London and Glasgow, 1969, p. 154.
17. Breuilly, *Nationalism*, Contents page.

18. Hugh Kearney, *The British Isles: a history of four nations*, Cambridge, 1989, passim.

19. Keith Robbins, *Nineteenth-century Britain: integration and diversity*. The Ford Lectures, delivered at the University of Oxford, 1986–87, Oxford, 1988, p. 185.

20. Rosalind Mitchison, *A History of Scotland*, London, 1970, p. 422.

21. This is the theme of Robbins, *Britain*. See also Anthony H. Birch, *Nationalism and national integration*, London, 1989, pp. 78, 80.

22. A slightly different observation was made by Rudolf Kjellén, quoted in Oscar Jaszi, *The dissolution of the Habsburg monarchy*, Chicago, 1929, p. 379: "A Great Power can endure without difficulty one Ireland, as England did, even three, as Imperial Germany did (Poland, Alsace, Schleswig). Different is the case when a Great Power is composed of nothing else but Irelands, as was almost the history of Austro-Hungary . . . . "

23. Christopher Smout, Time for a rethink of 1707 and all that, *The Sunday Times – Scotland*, 24 November 1991. For Breuilly, pp. 56–7, there is no "distinctive English nationalist ideology".

24. There is an alleged exception to this: Tony Benn, *Office without power: diaries 1968–72*, Hutchinson, 1988, p. 204, Sunday 5 October 1969, states that Anthony "Crosland has been given the job of Secretary of State for England, coordinating transport and housing and he is obviously very sick about it because he doesn't think there is anything in the job". There is, however, no reference to this in Susan Crosland, *Tony Crosland*, London, 1983, where it is stated that Crosland's new department "began under the name Local Government and Regional Planning", p. 208.

25. E. J. Hobsbawm, *Nations and nationalism since 1780: programme, myth, reality*, Cambridge, 1990, p. 177.

26. Mark Veblen Kauppi, Scottish nationalism: a Conceptual approach, University of Colorado at Boulder Ph.D., 1980, pp. 109–15; John Foster, Nationality, social change and class: transformations of national identity in Scotland, David McCrone, Stephen Kendrick and Pat Straw (eds), *The making of Scotland: nation, culture and social change*, Edinburgh, 1989, p. 36; Birch, *Nationalism*, pp. 92–3.

27. Ian O. Bayne, The impact of 1979 on the SNP, Tom Gallacher (ed.), *Nationalism in the nineties*, Edinburgh, 1991, p. 61.

28. Breuilly, *Nationalism*, p. 282.

29. A frank and sober assessment of Scotland's "problems as well as opportunities" in the European arena can be found in Isobel Lindsay, The SNP and the lure of Europe, Gallacher, *Nationalism*, pp. 84–101, especially p. 84: "For short-term expediency, the 'Scotland in Europe' concept was projected as an easy escape route from the problems of

seeking a constitutional settlement with England . . . ."

30. Kenneth O. Morgan, *Rebirth of a nation. Wales 1880–1980*, Oxford, 1982, pp. 400–1; Belle-Ann Abrams, Scottish nationalism and the British response: a critical analysis of the devolution debate, Brandeis University Ph.D., 1986, pp. 203, 236 note 45.
31. *Ibid.*, pp. 201–2, 234 n. 31, 235 n. 41.
32. Morgan, *Wales*, p. 338.
33. Smout, Time for a rethink.
34. Mitchison, *Scotland*, pp. 303, 305–8.
35. Abrams, Scottish nationalism, pp. 219–22.
36. James G. Kellas, *The Scottish political system*, Cambridge, 1989, p. 125; Jeremy Paxman, *Friends in high places*, London, 1991, pp. 73–84.
37. Mitchison, *Scotland*, pp. 161–5, 303–16.
38. Robbins, *Britain*, p. 184.
39. A. J. P. Taylor, *The Habsburg monarchy*, London, 1964, pp. 268–9.
40. Mitchison, *Scotland*, pp. 347, 357; Foster, Nationality, social change and class, p. 37; Birch, *Nationalism*, pp. 90–1.
41. Vernon Bogdanor, speaking on "The World This Weekend", BBC Radio 4, 1 December 1991.
42. Bell, *Origins*, pp. 165–6, 171–8. See also Paul Kennedy, *The rise and fall of the great powers: economic change and military conflict from 1500 to 2000*, London, 1988, pp. 338, 342–4, esp. p. 338: "during the first two years of the conflict, Russia and France took the main burden of checking the German military machine", with British participation crucial in the later stages of the war.
43. Brian Holden Reid, The second front in Europe, John Campbell (ed.), *The experience of World War II*, Oxford, 1989, pp. 74–7; Martin Gilbert, *Churchill: a life*, London, 1992, p. 777.
44. Kent and Young, The "Third Force", pp. 57–8; Reynolds, *Britannia*, pp. 180–2, 212–16.
45. Beloff, *General*, pp. 31–8; Barzini, *Europeans*, pp. 150–2.
46. *Ibid.*, pp. 58–60; Reynolds, *Britannia*, p. 198. Correlli Barnett puts it more pungently than most in *The audit of war: the illusion and reality of Britain as a great nation*, London, 1987, p. 304.
47. Kennedy, *Great powers*, pp. 401–11.
48. Jonathan Lewis and Phillip Whitehead, *Stalin: a time for judgement*, London, 1990, pp. 120–1 and, especially, figures detailing amounts of oil, metals, cotton, lumber and grain delivered to Germany, p. 227 n. 12; Jeremy Noakes and Geoffrey Pridham, *Nazism 1919–1945*, vol. 3: Foreign policy, war and racial extermination, *Exeter*, 1988, pp. 742, 781, 791.
49. On Britain's "continental strategy", see Kennedy, *Great powers*, pp. 125ff.

50. Blanchard Jerrold, *The wit and opinions of Douglas Jerrold*, London, 1859, p. 13, "The Anglo-French Alliance", Jerrold's riposte to a Frenchman who "said that he was proud to see the English and French such good friends at last".

51. Kennedy, *Great powers*, p. 124.

52. Pitt certainly said that "America had been conquered in Germany" (William Cobbett, *Parliamentary history of England*, 3, George III, debate in the Commons on the preliminary treaty of peace, 1762, p. 1267); earlier, in promoting the alliance with Prussia, Pitt had claimed that "[France's] interest in America, was the motive that drew their sword in Germany" (Cobbett, *Parliamentary history*, 30, George II, debate in the commons on the treaty with Prussia, 1757, p. 788). I am indebted to Professor H. T. Dickinson, University of Edinburgh, for these references.

53. Many of Norman Angell's pre-war writings were directed at allaying at times hysterical British fears of German aggression, on the grounds that there could be no material benefit for Germany in waging war against Britain, even if she were to win British colonies as a result. See *Europe's optical illusion*, London, 1909, and subsequent editions in which he refuted criticisms of this first one. See also J. D. B. Miller, *Norman Angell and the futility of war*, London, 1986, especially chapter 2, pp. 25–52.

54. Reynolds, *Britannia*, pp. 115ff. This has been my own expressed view for many years.

55. Sidney Aster, "Guilty Men": the case of Neville Chamberlain, Robert Boyce and Esmonde M. Robertson (eds), *Paths to war: new essays on the origins of the Second World War*, London, 1989, p. 242. See also Richard Overy with Andrew Wheatcroft, *The road to war*, London, 1989, pp. 79, 84.

56. Reynolds, *Britannia*, p. 142.

57. On the last two points, see Beloff, *General*, pp. 35–7, 156–8, 160–4, 169–71, 173. On de Gaulle's heavy dependence on Anglo-American aid in the war, which he "resented, even as he demanded more", see Kennedy, *Great powers*, p. 472.

58. Dennis Swann, *The economics of the Common Market*, London, 1990, pp. 205–7.

59. S. B. Saul, Industrialisation and de-industrialisation? The interaction of the German and British economies before the First World War, The 1979 Annual Lecture, German Historical Institute London, pp. 11, 29.

60. Chris Cook and John Stevenson (eds), *The Longman handbook of modern European history, 1763–1985*, Essex, 1987, pp. 228–9.

61. In 1985, 338,000 persons (1.6% of the workforce) were engaged

in agriculture, forestry and fishing. From Chris Cook and John Stevenson (eds), *The Longman handbook of modern British history, 1714–1987*, Essex, 1988, p. 156. Wiener's argument, in *English culture*, is not that Britain is not an urban society but that "The consolidation of a 'gentrified' bourgeois culture, particularly the rooting of pseudoaristocratic attitudes and values in upper-middle-class educated opinion, shaped an unfavorable context for economic endeavor" (p. 10).

62. Wilhelm Abel, *Agricultural fluctuations in Europe from the thirteenth to the twentieth centuries*, London, 1986, pp. 272–3.

63. Ian Kershaw, *Popular opinion and political dissent in the Third Reich. Bavaria 1933–1945*, Oxford, 1983, pp. 41–65, 242–6, 256, 282–96; Jill Stephenson, War and society in Württemberg, 1939–1945: beating the system, *German Studies Review*, Vol. VIII, no. 1, 1985, pp. 89–105; idem., Resistance to "no surrender": popular disobedience in Württemberg in 1945, in F. R. Nicosia and L. D. Stokes, *Germans against Nazism: essays in honour of Peter Hoffmann*, Oxford, 1990, pp. 351–67.

64. Roy Foster, *Modern Ireland 1600–1972*, London, 1989, p. 594, quoting a survey carried out by the Institute of Public Administration in 1971.

65. Swann, *Economics*, pp. 207–13, 308–9.

66. *Ibid.*, pp. 293–95.

67. Beloff, *General*, p. 59.

68. Barzini, *Europeans*, p. 59.

CHAPTER TWELVE

The New Europe: a new agenda for research?

Jude Bloomfield

"Nationalism cannot be overcome by internationalism, as many people have thought, for we speak languages. The answer is plurinationalism."

Elias Canetti, "1945", The Human Province

"Everything in Europe is minority, even the largest countries, the most multifarious religions and the most powerful political parties."

H. Brugmans

Introduction

National histories have come to dominate our understanding of European history and inflected our responses to the "New Europe", through an "additive" approach: Europe as the sum of nation states, or, more often than not, the sum of member states. Methodologically, the "international" dimension has entered the picture more as an external feature – as foreign policy and international relations which impinges little on the inner life of European countries, bar war! Where comparative method has poked its nose into the frame, it has often been through the empiricist abstraction of a variable common to two or more countries, such as peasants, policing, industrial take-off, torn from their location within internal social relations and in the international system, whether this be conceived as a world economy, international hierarchy of states, the so-called inter-state system, or an international society. There are other equally questionable concepts of European history, such as that of the West as the superior repositary of civilization, and these also find their echoes in the contemporary debate on the New Europe.

The belief in total determinacy, whether by external economic forces, the weight of cultural tradition or some historic destiny are subject to methodological criticism. I will contest the idea of a predestination for Europe rooted in an ancient legitimacy, unity and fixed identity as a mythology which can only function to exclude others and close off the possibility of change and adaptation to "outsiders", and thus preclude confronting and overcoming the "dark side" of European history: its conquest and domination of other peoples. Such exclusion violates the universalist premises of the Enlightenment, popular sovereignty and citizenship and threatens to reproduce an exclusive ethnic concept of the nation state at the European level.

This chapter attempts to take the debate on Europe beyond a dialogue of the deaf with parallel and scarcely interacting discourses – economic (1992 and the Single Market), political (national sovereignty, the federalist "F" word) and cultural (the "Idea of Europe" and European cultural identity among intellectuals). It aims to retrieve the relevance of the concepts of civil society and the public sphere for the debate on the New Europe. I will focus on the wider cultural debate (wider in the sense of raising historical and symbolic questions) and examine the political implications of different visions of Europe, proposing an alternative model for understanding European culture, articulated to practical policies, in relation to regional and local economies, industrial strategy, language and education, citizenship rights and nationality law.

European civil society

The radical new starting point of a history of the New Europe is the existence of a Europeanized civil society. The evidence of its emergence has been accumulating, in the economic and cultural spheres which are creating compelling pressures and fissures in the political domain. Its most obvious signs have been the integration of business and finance, through cross-border mergers, acquisitions, partnerships and joint ventures, the internationalization of finance and money markets, the concentration of intra-European trade which now accounts for the bulk of all European trade.[1]

A European-wide organization of business in the roundtable of leading industrialists was influential in formulating the Single Market programme for 1992. The impetus came from large producers with long production runs who would benefit from economies of scale, and were particularly concerned about the decline in European competitiveness in the face of US and Japanese rivalry.[2] However, the evidence of the London Business School shows mass production of uniform goods now runs contrary to the trend of most European industries and markets. Apart from a handful of high-cost technology industries like aircraft and chemicals, most manufacture is geared to diverse, high quality, customized products in smaller, flexible production units.[3] But the failed strategy of promoting "national champions" of the 1970s was transposed onto a continental scale to produce European champions fit for global contest. Many European Community industrial programmes such as ESPRIT for research in information technology, RACE for advanced telecommunications and BAP for biotechnology grew out of round tables or close collaboration between high-tech firms and "Europeanized agents" of the state, linked together in a European network integrating private corporate and bureaucratic interests.[4]

EC industrial policy was set on its course of market-led integration and promoting European-owned multinational IT, telecommunications and other companies against their world competitors. This choice of policy reflected the surrender of public policy and social regulation to neo-liberal orthodoxy. The alternative of focusing on closing the gap within Europe, between the richest and poorest regions, through a policy to encourage diffusion of new technologies, "which would enhance Community solidarity by reducing existing gaps in technology and industrial culture" and "tend to multiply resources by stimulating general improvements in quality and efficiency, rather than strengthening the strongest links in the chain",[5] would have marked a commitment to represent public interests across the whole Community.

The labour market has also undergone a degree of Europeanization particularly among managerial strata, financial executives, and in trade and leisure services. This trend will become marked among various categories of professionals – perhaps language teachers first of all, under the impetus of reciprocal recognition of qualifications

by member states after 1992.[6] But this only accentuates the social
and ethnic differentiation within the class structure. *Intra*-European
migration is growing rapidly, but against a background of ever
tighter controls on immigration from outside the Community. Since
the recession of 1973, a stop was put on recruitment of migrant
workers from the Southern Mediterranean countries, with "guest"
status. Thereafter, immigration was confined to family reunification
and refugees. Similarly quotas and queues were imposed by the
former colonial powers, Britain and France, on subjects seeking
to immigrate. The focus of ex-Community immigration has thus
shifted to refugees and asylum seekers, on the one hand, and
clandestine migrants, on the other. Young migrant workers are
concentrated in the twilight zone of the European economy, in
dirty, dangerous industrial jobs or shifting about in casual and
seasonal trades, labouring, cleaning, fruit picking, catering. If
they live a clandestine existence they are not only casualized
but also criminalized. This stands in stark contrast to the range of
opportunities for movement and migration of European citizens –
on career itineraries in multinational firms, on student exchanges or
in search of summer work, on tourist trips which turn into retirement
in the sun on the shores of the Southern Mediterranean. As Romero
summarizes the paradox:

> Substantial discriminations begin to apply at the frontiers of
> Western Europe rather than inside it. In the western Euro-
> pean area, however, the E.C. forms a privileged inner space
> whose lack of restrictions affects not freedom of movement
> as such, but rather the possibility of combining various types
> of movement.[7]

A European-wide civil society also structures the relationships
between cities, constraining them within a European urban
hierarchy. Cities are caught up within core-periphery relationships
across Europe which impose a distribution of functions and specialization, which reflects the balance of economic power territorially
and the international division of labour, and is thus difficult to
supersede. This leads to an allocation of key and subordinate
functions between cities – for example those that will host the headquarters and those the branches, those that will host the research end
of advanced industry with its knowledge communities and cultural

consumption and those the menial assembling of the screwdriver economy or the "no-tech, low-tech" low life – and so breeds fierce competition between cities – to be the leading cultural or financial capital, for example between Paris, London and Frankfurt. Cities are forced to adopt locational strategies in this competitive European environment, actively to manage restructuring and retraining. They have to become adept at marketing themselves or face losing out in the inter-urban competition to attract "footloose" capital, business and cultural tourism, trade fairs, academic conferences, EC funding for capital projects, and so on. The more innovative cities, particularly in Germany, have used an active urban policy to turn inter-city competition from a negative zero-sum game into a positive programme of regeneration, upgrading the environment through greening wasteland and retrieving derelict sites for social housing and cultural districts, creating new rapid transit links and putting on cultural programmes and festivals to animate the city throughout the year. But these generate tensions between the international demands of business or tourism and local or regional identity, between flagship prestige projects and pressing social needs.[8]

In the field of communication, a deregulated internationalized environment has grown up alongside national broadcasting channels. New delivery systems by satellite and cable in some countries, and the impact of increased competition and low-cost programming – cheap American imports, repeats, chat and gameshows – have put licence-funded public service broadcasting, accessible to the whole community, under threat. The shift to private subscription would definitively undermine any unified national public. Already video recording has enabled personal scheduling to override the national broadcasting schedules. Unregulated internationalization is bound to desynchronize the national community as members of it no longer move in homogeneous time.[9] The discourse of national sovereignty rings particularly hollow when combined with advocacy of deregulation in broadcasting.

But internationalization is a process and European broadcasting systems are in a transitional phase at the moment. While there is evidence of growing co-operation between the respective international broadcasting associations, including the European Broadcasting Union (EBU) in news reporting, and a degree of harmonization of professional codes, national channels still order material according to perceptions of national interest.[10] The EBU, which incorporates the national broadcasting authorities, has set up a programme exchange scheme between its own public broadcasting corporations and the former Yugoslavia, Tunisia and Israel and it also pioneered a satellite programme Europa T.V. which failed.[11] The French and Germans both have European cultural channels on satellite, but pressure of American competition led them to join up in November 1988 to co-produce one of them, Le Sept. It is beamed in high definition and reaches Switzerland, Benelux, Germany and, since German unification, even Central Europe some of the time, and has a four-language translation facility. Owing to the merger, it will have to adapt to the more pluralist approach of the Germans, adopting programmes which reflect social and regional diversity, contemporary conflicts and comment, rather than promoting national prestige and Francophone ascendancy through the traditional cultural heritage.[12] The *European* newspaper, although it has improved its coverage, is still confined to an international and largely business elite, and to sole publication in English.

Therefore, a European civil society of a rudimentary kind has come into being, but if Habermas's identification of a public sphere of rational critical debate, of informed public opinion, within civil society, alongside the economic and personal spheres, and capable of influencing or even shaping them, is accepted,[13] it is clear that at European level, a developed civil society in the fuller sense is lacking. Hence the term democratic deficit. Some of the consequences of the lack of a fully-fledged European public sphere are evident – the lack of public accountability: the weak powers of the European Parliament, the dominance of the executive over the legislature, areas of policy falling outside European or national parliamentary scrutiny, such as joint policing and immigration procedures, centralized decision-making without channels for public debate or wider representation of public interests, and the lack of public policy in industry, broadcasting, innovation, all of which have contributed to widespread public bewilderment and ignorance about key issues.

Theoretical approaches to the New Europe

The "New Europe" poses the need for a new theoretical framework which can grasp what is new in this Europe and not replicate it as an agglomeration of discrete entities – nation states, or what I have called the additive approach. This approach clearly cannot analyze the pan-European phenomena: those social, cultural and political activities which cross borders and escape the national boundaries of our thinking and paradigms.

European integration studies as a burgeoning "discipline" is not very developed theoretically. Functionalist and neo-functionalist political accounts take on a pragmatism, where politics follows economics piecemeal, through "spillover"[14] from one policy area to another, or expresses, as Dahrendorf has put it, "the curiously mechanical Cartesian view that if one begins at one corner, such as trade, one is bound to end up with political union and with the United States of Europe"[15] through a gradual consensus between states emerging to limit their sovereignty in the interest of greater gains, and breeding a "habit of co-operation". Although at a descriptive level functionalism may explain both the enlargement of the Community and growth of powers and policy areas which have come under its compass, it is not at a level of abstraction or theoretical generalization to account for the contradictory pulls and pressures to which European political integration has been subject. However, while this descriptive approach may not offer very fertile ground for theorizing the new Europe, grander global theories are also deficient.

World systems theory appears to offer a ready-made explanatory framework for understanding the process of Europeanization as part of the wider internationalization of economic relations and political and social organization. It is probably historically the most far-reaching and influential interpretation of globalization, based on the creation of an all-embracing world capitalist economy from the mid-sixteenth century through colonial conquest and expansion of the Atlantic seaboard states. This process incorporated the rest of the world in a single division of labour, global market and system of unequal exchange between the core and periphery, composed of what is commonly termed the advanced capitalist world and the Third World. This is the overriding and determining contradiction of every sub-structure, whether states or regional governments or social movements.[16]

This understanding of globalization is ill-suited to defining the complex links between regional, national, intra- and international political organization, because it totalizes the economic as an external all-powerful overdetermining force. The concept of the whole is not as an *interactive*, conflictual system made up of diverse constituent elements – what Theda Skocpol has defined as "intersecting structures (class structures, trade networks, state structures and geopolitical systems) involving varying but autonomous logics and different, though overlapping, historical times, rather than a single all-embracing system that comes into being in one stage and then remains constant in its essential patterns until capitalism meets its demise".[17]

By totalizing the power of international capital as an overwhelming, exogenous force, it downgrades the political capacity of states, by virtue of their insertion in the "inter-state system" to act autonomously, and likewise restricts the possibility of resistance and autonomy of political sub-structures such as regional and local government, political parties and movements, to zero. Anything less than opposition conducted at world level means incorporation and institutionalization by the state. Wallerstein pays lip service to the autonomy of the micro level in affecting the macro level of the system, but political power is essentially reduced to economic power, and even oppositional political manifestations such as "the anti-systemic movements" are considered as "institutional products of the capitalist world-economy".[18] But the global capitalist class is ascribed consciousness and subjectivity, the power to make up its collective mind, without any political mediation.[19]

The over-abstract and economically reductive nature of the world systems school has deleterious effects on concrete analysis of societies, cities, culture, people and places, verging on the comical. Indeed, Wallerstein disputes the concept of society, rather like Mrs Thatcher does.[20] After all, the market is all. Following in his footsteps, the concrete is on the point of disappearing, as cities become "placeless" intersections of flows, in the fanciful overstatement of globalization tendencies.[21] Furthermore the assumption of a single overdetermining global core-periphery contradiction leaves the only possibility of cultural resistance and critical forces arising to the Third World, as though there are no peripheries in Europe, and no heterogeneous and conflicting cultures within the core regions.[22]

However, the binary concept of core and periphery can account for the uneven economic development of capitalism and unequal distribution of power, political and cultural, as well as economic, across territory *within* Europe, unravelling it as an *internally* differentiated, conflictual but integrated system. Significantly, development economists such as Dudley Seers have applied the concept of underdevelopment to Europe. Seers found a number of useful empirical measures for core and periphery such as the concentration of headquarters of multinational companies, banks and financial institutions, high levels of consumption of electricity and of car ownership, attraction of migrants to and outflow of tourists from the core while the reverse applies to the periphery.[23] In addition, the latter is on the receiving end of the education and broadcasting systems, and of tourism.[24] It haemorrhages skills and the young able-bodied to the core. The dependence of the periphery is measured in terms of lower levels of capital investment and consumption, the weaker labour market and lack of control over communications and symbolic representation.

Therefore, a theoretical framework for analyzing the New Europe needs to grasp the regional realignments complementing internationalization. On the one hand, capital becomes more international in its operations, apparently more stateless and fancy-free (hence "footloose"), but, at the same time, it is registered in a homeland which gives it shelter and provides it with competitive advantages through enlarging the internal market, promoting technological innovation, discounting certain costs which the society as a whole pays for, such as training, for example through the EC Social Fund. So, at the same time, the US, Japan, the European Community have emerged at global level as rival regional blocs, which have conflicting relationships of competition and co-operation. But within the core blocs, the uneven distribution of power has created internal core and periphery regions too. "Regions" are political constructs, not only cultural communities and economic sub-systems. Where they are states or conglomerations of states, such as the EC, they face pressure to enhance the power of their multi-nationals, but peripheral regions within these blocs may mobilize their political power to resist being dominated by the core regions and global economy as a whole, through diversification and other strategies designed to strengthen their autonomy.

A theory of internationalization based on the concentration yet global spread of corporate power must also take account of the contradictory political pressures it sets up, both through regional differentiation and its own need for a political framework. The eclipse of the nation state as a regulatory order and the deregulation of the 1980s has ironically produced a growing demand for "re-regulation" especially in the chaotic financial markets. However, the nation state not only provided order but also the frame of reference for democratic political intervention, for imposing social priorities. Its erosion has created a vacuum in public debate and public policy. The weakness of collective mobilization at European level is reflected in the unrepresentative and undemocratic nature of European government. The real conflict over the form of a European order is between, on the one hand, a position of no international regulation or only a minimalist form to enable the market to operate, combined with strong national order for internal policing and symbolic functions and inter-governmental co-operation; and, on the other hand, a supranational regulatory framework which could also give expression to and seek to redress regional differentiation and inequality, both within Europe, and in the wider world through revision of the international trade and payments system. The shift in power to the European level has begun to crystallize out European-wide social movements and political groupings, networks across borders between trade unions, green movements, cities and regions, creating a web of international exchanges, communications, research and political co-ordination which constitutes an embryonic European civic culture and public sphere.

Cultural discourse: the Idea of Europe

The "Idea of Europe" has been a subject of cultural debate since the Enlightenment, some say even earlier, since Erasmus. Yet, the synthetic idea underlying Europe, in the minds of the founders of the EC was Christian. Schuman's vision of European integration was based on Christian individualism and moral values. Enlightenment rationalism and the Rights of Man were themselves attributed a Christian inspiration.[25] These values were shared by the Christian democratic founders of the Community. However, the resurrection of Latin Christendom as the cultural foundation for European unity is more influential in historiography,[26] and among Central European intellectuals who wish to rejoin Europe than among contemporary proponents of European unification.

Echoes of it in its latter-day form acknowledge the secular transformation of culture and its translation into vernacular in the Enlightenment. Hugh Seton-Watson historicizes the myth of Latin Christendom as the land of the true faith and of the civilized, by showing its mirror image in Russia in the sixteenth century: the Principality of Muscovy, once freed of Tartar control, became the sole Orthodox Christian ruler in the world and viewed itself as the only true keeper of the faith surrounded by Catholic schismatics and heretics. He recognizes that "In today's world, allegiance to Christendom, the land of the true faith, can have no meaning." And yet in response to the prosaic and piecemeal development of the European Community, he still yearns for a common cause and a "European mystique".[27]

It is rather a secularized version of the idea of Europe, as superior Western civilization which has infected the cultural debate and been used to give a moral justification to neo-colonial aspirations, still perceptible in the self-consciousness of the European Community. While Schuman saw a Christian justification and moral purpose in bringing "civilization" to "the immature nations" of Africa, Monnet believed the development of Africa was a major European task.[28] The belief persisted that Europe was the centre of the world, the magnet of attraction and the giver of good: as Paul Valéry put it "Everything came to Europe and everything, or nearly everything, has come from it."[29] This "eurocentric culturalism"[30] can still be traced in aspects of EC cultural affairs, especially relations with non-EC "third countries".

On the question of writing a history of Europe, although the EC was advised by its own cultural experts not to present an authorized version, for fear "it might lead to distortions or wrong interpretations", nevertheless the Commission gave its support to Duroselle's *History of the European Peoples*, simultaneously translated into eight languages.[31] Although this is a valiant effort, as the title indicates, to produce a non-racial and non-monoethnic narrative, it is not a history from the perspective of minority peoples or of the periphery. The Jews crop up when they are massacred in the Crusades and in the Holocaust, and the Dreyfus scandal is mentioned, but there is no history of them as a people with a long European history predating Chrisianity.[32] The Arabs in Spain are treated as separate and other, rather than an integral part of Europe, although their intellectual influence in transmitting the ancient Greek texts is acknowledged along with their impact on science and medicine, trade, language and architecture.[33] Decolonization is related to Europe's revised position in the world, not to the multicultural transformation of Western Europe from post-colonial migration. Some of the peoples in Europe command more attention than others, even in what purports to be a cultural anthropological account, rather than one focussed exclusively on state power.

The temptation to offer a grand meta-narrative of European history and culture still presents itself because of the "cultural deficit"[34] as well as the democratic deficit in European integration. The functionalist view of culture as a symbolic system which confers meaning on the social order, ensuring conformity to its basic values and countering the potential for social conflict, is predicated on the standpoint of the state, trying to reproduce given power relations, rather than on that of citizens or social and ethnic groups in civil society.[35] The lack of legitimacy and enthusiasm for the European idea among the populace at large has led to some efforts to create a single binding European cultural identity from above, but these should not be confused with the concept of a People's Europe, predicated on enlarging citizens' rights, not enhancing state power.[36] However, the predominant stress in Community writing tends to be placed on a shared democratic and pluralistic framework rather than on a cohesive, all-embracing identity. As a leader of the European Movement has remarked: "Apart from a shared perception of common democratic values, only students of history or the arts are likely to recognize that we have a common European heritage."[37]

While the EC cultural office has moved away from a monolithic concept of European culture and has increasingly stressed the multiple character of European cultures, it is still entangled in conceptual confusion by trying to fit them into some unity, other than the unity of a political framework which guarantees pluralism. The desire for common roots still intrudes into its thinking. The latest, post-Maastricht, EC cultural programme distinguishes a dual role for cultural policy – both "to respect the cultural diversity which constitutes the very essence and wealth of Europe and to highlight its common cultural heritage".[38] Yet the main emphasis has clearly shifted to cultural dialogue and transnational networks from below, with an attentive eye to the periphery. This implies that the post-modern critique of holistic conceptions of unity, whether it be unified space, history or identity, has led the EC in its cultural guise to reconceive European cultures as plural and non-homogenous, based on "polyphony" and "dialogic", reciprocal interaction and exchange.[39] Facilitating such cross-fertilization brings about a symbiosis creating something new – the kind of cultural convergence embodied in jazz.

However, the global pressures towards cultural homogenization come not from a common Christian heritage or a mystic "unity in diversity", but from the expansion of a capitalist technological civilization carried by electronic media, telecommunications and computers, controlled by vast international entertainment and information empires. A. D. Smith reminds us of the "fundamentally memoryless nature of any cosmopolitan culture created today".[40] Yet people respond and interpret its messages in the light of their experience and cultural perceptions and this homogenizing tendency is counteracted by an accentuated sense of place and difference, a sharpened sense of "one's own unmistakeable cultural identity".[41]

Homogenizing trends in the electronic media raise the problem of how to ensure diversity and experimentation in programming and high production quality. If EC intervention in the cultural field is examined, it is clear that it has only partially addressed the problem. Its actions have been directed at setting up a unified "European cultural space" in the advanced communications technologies, through such programmes as MEDIA and Eureka audio-visual. In broadcasting through "Télévison sans frontières", it tried to guarantee minimum quotas of European produced programmes for national networks, though this was contested. In film through Edfo it has set up a distribution network for European low-budget films which, through offsetting dubbing and marketing costs, enables films to realize a European-wide audience potential, and through the Script fund it encourages and rewards new writing.

This policy has been criticized as a kind of "media equivalent of an externally imposed educational system on a European scale"[42] imitating the uniformity which the nation state tried to achieve at national level. But this criticism is really misdirected in a wildly deregulated media environment, which treats cultural products like any other commodity and seeks to cut production costs. The media policy derived first and foremost from an industrial policy, and its limitations as a cultural policy are discernible from that point of view.[43] Indeed, the EC is assiduous in avoiding the term cultural policy, as its treaty obligations are only to treat cultural products, services, and workers, in the same way as any other category of commodity or worker, i.e. to guarantee their free movement.[44] The intervention in the audiovisual field is aimed at giving some protection to European cultural products over American TV imports and the dominance of Hollywood, although its impact remains slight. The industrial policy of promoting "European champions" to compete with their Japanese and American telecommunications rivals – for example in the field of high definition television – can certainly be questioned as an appropriate policy objective for the European Community. But this is not the same as prescribing cultural content. Ferry blurs the distinction between creating a space and specifying what will fill it.

It is true the EC believes a common market in broadcasting will "help to develop a people's Europe through reinforcing the sense of belonging to the Community composed of countries which are different yet partake of a deep solidarity"[45] but this only expresses a hope that cultural exchange and exposé will help people identify with others in Europe, not a state programme of supranational indoctrination. A People's Europe focuses on the enhancement of positive rights of citizenship within an integrated Europe, some actual – such as a form of workers" participation written into the European companies" statute, educational exchanges for 15 to 25 year olds in the Youth for Europe programme, with a young people's pass for access to cultural facilities while abroad,[46] some speculative – a study year spent abroad in another EC country either as part of an international baccheaulauréate or spent after leaving school[47] – a kind of Erasmus programme for schools – a European Equal Opportunities Commission to counter discrimination[48] and a Constitution, drawn up by the European Parliament guaranteeing citizens' rights.

A multi-cultural European society, as conceived above , does have manifold policy implications though and I would like to mention two of them here – language and education. Multilingualism is accorded a central role in European integration by the EC except for Britain, in the Lingua programme, educational exchanges, training of linguists and translators and the European Translation Fund.[49] But it is not spelt out whether the Asian and African languages spoken in immigrant communities in Europe count as indigenous, as "the languages European citizens speak". As has been pointed out:

France's centralist view of French as the only legitimate language of that country and the closed attitude towards Arabic as a second lingua franca do not necessarily bode well. The authors ask pertinently "How pluralist will European pluralism be?"[50]

A multilingual European language programme if it is to be pluralistic, would, therefore, include the full range of languages spoken in Europe, extending beyond the minority languages of the regions, such as Welsh, Catalan and Breton, to ethnic communities. The implication for national education systems is to make minority languages available options on the syllabus of the state system, not outside of it as in the Netherlands,[51] with the opportunity to be examined in them. The same argument applies to the teaching of cultures and religions. With the separation of Church and state and religious toleration as keystones of the Enlightenment, the curriculum of a multi-cultural, multi-ethnic society would reflect this in the comparative anthropological study of religions and cultures. It would also preclude schools from imposing cultural uniformity in the way that has been done in France and Germany in conflicts over Muslim schoolgirls wearing headscarves and in an earlier era in Britain over Sikhs wearing turbans.

Some contemporary intellectuals have protested at the prosaic and impoverished vision of Europe which reduces its great culture, cities and writers to the banality of economic exchange, a steel and coal treaty, the 1992 programme.[52] In Enzensberger's provocatively titled essay "Brussels or Europe – one of the two", he dramatically counterposes the single "idea of Europe" emanating from Brussels to a Europe of the mind. On the one hand, the 1992 programme is a petty bureaucratic concoction, the "idea of Europe" a purely idealistic gloss to cover up the simple reassertion of a colonized Europe in the world economy. On the other, there are a multitude of European ideas, which, no sooner voiced, become universal.[53] This echoes a more widely felt disquiet with the lack of a cultural concept in piecemeal functional integration of Europe, even expressed by Jean Monnet, a founder of the EC resigned to functionalism. But this view is outdated in a number of respects – taking a very restricted view of culture as a sacred sphere of high culture, cut off both from the economy, electronic media and wider popular culture, and it shows silent disregard for Strasbourg, the seat of the European Parliament and political sphere. By default, it reverts to a national perspective. Some of the French cultural critics have even retrospectivey rehabilitated De Gaulle's *"Europe des patries"*.[54]

Enzensberger's exquisite portrait of Europe, "Ach Europa" (a sigh from the heart in German) synthesizes national cultural differences in cameos of daily life. However, as Europe is seen from the viewpoint of the periphery, and "from below", through what the symbolic incidents of everyday life reveal of the national culture, it has fuelled the idea of "Europe of the Regions". In this Europe, Sweden and Italy stand at two extremes, the one of statist regimentation and bureaucratic regulation, the other of maddening but endearing chaos – and productivity. His colourful picture of Italy attributes its problems to its corrupt, self-serving political system and its virtues to the autonomous initiative of the people. Yet, while this picture is painfully funny and accurate as far as the central state is concerned, it sets up its own myth of authenticity, of the pure people, spontaneously creative and innovative when unshackled and set free of stifling bureaucracy:

> While state activity has left behind nothing but the grand ruins of obsolescent heavy industry, efficient small and medium-sized industrial companies have sprung up spontaneously in furniture-making and tourism, fashion and precision engineering. The country's present affluence depends on this swarm of heterogeneous initiatives.[55]

The energy and innovativeness of civil society are romanticised without recognition of the public sphere. The "Third Italy", that unexpected economic miracle of the centre and north-east of the country, supplementing and even surpassing the Northern industrial triangle in output and earnings, in stark contrast to the warped development of the southern Mezzogiorno, is not, however, a politically virgin and immaculate conception. It grew up in an intensely political environment which nurtured a dense undergrowth of small firms with soft loans, technical support and social infrastructure. Strong regional and local government, whether of the Social-Communist left in Emilia Romagna or the Christian Democratic right in the Veneto, provided the co-ordination of resources and the social framework in which competition could combine with co-operation – to share overheads, expertise, marketing and research costs, and provided the high quality social services, health and childcare which enabled women to participate fully in economic life and the resources of the family and kinship networks to be mobilized.[56] The "Third Italy" stands in stark contrast to the systemic corruption, inefficiency and irrationality of the national state, but as a different model of politics, of the relation between public authority and private, though often co-operative, initiative. It cannot be represented as an apolitical, economic model and certainly not imitated as such, because central to its success has been the functioning of local democratic self-government with some financial autonomy.

Others seek to harness diversity to a wider political framework for Europe. Here a cultural community or economic region would exercise effective autonomy within broader political boundaries. Peter Glotz, the leading thinker of the German SPD, has argued that "We must move both down to the 'tribes', to regional autonomy, and up to 'supranational' structures . . . for a pan-European federal state with maximum guarantees for ethnic groups and minority rights." This concept has been criticized as a return to tribalism, as threatening the Balkanization of Europe.[57] Firstly, one should note the ironic quotation marks: "Tribe" is a misnomer. The complex and multifarious formation of regions based on culture and local economies means, of course, that they are not tribes in the original sense of kinship groups, nor in the acquired pejorative sense of being at war with each other. True, some national movements – the Scots and the Catalans most notably – have seized upon the idea of Europe of the Regions as a means of achieving their independence as small nations within a unified Europe. What distinguishes them from the real Balkanization going on in the former Yugoslavia, is their acceptance of a civic basis of nationality, of a civil society with social space for minorities, where belonging to the nation is not defined by an exclusive ethnicity. The resort to tribalism, when people fall back on ethnic identity or kinship as the exclusive key to territorial right and national belonging results from the erosion or absence of civic politics, not from its federal, decentralized expression. Kinship can be a source of strength and support when it is allied to a democratic political framework and acts as an informal redistributive network, absorbing social shocks like unemployment and sharing good fortune within the family and community.

But Dahrendorf's more substantive argument is that the nation state constitutes the sole existing framework of citizenship, the only guarantee of constitutional rights. Therefore it is necessary to specify the constitutional and political framework of a Europe of the Regions which would not only guarantee constitutional rights, but realize them more fully.

The first prerequisite is powerful local/regional self-government, particularly strong regional assemblies with financial autonomy and federal representation. In a federalist Europe of the Regions, the regions would also be represented at the kernel of Europe, perhaps in a second chamber resembling the *Bundersrat* in Germany, which is composed of representatives of the Länder.[58]

Secondly it requires a redistributive mechanism at the centre, if the regions are to hang together as a unified entity, a genuine community. Overcoming regional disparities was laid down as an objective in the Treaty of Rome, but it was assumed that it would be realized as a by-product of the free market and "trickle down" from the richer to the poorer regions. Contrary to this happening, with the slowing down of economic growth since the 1970s and the incorporation of fragile peripheral economies in the Community, the gap has widened.[59]

The setting up of the Regional Development Fund in 1975 was de facto acknowledgement of the need for intervention. Under the 1992 programme for single market unification, the structural funds to promote social and economic cohesion have been doubled to 13 billion ECU, accounting for 30 per cent of the EC budget, from their 18 per cent level in 1988, but the Common Agricultural Policy still swallows up the lion's share of the budget.[60] Despite the current disfavour with which redistributive mechanisms are viewed, under the immediate pressures of recession and the unaccounted costs of German unification, and the longer term disenchantment with the centralized state, if the objective of social and economic cohesion is to be met, it will require a greater scale of budget with new priorities of allocation within it.

Endogenous growth is a policy objective designed to build up the resilience of a region in the face of pressures from the world economy, to insulate itself to some degree from uncertainty and sudden shock, such as a major multinational company pulling out, to reduce dependence by diversification and to encourage adaptiveness but in keeping with the traditions and strengths of the region. Regional economists have sought in this way to maximize the autonomy of the region to resist being subordinated and marginalized. For while the tendency has become pronounced of international mobility of capital and other production factors, this has only accentuated the contrast with the immobility of the regional environment: traditional skills, technology, social and institutional structure.[61] They highlight the role of self-government in social regulation of the market, in mobilizing fully the region's resources, in creating social networks and infrastructure which can externalize and pool costs, in adapting and updating skills, stimulating entrepreneurship and applying creative intelligence to a commercial environment.[62] Culture has itself become an industrial sector, strategic to modernization strategies because of the shift from producing material to symbolic products – data, design, languages, graphics, text, in knowledge-based industries, and because creativity applied to product innovation and design creates higher added value than can be achieved by lowering production costs. Where regional specialization is incubated in a socio-political shell of the kind described in Italy and acquires a certain critical mass, it guarantees a degree of social autonomy and cultural diversification which, if they could be reproduced elsewhere, would prove attractive features of a Europe of the Regions.[63]

In addition to local democratic self-government and redistributive justice, a Europe of the Regions, no less than any other popular conception of the New Europe, also requires the democratic legitimacy of the central institutions. The relevance of the overarching federal authority would become transparent to communities if regional and industrial policy enhanced social autonomy and local control, but also to individual citizens if the European Parliament underwrote a Bill of Rights, giving positive meaning to European citizenship.

Europe of the Regions is a map of the political imagination, derived from a new form of regionalism which is articulated to a European-wide democratic political project. It stands in sharp contrast to an older kind of regionalism which is being mobilized against European integration by the fascist Right. Others, like the Lega Lombarda in Italy, though "pro-European", also advocate retrenchment against outsiders, whether they be Brussels bureaucrats, mafioso Southerners, migrants from the Mahgreb or foreign competitors. The real test of a community is how it treats strangers and relates to the needs of others. This poses a particularly acute challenge for so composite a community as the European Community. By enhancing local autonomy and decision-making power, in a positive fight to modernize, regions would capitalize on their specificity, renewing their identity in a cosmopolitan setting, sometimes competing and more often co-operating and co-ordinating efforts with other regions.

In the attempt to stimulate moral and civic renewal of Central Europe, when the state dominated personal and political life under Soviet-styled regimes, the concept of anti-political politics was evolved.[64] Vaclav Havel stressed authentic needs as the starting point of genuine, meaningful politics. In his view, these are bounded by the *Lebenswelt* or *Naturwelt*, a concept borrowed from Husserl, with which he defines a personal realm of experience and responsibility, derived from an unalienated relationship to nature which confers an inherent moral sense, a kind of childhood or rural innocence. His choice of words – "gründlich" (from the earth) – and of examples of when he was a boy, and of peasant life are telling: he wishes to convey the abiding, organic links between human beings, nature and the Infinite.[65] This world stands in sharp conflict with the technological domination, centralized state control and "global automatism" which Havel sees as the underlying sickness both of totalitarian systems of power and Western industrial-consumer society.[66]

The boundaries of political concern and responsibility are defined too narrowly to confront the needs of the variety of others who are foreign to one's personal world, particularly if it is the slow-changing world of idealized rural stability. It is in the city that the confrontation of differences and interaction of strangers comes about, and where the basis of a civic, inclusive framework for politics is being forged. Some West European writers have seen modern-day social movements – such as the women's and environmental movements – arising out of the needs of everyday life, as a sign of the renaissance of civil society, and the foundation of a radically redefined politics, not rooted in organic relationships but in the contingencies of urban existence and co-existence.[67] In Richard Sennet's essay "Exposure", he finds in the fragmentary quality of the city the moral basis of a new kind of civil society, and one could add political renewal, in empathy with strangers, with those who are not familiar, not linked through kinship or tongue, who are other than oneself:

The modern city can turn people outward, not inward; rather than wholeness, the city can give the experiences of otherness. The power of the city to reorient people in this way lies in its diversity; in the presence of difference people have at least the possibility to step outside themselves.[68]

Migration, citizenship and borders: who is a European?

The siege mentality of "Fortress Europe", which combines increased internal unification with growing protectionism and closure towards the outside world, is not directed primarily against the EC rival trading blocs of the United States and Japan, as the term originally implied, since their companies have already penetrated deep into the European economy. Its impact is felt most immediately on the countries which lie at the edges of the EC trading bloc in Eastern Europe and in the Maghreb – which lost EC trade preferences when the European Southern Mediterranean countries joined the Community and whose trade has stagnated since then.[69] Fortress Europe does not only have ramifications for access of products to the European market but also for people, especially from Third World countries.

The discrimination between European and non-European citizens is highlighted in the double standards of treatment of those residing in Europe, and in the rights of entry applied by nationality law. The legal position of people of non-European descent living in Europe is highly differentiated – going from illegal immigrants with no rights at all, through refugees and asylum seekers, to those with temporary but renewable settlement rights based on bilateral agreements between the host and sender countries, and their second-generation born in Europe but "denizens" without legal rights, to naturalized, Commonwealth or ex-colonial citizens and second generations born in Europe who live in well-established communities.[70] The gradations are further compounded by social differentiation by gender, culture and occupation.[71]

The discrepancy in treatment becomes clear between that of migrants who are EC nationals and those who are non-EC nationals. In 1990 there were nearly 5 million migrants of EC origin in Europe, and their number is growing fast, and 7.75 million migrants of non-EC origin excluding those who have acquired citizenship rights.

In the first case, Europe has open doors, extending the rights an EC national enjoys in his or her native state to all other member states with reciprocal residence right for individuals and their families, recognition of qualifications, access to jobs, social security and educational exchanges. Member states are obliged under EC law to provide teaching of the language and culture of the country of origin as part of the normal education of children of EC nationals. They will also soon have voting rights in local elections in the host country as the first step to full political participation. By contrast, non-EC nationals have no free movement between EC states and national labour markets, they suffer restricted rights to family reunion and endure tight screening of marriages to weed out "marriages of convenience", and they enjoy none of the benefits, educational opportunities or political rights of their EC national counterparts.[72] Within the host country Germany, migrant workers have been labelled "guests" because of its self-perception as a non-immigration country, despite the massive contribution migrant labour made to its post-war prosperity. As a result Turks have lingered in a state of prolonged transitoriness, lasting over twenty years in some cases, with children born and educated in Germany, whose first language is German and yet who have no citizenship rights. Under German laws such migrants must satisfy the subjective whim of a judge that they are useful members of German society and they must occupy a minimum amount of space which does not take into account the different size and structure of the Turkish family or their housing problems. The framing of cultural norms which have to be met to acquire citizenship is designed to exclude those who are "different". As a conservative German paper expressed it in December 1982, "the interchange between Slav, Romanic, Germanic and other Celtic peoples has become a habit. A tacit 'we' feeling has arisen in one and the same European culture. But excluded from this are the Turk-peoples, the Palestinians, North Africans and others from totally alien cultures. They, and only they, are the 'foreigner problem' in the Federal Republic."[73] It is perhaps not surprising that only 0.13 per cent of the 1.5 million Turkish population have become German citizens.[74]

Finally, rights of entry of Third World migrants have been progressively wittled away or removed altogether, including from refugees and asylum seekers, through extending visa requirements to the countries which generate most of the refugees and imposing penalties on air and shipping lines which carry passengers whose papers are not in order. In addition an informal structure has evolved outslde of the EC institutions and the scrutiny of the European Parliament to co-ordinate the efforts of the major core states Germany, France, Belgium, the Netherlands and Luxemburg. The Schengen agreement of 1990 provided for co-operation on visa requirements and illegal immigration, drugs, arms and anti-terrorist operations, thus bracketing immigration with international crime in a potent ideological mix. It has set up a permanent mechanism for overseeing the issuing of visas, compiling a list of undesirable aliens and pooling information between the states concerned, so that rejection of an asylum application by one state will meet the same fate in all other states in the group.[75] Again the double standard at the heart of nationality law has been exposed by the wave of immigration of 800,000 ethnic Germans over the last three years. German nationality law, based as it is on ethnic belonging (*Volkszugehörigkeit*), granted automatic citizenship to East Germans, having defined in the constitution the spouses and descendants of those who lived in the Nazi Reich at the end of 1937 as German and to all those of German ancestry who settled in the East.[76] The precedence Germany gave to an ethnic criterion of citizenship in the largest movement of population probably since the return of refugees in the late 1940s undermined the "constitutional patriotism" which had marked the waning of a racially exclusive sense of the German nation in West Germany.[77] It set a bad precedent for the newly emergent states in Eastern and south-eastern Europe. The adoption by Croatia of the German ethnic concept of citizenship jeopardized the position of the 17 per cent of the non-Croat, mainly Serb population who were deprived of passports.[78] The fruits of imposing an ethnic basis to citizenship where there are large minority populations have been brutally exposed and ruthlessly gleaned in the Yugoslav civil war. It is the exclusion of ethnic groups from civil society, denying them constitutional rights and the political influence that derives from organising politically, which is resulting in the Balkanization rather than unification of Europe.

Studies show how universal it is for nationalism to search for origins to legitimate present claims of belonging to a common lineage and cultural heritage and, of course, "by right" to a specific territory.[79] These myths may be essential to achieve a unified will for political action among one group of people, but their effect such as the Protestant annual symbolic replay of the Battle of the Boyne, or Serbia's avenging the Battle of Kosovo of 1389, may be highly destructive of others. Historical scholarship must of course take account of the power and effectiveness of myths without itself reproducing them in writing the history of European unification.

Whether the "ethnic core"[80] was real or a fiction of the modernizing state, the aim was to create a monoethnic state with uniform culture, literacy, and social values, which, according to functionalists, was adapted to the technological and bureaucratic needs of industrial society. Cultural homogeneity and social mobility, in this view, are "not merely the norm of advanced industrial society, but also . . . a condition of its smooth functioning".[81]

However, the myth of monoethnicity was only realized through marginalizing and suppressing other cultures and peoples by force. Where the state constructed the nation "from above" for the purpose of consolidating its power, it imposed administrative and linguistic unification, not only driving out other dialects but expelling misfit communities: for example, the Edict of Nantes in 1685 withdrew the statute of religious toleration of the Huguenots that led to their expulsion.[82] In Italy, the unified language, the literary language derived from Tuscan, was imposed on a dialect-speaking population, only ten per cent of whom spoke it and less than one per cent of whom could write it. The attempts at Fascist national integration notwithstanding, in 1951 two-thirds of Italian people over the age of 15 still spoke in dialect and did not understand the language they were taught in schools.[83] The forcible imposition of national homogeneity fractured cultural identity, driving dialects and reject cultures into an, inner migration, confined to the private world of familial or communal discourse, separate and not understood by the outside world of power and officialdom.

If the national myth of monoethnic culture becomes the criterion for a unified Europe, it would reproduce on a larger scale the violence and suppressions which "minority" cultures, languages and people have undergone. If the myth of monoethnicity is taken for reality, then the history of those suppressions and violence is passed over in silence. One is reminded of Walter Benjamin's warning of the danger in historicism of empathizing with the victor.[84]

Chaotic unregulated internationalization of capital, communications and culture without popular participation in the European public sphere is producing disorientation, unpredictable and irrational reactions: a reversion to old, even buried ethnic and religious identities and their fundamentalist assertion, sometimes leading to violently imposed segregation, racist assaults and annihilation. Only a framework which addresses inequalities and guarantees cultural autonomy, self-recognition, the recognition of others, and minority rights can enable ethnic and cultural pluralism and democratic, civic politics to flourish.

It is timely to remember that Europe's namesake, Europa, came from the Levant on the shores of the Mediterranean. The mosaic of the Mediterranean, which is "less a cultural unity and more a collection of communities and cultures . . . shifting and making new patterns like the pebbles in a kaleidoscope"[85] offers a vivid multiethnic picture of Europe's past and an attractive alternative future to xenophobia and "ethnic cleansing".

Notes

1. See for example, P. M. Wijkman, Patterns of production and trade, in W. Wallace (ed.), *Dynamics of European integration*, Pinter, 1990, pp. 89–104.
2. See J. Pinder, *European Community: the building of a union*, Oxford, 1991, p. 208; for the political background to the act, see J. Grahl and P. Teague, *1992: the big market*, Lawrence and Wishart, 1990, pp. 17–24. K. Richardson, Europe's industrialists help shape the single market: the European Round Table works to encourage Europe's integration and to strengthen its economies, *Europe: magazine of the European Community*, 1989, pp. 18–20.
3. See P. Geronski and J. Haskel, Beyond the hype: the effects of 1992, London Business School, Working Paper Series, Number 69.
4. E. Wistrich, *After 1992: the United States of Europe*, Routledge, 1989, pp. 57–9; R. Keohane and S. Hoffman, Community politics and institutional change, in W. Wallace (ed.), *Dynamics of European integration*, p. 281.
5. J. Grahl and P. Teague, *1992: the big market*, pp. 177–83.
6. Regulation Dir 89/48, 21 December 1988, *Official Journal*, 1989 119–16.
7. F. Romero, Cross border population movements, in W. Wallace, *Dynamics of European integration*, p. 189.
8. See R. Rogers, London: a call for action, in R. Rogers and M. Fisher, *A new London*, Penguin 1992, p. xiv. and F. Bianchini, Urban cultural

policies in Western Europe: an overview, in M. Parkinson and F. Bianchini (eds), *Cultural policy and urban regeneration: the West European experience*, Manchester University Press, 1993.

9. See W. Benjamin for concept of empty homogeneous time in *Illuminations*, Cape, 1970 and B. Anderson's application of it to the creation of a unified nation in *Imagined communities*, Verso, 1991 edition, pp. 22–36.

10. P. Dahlgren and C. Sparks (eds), *Communication and citizenship: journalism and the public sphere in the new media age*, Routledge, 1991.

11. B. De Witte, Cultural linkages, W. Wallace (ed.), *Dynamics of European integration*, pp. 201–2.

12. S. Emanuel, Culture in space: the European cultural channel, *Media, Culture & Society*, vol. 14, 1992, pp. 281–99.

13. J. Habermas, *The structural transformation of the public sphere*, Polity, 1989.

14. For recent exposition of spillover see R. Keohane and S. Hoffman, Community politics and institutional change.

15. R. Dahrendorf, in *Whose Europe? Competing visions for 1992*, Institute of Economic Affairs, 1989.

16. I. Wallerstein, *The modern world system*, Academic Press, 1974 and 1980; T. K. Hopkins and I. Wallerstein, *World systems analysis: theory and methodology*, Sage, 1982.

17. T. Skocpol, Wallerstein's world capitalist system: a theoretical and historical critique, *American Journal of Sociology*, vol. 82, no. 5, 1977, pp. 1087–88.

18. I. Wallerstein, Crises, in *Unthinking social science: the limits of nineteenth century paradigms*, Polity, 1991. p. 27.

19. For example, "the bourgeoisie, or if you prefer the capitalist strata, or if you prefer the ruling classes, drew two conclusions from the 'French revolutionary turmoil.'" . . "The world bourgeoisie . . . drew a second and logical inference", in The French revolution as a world historical event, in *Unthinking social science, ibid.*, p. 15; For a critique, see also A. Giddens, *The nation state and violence: volume two of a contemporary critique of historical materialism*, Polity, 1985, pp. 161–71.

20. I. Wallerstein, Societal development, or development of the world-system? in *Unthinking social science*, pp. 74–6.

21. M. Castells and J. Henderson, Techno-economic restructuring, sociopolitical processes, and spatial transformation: a global perspective, in Castells and Henderson (eds), *Global restructuring & territorial development*, Sage, 1987.

22. S. Amin, *L'Eurocentrisme: critique d'une idéologie*, Anthropos, 1988, pp. 90–91.

23. Dudley Seers, *Underdeveloped Europe*, Harvester, 1979.

24. D. Urwin and S. Rokkan, *Economy, territory, identity: politics of the West European peripheries*, Sage, 1983.
25. R. Schumann, *Pour l'Europe*, Nagel, Paris, 1963, pp. 57–63; P. Stirk, *The making of the New Europe*, Gower, 1990.
26. See A. Bance, The idea of Europe: from Erasmus to Erasmus, *Journal of European Studies*, xxii.
27. H. Seton-Watson, What is Europe? Where is Europe?, in G. Schöpflin and N. Woods (eds), *In search of Central Europe*, Polity, 1989.
28. R. Schuman, *Pour l'Europe*, pp. 70–71; J. Monnet, *Memoirs*, p. 300.
29. Quoted in G. Lejeune, *Culture in Europe*, Commission of the European Communities, DG Research, Science and Education, 1 March 1978, pp. 28–30.
30. The term is S. Amin's in *L'Eurocentrisme: critique d'une idéologie*.
31. *New prospects for community cultural action*, Commission of the European Communities, 29 April 1992, Annex B Report on Consultation Meetings with Professional People, Committee of Cultural Consultants. J. Duroselle, *Europe: a history of its peoples*, Viking, 1990, see F. Delouche's Introduction.
32. J. Duroselle, *Europe: a history of its peoples*, pp. 203, 332.
33. J. Duroselle, *ibid.*, p. 20.
34. J. Domenach, *Le Défi Culturel*, Gallimard, 1990.
35. Talcott Parsons, *The social system*, Beacon, 1951.
36. See B. De Witte, Cultural linkages, in W. Wallace (ed.), *Dynamics of European integration*, p. 193.
37. E. Wistrich, *After 1992. The United States of Europe*, p. 78.
38. *New prospects for community cultural action*, Brussels, 29 April 1992; See also *A fresh boost for culture in the European Community*, Memorandum from Mr. Ripa di Meana to the Commission, X/9/87, p. 3.
39. J. M. Benoist, *Pavane pour une Europe Défunte*, pp. 137–149; E. Morin, *Penser L'Europe*, Gallimard, 1990, I. Chambers, *Border Dialogues*, Commedia, 1992, p. 9.
40. A. D. Smith, National identity and the idea of European unity, *International Affairs*, 68, 1, 1992, p. 66.
41. W. Maihofer, Die Einheit der Kultur Europas in der Vielfalt der Kulturen, in A. Rijksbaron (ed.), *Europe from a cultural perspective*, Nijgh & Van Ditmar University Press, 1987, p. 5.
42. J. M. Ferry, Pertinence du post national, *Esprit*, November 1991.
43. For example Edfo is confined to distribution and prevented from giving production subsidies because of EC competition policy.
44. L. Missir de Lusignan, *Pour une Politique Européenne de la Culture*, under the direction of J. Delcourt and R. Papini, *Economica*, 1987, p. 78.
45. European Commission, Towards a large European audio-visual market, *European File*, 4, 1988.

46. *Official Journal*, C348, 31 December 1985.
47. W. Hutton, *The future of Europe: a British-German discussion*, Goethe Institut, London, February 10 1992, volume 6, p. 38; J. Domenach, *Le Défi Culturel*, p. 117.
48. E. Wistrich, *After 1992. The United States of Europe*, p. 82.
49. See CEC *A fresh boost for culture in the European Community*, pp. 16, 23, 31–2; CEC *Books and reading: a cultural challenge for Europe*, Brussels, 3 August 1989, pp. 3–4, 9–12.
50. N. Reeves and S. Wright, Languages and pluralism in Britain: the challenge of multi-culturalism, *The Linguist*, vol. 31, no. 4, p. 110. See also nos. 2–4, 1992.
51. J. Rex, Race and ethnicity in Europe, in J. Bailey (ed.), *Social Europe*, Longman, 1992, pp. 112–15.
52. H. Enzensberger, Brüssel oder Europa – eins von beiden, in *Der Fliegende Robert*, Suhrkamp, p. 117; J. M. Benoist, *Pavane pour une Europe Défunte*, pp. 18–19.
53. H. Enzensberger, Brüssel oder Europa, *ibid.*, pp. 117–25.
54. J. M. Benoist, *ibid.*, pp. 55–76; J. M. Ferry, Pertinence de post national.
55. H. M. Enzensberger, *Europe, Europe*, Picador, 1990, pp. 80–81.
56. See F. Pyke, G. Beccattini, W. Sengenberger (eds), *Industrial districts and inter-firm co-operation in Italy*, International Institute of Labour Studies, Geneva, 1990, especially pp. 2–6, 24–8, 155–6; C. Sabel, *Work and politics. The division of labour in industry*, Cambridge, 1982, pp. 270–71; S. Brusco, Small firms and industrial districts; the experience of Italy, in D. Keeble and E. Wever (eds), *New firms and regional development in Europe*, pp. 187–94, and S. Brusco, The Emilian Model; productive decentralisation and social integration, *Cambridge Journal of Economics*, 6, 1982.
57. R. Dahrendorf, *Reflections on the revolution of 1989*, pp. 123–38.
58. On political reform, see J. Lodge, *The European Community and the challenge of the future*, Pinter, 1989.
59. The ratio of income levels between the richest and poorest regions rose from 5 to 14 with the accession of Greece, Spain and Portugal. See W. Molle R. Cappellin (eds), *Regional impact of Community policies on Europe*, Avebury, 1988, p. 2.
60. H. Wallace, *Europe, the challenge of diversity*, Royal Institute of International Affairs, London, 1985, pp. 24–6; J. Grahl and P. Teague, *1992: the big market*, Lawrence & Wishart, 1990, pp. 223–33.
61. W. Molle and R. Cappellin, *Regional impact of Community policies on Europe*, pp. 6–7.
62. See also: The Marshallian industrial district as a socio-economic notion, in F. Pyke, G. Beccattini, W. Sengenberger (eds), pp. 37–51; C. Sabel,

Flexible specialization and the re-emergence of regional economies, in P. Hirst and J. Zeitlin, *Reversing industrial decline*, Berg, London, 1989.

63. See especially C. Trigilia, Work and politics in the third Italy's industrial districts, in F. Pyke, G. Beccatini and W. Sengenberger (eds), pp. 160–79. The debate over whether these "industrial districts" can be reproduced in different conditions, for example where there is no communal tradition of husbanding resources as there was among sharecroppers or artisans, is rather misguided. The range of contexts in which such clusters arise has been shown to be wider – including non-agrarian ones – than was originally assumed. In addition, isolating the broad range of variables which influence the viability and staying power of these local economies in different cases does not mean that all the variables have to be present at all times. See F. Pyke and W. Sengenberger, Introduction to F. Pyke et al., pp. 2–6.

64. See V. Havel, Anti-political politics, in J. Keane (ed.), *Civil society and the state*, Verso, 1988, pp. 381–98, and *The power of the powerless*, pp. 23–96, Hutchinson, 1985.

65. V. Havel, Anti-political politics, *ibid.*, p. 382.

66. V. Havel, The power of the powerless, pp. 89–91.

67. See for example, A. Melucci, *Nomads of the present: social movements and individual needs in contemporary society*, Hutchinson, 1989; A. Pizzorno, in *Changing boundaries of the political*, Cambridge, 1987.

68. R. Sennett, in *The conscience of the eye*, Faber, 1990, p. 123.

69. See R. Aliboni, The Mediterranean dimension, in W. Wallace (ed.), *Dynamics of European integration*, p. 158–5g.

70. L. Balbo, Cittadini, Cittadini-Dimezzati, Non-Cittadini, in *Inchiesta*, vol. XX, no. 90, October–December 1930, p. 25.

71. In J. Andall, Women migrant workers in Italy, *Women's Studies International Forum*, vol. 15, no. 1, 1992, p. 43.

72. Centre for Research in Ethnic Relations, Unequal migrants: the European Community's unequal treatment of migrants and refugees, Policy Papers in Ethnic Relations, no. 13, May 1989.

73. Frankfurter Allgemeine, quoted in F. Webber, From Ethnocentrism to Euroracism, *Race & Class*, vol. 32, no. 3, 1991.

74. W. Meys and F. Sen (eds), *Zukunft in der Bundesrepublik oder Zukunft in der Türkei?*, Dağyeli Verlag, 1986, p. 169.

75. T. Bunyan, Towards an authoritarian European state, *Race and Class*, vol. 32, no. 3, January–March 1991, pp. 19–31.

76. F. Franz, Das Prinzip der Abstammung in der deutschen Staatsangehörigkeitsrecht, in *Rassismus und Migration in Europa* (Beiträge des Kongresses, "Migration und Rassismus in Europa", Hamburg, 26–30 September 1990), Argument, Verlag 1992.

77. J. Habermas, Yet again: German identity, *New German Critique*, no. 52, Winter 1992.
78. N. Beloff, An analysis of Germany's Yugoslav policy, unpublished paper, p. 4.
79. J. Breuilly, *Nationalism and the state*, University of Chicago Press, 1982, pp. 338–44; A. Giddens, *The nation-state and violence*, pp. 215–21.
80. A. D. Smith, *National identity*, Penguin, 1991.
81. E. Gellner, *Nations and nationalism*, Blackwell, 1990, p. 69.
82. A. D. Smith, State-making and nation-building, in J. A. Hall (ed.), *States in history*, Oxford, 1986, pp. 247–8.
83. See J. Steinberg, The historian and the *Questione della Lingua*, in P. Burke and R. Porter (eds), *The social history of language*, Cambridge, 1987, pp. 204–5; See also U. Østergård, "Denationalizing" national history, *Culture & History*, 9/10, 1991, pp. 19–20; B. Anderson, *Imagined communities*, pp. 37–46.
84. W. Benjamin, Theses on the philosophy of history, in *Illuminations*.
85. R. Fox, *The inner sea*, Sinclair-Stevenson, 1991, p. 16.

Epilogue: Historians, nations, and the future of Europe

Douglas Johnson

At the time of the conference which concluded the Maastricht agreement, everyone was faced with an important dilemma. But for historians the dilemma was particularly acute. We were told that the most fundamental change was taking place in European history, we were faced with the prospect of a federalist western Europe. This was not only an innovation, but it was the denial of British foreign policy as it had existed, some would say successfully, since the days of Elizabeth I. That is to say that there had been every reason to prevent European unity under Spain, or France, or eventually Germany. But to put forward such an objection was to suggest that one had sunk into an unfortunate historicism. The objector would be described as a Little Englander, or a Palmerstonian, or someone imbued with a haughty, senior-officer mentality that showed contempt for foreigners, hostility to the people on the other side of the hill. As in the famous Cavafy poem, in this context one is waiting for the barbarians, or, to extend a famous phrase, one is contemplating faraway countries about which one knows nothing.

But at the same time as the historian was obliged to accept the possibility of a federalist western Europe, it was obligatory to realize that an important phenomenon was taking place: the independence of the Ukraine. If one was critical of this, then one was guilty of seeing only the bad side of nationalism; one equated it too easily with the characteristics of war, chauvinism, fascism, intolerance, repression and, sometimes, racism. Thus it was difficult to accept or reject Maastricht.

But the dilemma also affects historians in their professional capacity. They might have to make up their minds as to the importance of historical studies. Does the study of the past help one the better to understand the present? Many historians, A. J. P. Taylor *"en tête"*, have rigorously denied this. Does the study of the present help us better to understand the past? It is said that the greatest danger for the historian is to be over-influenced by his or her own times and to give credence to the anachronisms of others.

The historian contributes to the debate in a number of ways. In the first place a school of history exists which emphasizes the existence of Europe as an entity over many centuries. Therefore the creation of some sort of federation in present-day western Europe can be seen as a return to source rather than as a sudden invention. It is no accident that in the early days of the Community it was frequently stated that it resembled the empire of Charlemagne.[1] The notion of Christendom, bringing together a communion of peoples within a geographical area, is fundamental to this view. One can argue about dates and detail. It can be said to have begun with the granting to Christians, by the Emperor Constantine, of equal rights with other religions. From this Christianity acquired an exclusive status as the religion of the Empire. It became an ideal and an organization that could transcend territorial and feudal loyalties, an idea that became all the more powerful as it became involved in a conflict with Islam. Or it can be said that the foundations of Europe emerged from the ninth century. Then, inspired by economic prosperity, ethnic and linguistic diversity was tempered by Christianity, by a uniform educational system, by the liturgical language of Latin. Professor Georges Duby assures us that an educated man was as much at home in Königsberg as he was in Valence, or Edinburgh, as in Prague. Even in periods of economic depression or stagnation, such as followed the Black Death or such as marks periods in early modern times, the cultural substructures persisted; the idea of a European community, it is argued, remains.

This sentiment is all the more remarkable when the vitality of Europe is contrasted to the somnolence of other areas, such as the Ottoman Empire. Reason accompanied faith, and Europe became the world's leading scientific laboratory and industrial workshop. There were, of course, differences between countries, and historians, such as Fernand Braudel, have always seen a fundamental difference between the *continental* and the *marin*,[2] but there was an essential European community, with its culture, its system of values, its set of ethics. The story of Robinson Crusoe became a cultural symbol for this Europe, the story of how man can transform nature (although, it is said, not all Europeans went down on their knees to give thanks to God).

Such a view of history fits in to the fashion that seeks to see history studied over long periods of time and wishes to see the important issues examined, that is to say, how people lived, what they believed, what they wanted. Historians should see the history of western Europe in terms of navigation, of steam, of textiles rather than lose themselves in the intricacies of frontiers and royal inheritances which led to futile conflicts.

As in the discussion that took place between Old Kaspar and Little Peterkin about the battle of Blenheim, the historian has too often been saying that it was a glorious victory without knowing what it was all about. It is interesting to note that associations of young historians are springing up that attack what they call *"l'hyperspécialisation"* which has characterized much of historical research, so that only details are studied, and which attack what they call the narcissism of national historical studies. They seek to study on a European scale, the state, the family, the progress of reason.[3]

A second means whereby historians make their contribution to the debate on the future of Europe, engendered by the Maastricht treaty, is to emphasize the difficulties with which national states were created. The distinction is between the national state and the nation state, the latter being a very rare phenomenon that encompasses a single, culturally homogenous people. There was a time when received history assumed that it was natural that national states should emerge. Every O-leveller knew that those who endeavoured to prevent their formation, such as Metternich, were foolish and their efforts were doomed to failure. Equally futile were the efforts of those who strove to unite, in one state, peoples who were not allied as nations. Hence the unified Kingdom of Belgium and Holland, created in 1815, inevitably broke up. Right-thinking people wept at the suppression of the Poles, or even rioted in the streets of Paris when they learned the official version of events, that order had been restored to the streets of Warsaw. Mr Gladstone was indignant that the populations of Alsace and Lorraine should have been transferred to German rule as if they were cattle, and the infant Winston Churchill, when shown the shrouded statues in the Place de la Concorde, earnestly wished that the provinces should be restored to France.

But whilst the traditional teaching of nineteenth-century history concentrated on the story of the unification of Germany and Italy, and presented the first as a triumph of Bismarck's skill and the second as a tribute to the force of Liberalism, nowadays the emphasis is on the inadequacies of these unifications. Cynicism prevails. The political malaise that existed in unified Germany is seen as vital in the creation of further crises, whilst examination questions now highlight the failures of united Italy. "'We have made Italy; now we must make Italians'. Discuss" is only rivalled as a more popular examination question by "What went wrong with the *Risorgimento*?".

But perhaps the most remarkable revision is that of the history of France. It used to be said that the making of the French nation was *"une merveilleuse histoire"*, one that stretched backwards to the very beginning of time, but that the familiar visage of France was always there if only in *"filigranne"*, a distant image that was destined to become a reality. Was the key point when the French nation emerged to be associated with Clovis, the king of the Franks, who established his royal residence in Paris, or was it from Charles the Bold, the grandson of Charlemagne, or from Capet who became king in 987? He founded the dynasty which, from its origins until 1792 (or, some would claim) until 1848, established a great continuity in French history.

But nineteenth-century historians, such as Guizot and Michelet, believed that one had to look elsewhere before one could talk of the emergence of French sentiment. More recent historians have rejected their claims to have discovered the awakening of national sentiment in such events as the wars with the English. They see French history as a history of diversity and divisions, in which there is little sense of nation until modern times. The emphasis is on inner conflict, regionalism, the growth of population and the pressure on food resources, the rejection of monarchy and of Catholic orthodoxy, the breakdown of government. The amalgam of confrontations, attitudinization, and innovation were the features out of which the French nation emerged and was, it is suggested, not secure until the 1880s. The symbol of France might be the Marseillaise, but it is now said that those soldiers who marched on Paris and for the first time sang Rouget de l'Isle's masterpiece did not speak French among themselves.[4]

The question has been asked, was it the kings of France who created the French nation or was it the contrary, a geographical reality which created the kings of France? In pre-Roman Gaul, and ever afterwards, there was a geographical unity which corresponds, after certain adjustments to the frontiers, such as Alsace-Lorraine and Dunkirk, with a modern conception of France. In this sense it is suggested that there was, geographically speaking, a Gallo-Roman predestination of the country, however vague it might have been. France could not be created just anywhere. But geographers these days are anxious to deny this form of determinism. Faced with a map, from which all political frontiers have been removed, no one, it is argued, could identify France. The so-called natural frontiers of France are not barriers at all, and never were barriers. The Rhine meant trade, the Channel was a means of transit, the Pyrenees, the Alps and the Jura never prevented the movement of peoples, and the river Loire helped to link the north and south together. Whilst rejecting the theory of France's natural frontiers as pure imagination, some historians have claimed that the France which did eventually emerge was an accidental creation and they have amused themselves by imagining the different types of France that might well have evolved had circumstances been different. Thus there would have been a southern Mediterranean France, a Franco-English empire, or a Burgundian France.

This last, rejection of a myth, brings me to the question of nationalism. Marx thought that it was related to class and would disappear with socialism, and it is certain that, for a time at least, it could be suppressed. Professor Kedourie has called nationalism a doctrine invented in Europe at the beginning of the nineteenth century, suggesting that humanity is naturally divided into nations, that nations are known by certain characteristics which can be ascertained, and that the only legitimate type of government is national self-government. However, he also accepts that at its simplest, nationalism derives from the need to belong to a stable coherent community. This need may be satisfied by a variety of loyalties to family, village, region, language or religion. Nationalism is only one of the nostrums which seem to offer a sense of community and purpose. There is therefore no reason to suppose that a European community, engulfing regions, states, markets and economic activity should not also serve the same purpose. There is no law of history, politics or nature which states that people of different beliefs and cultures must be divided into nation states and be led by representatives of their own group.[5]

In a more recent work Professor Eric Hobsbawm has been more dismissive of the imagined communities that have been cobbled together in comparatively recent times, and which have invented retrospective illusions of continuous physical identity, of manifest destiny, of dynamic particularisms. History, folklore, traditions that are discovered and re-discovered are only part of the process of ideological engineering which is the basis of national construction. Ethnicity bears no relation to the function of nation states (think of the Basques, the Jews, the Kurds). Language can be relevant to national identity, but this is recent, and not central. *Pace* the story of those who sang the Marseillaise, Hobsbawm tells us that Manzoni, whose novel *I Promessi Sposi* created a national language for Italy, spoke French at home and Milanese dialect in the street. We must not be taken in by linguistic imperialisms. The conclusion to all this is that the historical significance of nationalism is in decline.[6]

All historians of the subject see the importance of war in the formation of the structures of national states. Countless memorials throughout Europe testify to how people were prepared to die for their country, whether its cause was right or wrong. Countless Englishmen, carrying in their hands equipment which was more valuable than anything that they had held in their hands before, were prepared to die for a flag. As the poet put it:

> In the nightmare of the dark
> All the dogs of Europe bark
> And the living nations wait
> Each sequestered in its hate.

History shows us that as war looms peoples in Europe have become more and more hateful of each other. There is no great movement to preserve peace and the fraternity of Europeans. There was a celebrated palmist who was consulted by many in the months before the outbreak of war in 1914 (it was said that Winston Churchill was one of her customers). She was bewildered as she studied the palms of young men and found that their life-lines were stopping shorter than was usual. She did not understand. Nor did the young men; but they marched, they sang, they killed and they were killed.

We are told that this is no longer possible in western Europe. The issues for which people fought for so long and so bitterly, no longer exist. The Rhine, the Low Countries, the Alps, the Pyrenees, the Channel, the Mediterranean, none of these sets one western European state against another. Each of the states, once at war, has received as tourists, as business associates, as technical, political or cultural collaborators, the inhabitants of those states which were once considered to be enemies. Frontiers no longer exist, neither for television programmes, nor for the cloud that rose from Chernobyl. Indeed the very nature of war has changed. Men no longer charge with bayonets fixed and bugles sounding and national flags cannot be affixed to Exocet missiles. Nuclear weapons mean that war is totally catastrophic, and everyone knows this. It is also catastrophically expensive.

It is also claimed that nations persist in their nationalism because of economic rivalry. Once again, the historian of today has a word to say. Whereas in the past the industrialization of Europe has been viewed as a series of separate industrial revolutions, each country treated as an economy which has its own progress and record, it is suggested that industrialization in Europe was a single process, and indeed, is linked to the world beyond Europe.[7] No European government can control the economy that exists within its frontiers, without reference to other countries, any more than it can prevent its inhabitants from watching television programmes made outside its frontiers or listening to the international radio.

If programmes made in the USA, in Britain or in Australia circulate throughout Europe, this, it can be argued, is in accord with a certain cultural history. If one considers, for example, painting in Spain, during the country's golden age, then one is obliged to realize how much of the art produced in Spain came from those who were not Spanish. There were Titian, Caravaggio, Bosch and Rubens. There was Sittow who came from Estonia and who was trained in Bruges. Pedro de Campania was from Brussels, Vincente. Carducci from Florence. And there was El Greco.

At most it can be said that nationalism only enters private life through sport. This gives satisfaction to the individual without disturbing society, as when the recent defeat of the French ice hockey team at Albertville was reported in the French newspaper *L'Équipe* as a triumphant defeat. In such encounters there are no bugles calling from sad shires.

Lastly, there is the question of empires. Should we study European history in terms of these great empires? The Spanish, the Portuguese, the Habsburg, the Ottoman, the French, the British – Paul Kennedy's book put forward the theory that, from time immemorial, certain societies or states have risen to prominence, or dominance, have carved out a regional or global sphere of influence, and have then fallen away from that position. Whilst they regarded their rise as natural, perhaps even predestined, none of them ever welcomed their decline and most sought to reverse it by adopting new strategies, blaming former policies, criticizing particular leaders. But no change of tactics, no renewal of government, has ever restored a declining empire to its former status, although it might, in certain circumstances, have gained a temporary delay. The argument as put forward by many is that the place that any nation holds in the world is affected far less by statesmen than by economic and geopolitical factors that are beyond the control of individual statesmen. The argument as put forward by Kennedy is that the decline of these empires was hastened by imperial overstretch – Spain was unable to digest the windfall of the new world, Charles V ate up his resources by trying to do too much, Napoleon fought brilliant battles but he could not defeat so many enemies at once.[8] Kennedy's arguments are not always acceptable, but even the case against him makes the story of empires still less important. The greatness of the Spanish empire is exaggerated; the Habsburgs might not have been able to establish an order of priorities for their empire, but they were well able, even if left to themselves to get into trouble; the power of Napoleon was always fragile. And is it true to suggest that certain states were dominated by the idea of promoting, or defending, their status, as a power? This is almost to treat states as if they were persons. Disraeli, as he helped John Bright on with his overcoat, shocked him by whispering in his ear that they had both been brought to the House of Commons by the same ambition. "We came here for fame", he said. Should we transfer such a conversation to international relations?

All this suggests that historians are agreed that the traditional method of teaching and studying history in terms of nation states has ended, is ending or ought to end. Even a French writer has ridiculed French nationalism which is opposed to economic modernization because it will ruin the French economy, which believes that French culture is the best in the world, which is ecological in believing that the Vikings will come and deposit their rubbish in their gardens, and which is paranoiac, convinced that the whole world hates them.[9]

Yet, the historian is obliged to acknowledge that since 1989 we have been living through the biggest explosion of nationalism that the world has ever seen. We were accustomed to Jews and Palestinians claiming that only through possession of national states of their own could they exist in security, and to 800 million Indians claiming to be a nation in spite of their considerable internal divisions and their lack of any past nationhood. The Soviet Union has split up; Czechs are disowning Slovaks; what the Carnegie Peace Foundation denounced as the Balkan religious wars have been rekindled.[10] The problem of Macedonia, a unit without an agreed name, involves Serbs, Albanians, Bulgarians, Romanians, Greeks and Turks. All talk is of frontiers, minorities, ethnicities and military intervention. And are these states part of Europe? Where does Europe end?[11]

It is clear that we still have to describe and to explain nationalism. This is where the historian came in. It could be that in the west there will come a time when people will say, "I am a European of Belgian origin" (or French, or German, or Italian) or they may say "I am a European of Lombard origin" (or Breton, or Welsh, or Bavarian). But historians must never prophesy.

Notes

1. See, for example, Lord Gladwyn, *The European idea*, London, 1966.
2. Braudel attributes to Charles V the idea of creating a European entity, which was abandoned by his son Philip II who was more ibero-atlantic. *Écrits sur l'histoire*, volume 2, Paris, 1990.
3. Some of these have formed the Association des jeunes historiens, 48 Boulevard Jourdan, Bureau 13175, 75014 Paris.
4. Amongst many authors one should note Colette Beaune, *Naissance de la nation France*, Paris, 1985; Emmanuel Le Roy Ladurie, Ces mythes qui out fait la France, *L'Express*, 20 September 1985, pp. 68–9.
5. Elie Kedourie, *Nationalism*, 2nd edition, London, 1961.
6. E. J. Hobsbawm, *Nations and nationalism*, London, 1991.

7. J. A. Schumpeter, *Business cycles*, New York, 1939; William Woodruff, *Impact of western man*, London, 1966.

8. Paul Kennedy, *The rise and fall of the great powers*, London, 1985.

9. Yann de l'Écotais, *Naissance d'une nation*, Paris, 1991.

10. Lord Courtney (ed.), *Nationalism and war in the near east*, Carnegie Endowment for International Peace, Oxford, 1915.

11. Alain Prate, *Quelle Europe?*, Paris, 1991. See the interview of the geographer Michel Foucher, Géopolitique, *Le Monde*, 7 May 1992, p. 2. Robin Okey, Central Europe / Eastern Europe: behind the definition, *Past and Present*, no. 137, November 1992, pp. 102–33, and other articles in this special number.

Index

Index